HELL IN THE

A MARINE RIFLEMAN'S JOURNEY

PACIFIC

FROM GUADALCANAL TO PELELIU

JIM McENERY
with BILL SLOAN

SIMON & SCHUSTER

NEW YORK   LONDON   TORONTO   SYDNEY   NEW DELHI

Simon & Schuster
1230 Avenue of the Americas
New York, NY 10020

First Simon & Schuster hardcover edition June 2012

SIMON & SCHUSTER and colophon are registered trademarks
of Simon & Schuster, Inc.

For information about special discounts for bulk purchases,
please contact Simon & Schuster Special Sales at
1-866-506-1949 or business@simonandschuster.com.

The Simon & Schuster Speakers Bureau can bring authors
to your live event. For more information or to book an event,
contact the Simon & Schuster Speakers Bureau at
1-866-248-3049 or visit our website at www.simonspeakers.com.

Designed by Ruth Lee-Mui
Maps by Paul Pugliese

Manufactured in the United States of America

10 9 8 7 6 5 4 3 2 1

Library of Congress Cataloging-in-Publication Data
McEnery, Jim.
   Hell in the Pacific : a Marine rifleman's journey from Guadalcanal to Peleliu / by Jim
McEnery with Bill Sloan.—First Simon & Schuster hardcover edition.
      p.   cm.
   Includes index.
   1. McEnery, Jim.   2. World War, 1939–1945—Campaigns—Pacific Area.   3. World
War, 1939–1945—Personal narratives, American.   4. United States. Marine Corps—
Biography.   5. Marines—United States—Biography.   I. Sloan, Bill.   II. Title.
   D767.9.M393 2012
   940.54'5973092—dc23
   [B]   2011052985

ISBN 978-1-4516-5913-9
ISBN 978-1-4516-5915-3 (ebook)

I wish to give heartfelt thanks to my wonderful family—
my wife, Gertrude McEnery; our daughter, Karen;
and our grandsons, Brendan and Erik Cummins—
and also to my coauthor, Bill Sloan, a true and special friend,
without whose knowledgeable help this book
might not have been completed.

CONTENTS

1. A NICE DAY FOR A BOAT RIDE   1

2. ALWAYS A MARINE AT HEART   21

3. DISASTER AT SEA, SLAUGHTER ASHORE   47

4. BUSHIDO TAKES A BEATING   71

5. JAPAN'S OFFENSIVE HITS A WALL   99

6. "WE'VE GOT THE BASTARDS LICKED"   127

7. RED MUD, RED BLOOD, GREEN HELL   153

8. THE CRAB AND COCONUT WARS   183

9. PELELIU—"A TERRIBLE MISTAKE"   207

10. THE WORST NIGHTMARE YET   235

11. GOING BACK TO THE REAL WORLD   267

    Epilogue   285

    Index   293

HELL IN THE PACIFIC

1

A NICE DAY FOR A BOAT RIDE

IT WAS ABOUT 8:30 AM, August 7, 1942, when I got my first good look at the island where we were going. To me, it seemed pretty much like every other island I'd seen in the Pacific during the two months I'd been there: white sand beaches framed by clusters of dark green palm trees, with dense jungle undergrowth just behind and blue-green hills rising up in the distance.

But this island was different, and every one of us knew it. This one was supposed to be crawling with Japs, all of them itching to blow us to hell.

We were bound for a section of shoreline designated as Beach Red. We didn't care much for that name. It made us think of blood— our blood.

Until our officers and senior NCOs started drumming how dangerous this place was into our heads, the name of the island hadn't meant a damned thing to me or any of the other guys in my platoon. I doubted if anybody back in the States had ever even heard of it.

Just for the record, it was called Guadalcanal.

The brass had warned everybody to expect the worst. They said some of us who were climbing down the cargo nets on the side of the troopship and trying to keep from stepping on each other's hands as we boarded our Higgins boats were going to get killed today. The letter we'd received from Colonel LeRoy P. Hunt, our regimental commander, had tried to be reassuring, but it didn't quite make it.

"God bless all of you," it said at the end, "and to hell with the Japs."

The troops respected Colonel Hunt. As a young lieutenant in France in 1918, he'd earned both a Navy Cross and a Distinguished Service Cross for heroism under fire. He knew what hard fighting was all about, and he was telling us this fight was going to be as hard as they came.

We were the men of the First Marine Division, but except for Hunt and a few other holdovers from World War I, we were all as green as gourds. Almost none of us had ever fired a shot in anger, and the grim warnings we'd been hearing the past few days made us jumpy.

The word spread through the ranks like some kind of epidemic. "Somebody's gonna get hurt! Somebody's gonna get hurt!"

Actually, though, if so many of us hadn't been so nervous and on edge, it would've been a pretty nice day for a boat ride. The sky was pale blue with some big, puffy clouds that looked like gobs of whipped cream. And as our Higgins boat headed for shore—less than a mile away now—there was hardly a ripple in the sea around us.

But even this early in the morning, the air was already uncomfortably warm and steamy. Our dungaree uniforms stuck to us like glue, and most of us were dripping with sweat by the time we made it down the nets. By afternoon, it was sure to be hot as blazes.

Like the rest of the fifty guys in my boat, I was tense and excited, and my pulse was going pretty fast. But I wasn't really scared. I don't scare easy. Never have. I don't know why; I just don't. I probably *should've* been scared but just didn't have enough sense to be, and I sure as hell didn't blame anybody that was.

While most of the others in the boat stayed huddled down behind the gunwales in case the Nips opened up on us, I kept my eyes on the island, watching it get closer and closer. Maybe I wanted to seem more confident than I really was to help encourage the rest of the men, especially the young ones in my squad.

I call them men—and they got to be men in a hurry if they lived long enough—but most of them were really still just boys that day. I was almost twenty-three, and that was four or five years older than most of the kids in my squad. I'd been promoted to corporal a few months ago and appointed a squad leader a little later on. So I felt like it was part of my job to, you know, set a good example and try to reassure these younger guys.

Spread out around us were a half-dozen other Higgins boats, carrying the 300-plus first-wave troops of the First and Third Battalions of the Fifth Marine Regiment. The guys in my boat were all from K Company, Third Battalion, Fifth—better known as K/3/5. We were assigned to anchor the left flank of our line once we got ashore.

Following in our wake were boats carrying another 300 or more men from two battalions of the First Marine Regiment. This meant that, in all, the whole first wave of Marine assault troops assigned to land on Guadalcanal's Beach Red was only 600 or 700 guys. This didn't seem like very many, considering this was America's first offensive ground action of World War II in the Pacific.

Of course, this first wave was only a small part of our full invasion force. Within the next couple of hours, all 5,000 men in the three waves of the First and Third Battalions, Fifth Marines, and First, Second, and Third Battalions, First Marines, would be ashore.

Our division commander, General Alexander A. Vandegrift, figured at least 5,000 Japs were waiting for us on shore. That may sound like a fairly even matchup, but it really wasn't. We could expect the Jap defenders to be well dug in while we'd be out in the open, if you see what I mean.

(I should stop right now and explain something to you. Any time I say "First Marines" or "Fifth Marines" or "Seventh Marines" and so forth, I'm talking about regiments. In this case, infantry regiments with about 3,000 riflemen apiece. If I'm talking about a Marine Corps division, I always use the full name, like "First Marine Division." It's kind of confusing, and I want to clear it up now so you don't get the First Marines, a regiment, mixed up with the First Marine Division.)

THE FIRST ASSIGNMENT for us in the First and Third Battalions, Fifth Marines—known as Combat Group A—was to secure a beachhead 2,000 yards long and 600 yards deep along the north coast of Guadalcanal.

When we finished landing, all three battalions of the First Marines—Combat Group B—would pass through the Fifth Marines' position and advance a couple of miles west toward a piece of high ground called the Grassy Knoll. Then they were to set up three separate circular defensive perimeters on either side of the Tenaru River and on the east bank of another stream called Alligator Creek.

If we were lucky, this was all supposed to happen on the first day. If we weren't lucky, nobody knew what would happen. Even at best, our defenses would be widely scattered and thinly stretched.

Meanwhile, other elements of the division had already landed earlier that morning on the small island of Tulagi about twenty miles north of Guadalcanal. The Second Battalion, Fifth, and the First Marine Raider Battalion ran into a major firefight on Tulagi right away. About 120 Marines were killed or wounded there before the island was secured, and about 350 Jap defenders were killed. Only three Japs lived to surrender.

Other Marines were hitting the twin islands of Gavutu and Tanambogo and the larger island of Florida just across Sealark Channel from Beach Red. As it turned out, there weren't any Jap defenders at all on Florida, but there were plenty to go around on the other islands. The First Marine Parachute Battalion landed from boats on Gavutu and got in one helluva scrap. One in five of their guys were being killed or wounded in the battle that morning, but at the same time the Japs were losing 516 killed on the two islands.

It was a good thing for us on Guadalcanal that we didn't hear any of these casualty figures until later on. If we'd known what was happening on those other islands, we'd have really been spooked.

The total strength of all First Marine Division units in the

Guadalcanal amphibious operation was 956 officers and 18,146 enlisted men. But at least half of them were rear-echelon support and supply troops. Most of the front-line combat troops were in infantry companies like K/3/5.

Backing up our landings was a huge convoy of Navy ships. They called it Task Force 62, and it included seventy-five ships in all—transports, destroyers, and cruisers—and it was protected by four U.S. carriers with full complements of combat aircraft.

Since dawn, the cruisers and destroyers had been pounding the shores of the target islands with their heavy guns. I'd heard them blasting away when I went above decks just as the sun was coming up.

Flocks of carrier-based F4F Wildcat fighters and Douglas Dauntless dive-bombers also made bombing runs over the beaches and adjacent jungle to "soften up" the Jap defenses. Unfortunately, though, there weren't any Jap defenses there. I doubt if all that wasted firepower killed or wounded—or even scared—a single enemy soldier. But none of us knew that going in.

BASED ON WHAT we'd been told, we expected to come under heavy fire from Jap mortars, machine guns, and artillery at any second. But instead it was totally quiet. Unnaturally quiet. Quiet as a tomb, you might say.

We were only a few hundred yards from shore now, and some of my platoon mates were staring toward the approaching beach with grim expressions and glassy eyes. Others were bowing their heads and moving their lips in silent prayer.

For a second, I had a mental picture of my mother and sister, and I remembered the last letters I'd gotten from them. I figured other guys were thinking about their families, too, and wondering if they'd ever see them again. It made me glad I didn't have a wife and kids back home, or even a steady girlfriend, to grieve for me if anything happened.

On either side of the bow of the boat, a pair of Marines with Browning Automatic Rifles (BARs) manned two forward gun ports, but they had nothing to shoot at. Not yet, anyway.

I shifted my eyes from the island to glance at PFC William Murray, a pint-sized kid of eighteen who served as a scout in my platoon. He was crouching next to me and fidgeting with one of the two hand grenades that each rifleman had hooked to his belt. Then, just as I turned toward him, I saw a look of total terror flash across his face.

"My God!" he blurted. "I think I dislodged the pin."

Without even thinking, I lunged forward in time to grab the grenade and push the pin back into place.

"What the hell you trying to do?" I said. "You want to blow up the whole damn boat?" If the grenade had gone off, it would've done exactly that. I didn't know it at the time, but accidents with dislodged grenade pins would kill and maim a lot of Marines before the war was over.

Murray was white-faced and shaking, even after I secured the grenade. "I don't want this thing on my belt anymore," he said. "I'm scared of it. I'm gonna throw it over the side."

"No, you're not," I told him. "Hand it to me. I'll give you one of mine to replace it."

"But—"

"Just calm down and give it here," I said. "It'll be okay. That one grenade might save your life this morning."

After Murray and I swapped grenades, everything got deathly

silent again. The only sound you could hear was the sea gently lapping at the sides of the boat and the low rumble of its engine. It was as if every guy there was expecting all hell to break loose any second. It was more than Sergeant Norman "Dutch" Schantunbach, one of K/3/5's squad leaders, could take.

"Knock it off, you guys!" he said. "You ain't dead yet, for Chrissake, so look lively! Let's make some noise. Let's sing a song."

"I don't know no songs," somebody mumbled.

"Well, hell, I do," said Schantunbach, one of the company's most dedicated beer drinkers. "How about 'Roll Out the Barrel'?"

A Marine next to Schantunbach shrugged. "Okay, hit it," he said.

Seconds later, a couple of dozen off-key male voices echoed across the water: I almost laughed. It sounded bad enough to scare off any Jap within five miles.

> *Roll out the barrel,*
> *We'll have a barrel of fun!*
> *Roll out the barrel,*
> *We've got the blues on the run!*

AT EXACTLY 9:06 AM, without further incident or a single shot being fired in our direction, our Higgins boat bumped against the beach, and we started scrambling over the gunwales and jumping to the ground. Later on, our landing craft would have ramps in front that dropped down so you could run straight onto the beach, but at Guadalcanal, we did it the hard way. The wet way.

Besides those two grenades everybody carried, each of us waded ashore with just one "unit of fire" for our bolt-action 1903

Springfield rifles. It had been six years since the new semiautomatic Garand M-1s were introduced, but hardly any outfits in the Pacific had the M-1s yet. Our government in Washington had decided to send all the best weapons and equipment to the European Theater of Operations first. That's how we ended up fighting with obsolete forty-year-old stuff in the Pacific. We'd even been using those British-style World War I helmets until they issued us some new replacements a few weeks before we headed for Guadalcanal.

By the way, in typical combat conditions, that "unit of fire" I was talking about equals just one average day's worth of ammunition. In other words, it ain't much.

So you tried not to wonder what would happen if a bunch of Japs came charging out of the jungle and we got in a firefight that lasted half a day. Only it wouldn't. It couldn't. With what little firepower we had, we'd be lucky if it lasted half an *hour*.

If we'd run into any hornet's nests like the ones on Gavutu and Tulagi, we'd have been out of ammo, out of luck, and maybe out of blood, too.

We didn't even have any food. I went ashore without a pack or rations of any kind, and most of the guys in my platoon were in the same shape. Besides my rifle, I had a canteen with a quart of water in it, the two grenades on my belt, my bayonet, and that one unit of fire.

I didn't even have a trenching tool to dig with. All I had was a pair of wire cutters that some joker thought we'd need to cut barbed wire. Of course, there wasn't any barbed wire, but there was an awful lot of dirt to dig.

The Navy was supposed to be sending the rest of our supplies in by boat. That's all we knew. When and where was anybody's guess. So was how we were going to retrieve them once they got there.

"Get off the beach and into the trees as quick as you can!" yelled Lieutenant Arthur "Scoop" Adams, our platoon leader. "Dig in, form a skirmish line, and hold your ground against whatever comes!"

Oh sure! I thought. *Fat chance!* But I took a firm grip on my '03 Springfield, waved my squad forward, and ran for the trees like I was told. So did everybody else. That's what Marines do.

It was August 7, 1942—eight months to the day since the Japs had pulled their sneak attack on Pearl Harbor and crippled our Pacific Fleet. That "stab in the back," as the newspapers called it, made the American people madder than hell. They were aching to strike back, but I think it also made them feel more scared and helpless than anything that had ever happened before.

Back in April, we'd started making the Nip bastards pay for what they'd done when our Army pilots gave them a wake-up call by bombing Tokyo. Then, in June, our Navy and Marine fliers had kicked their butts and sunk their carriers in the Battle of Midway.

Now we were finally ready to get after the Japs on the ground—if we could find the so-and-sos. By landing on Guadalcanal, the First Marine Division was carrying out the first amphibious assault by U.S. forces since the Spanish-American War. But so far, this invasion was no big deal. Hell, a Girl Scout troop could've made the landing we'd just made!

If there were any Japanese soldiers on the island, they were totally silent—and invisible.

The beach where we landed was very narrow. A fringe of coconut palms started maybe fifteen or twenty yards from the water's edge, and within another ten yards or so, we were facing a wall of brushy jungle undergrowth.

Our first objective was a low ridge that rose up about a hundred yards inland. We had to hack our way to it through the bushes, but once we got there, it gave us a natural line of defense with a good view of the beach.

We started digging foxholes as fast as we could while some of the guys took cover in the trees and brush and kept their eyes on the jungle and their rifles at the ready. Other guys hacked at the undergrowth with bayonets and machetes, but it took a lot of hacking to make even a small dent in the stuff. I borrowed a shovel from one of the guys keeping watch. We saw nothing, and the only sounds we heard were our own grunts and heavy breathing from all that digging.

We knew from our maps that Guadalcanal was a pretty damn big island—roughly ninety miles long from east to west and thirty miles wide from north to south. It lies near the southwest end of the Solomon Islands chain, and it had been a British possession until the Japs decided to invade it in the spring of 1942. As it turned out, that was one of the worst mistakes they made in the war. But when we decided to go in and take it back, that came awful close to being just as big a mistake.

According to our intelligence, which wasn't exactly famous for its accuracy, the only fortified or inhabited areas of Guadalcanal were along a strip of the north-central coastline. That was where the unfinished Jap airfield that was our first main objective was located.

There were some small native settlements scattered over the rest of the island, but it was mostly an uninhabited wilderness of impenetrable jungles and rugged mountains. As far as we knew, the nearest enemy troops could be anywhere on it. They might be a two-day hike away, or they might be hiding just a few yards into the undergrowth. It didn't make you feel very secure to think about it.

We paused now and then to look at each other, shake our heads, and ask a question that none of us could answer:

"Where the hell are the Japs?"

WE DIDN'T GET a bite to eat that first day on Guadalcanal. That was the bad news. If the Japs had been close enough, they could've heard guys' stomachs growling like banshees up and down the line. By late afternoon, we were even running low on water because of the heat.

We'd been served the traditional "warrior's meal" of steak and eggs for breakfast that morning aboard ship. But that had been the middle of the night—about 2 AM—and by sundown that evening it was nothing but a distant memory.

The only casualty in the Fifth Marines that day was when some hungry private tried to stab a hole in a coconut with his bayonet to get at the meat and milk inside and cut his hand.

I guess that was the good news.

There was a really bad shortage of food on Guadalcanal, and for reasons I'll explain later, it lasted long after that first day. We didn't know it then, but K/3/5 would be fighting on Guadalcanal for over four months, and we stayed hungry most of the time.

A well-known author named Eric Hammel wrote a book about the Guadalcanal campaign more than forty years after the battle. He called it *Guadalcanal: Starvation Island*. As far as I'm concerned, he hit the nail right on the head.

Except for millions of coconuts on thousands of coconut trees, the only edible things I ever saw growing on the island were some stunted pineapples and a tree full of limes. Once in a while I saw a

Marine with a stalk of bananas, but I never knew where they came from, and I never actually saw any bananas growing on trees.

We never got lunch the whole time we were there, and our breakfasts were mostly black coffee and nothing else. Our only real meal was at night, and we wouldn't have had that during those first few weeks if we hadn't found several tons of rice the Japs had stored near the airfield and left behind.

About 12:30 PM that first day—right in the middle of our "lunchless hour"—we saw our first Jap air raid. Their planes flew right over our positions. There were thirty or forty of them, and they were less than a hundred feet off the ground. But they didn't even slow down or take a second look at us. They were after our ships out in the Sealark Channel.

We stopped digging in long enough to watch the fireworks. We'd been trained to hit the deck when enemy planes showed up, but I could see hundreds of Marines up and down the beach just standing there gawking at the planes like they were watching a damn ball game. You'd have thought they were in the bleachers at Yankee Stadium, for Pete's sake. If any of those Jap Zeros had decided to make a few strafing runs along the shoreline, it could've been one helluva slaughter.

Fortunately, the Nip pilots ignored us completely. They didn't even do much damage to our ships in that first raid. Not a single one of our ships was sunk in that raid, and only one destroyer was damaged. But, of course, from our vantage point we couldn't see anything that was going on in the channel. All we saw was the Jap planes flying over.

The biggest problem for us, though, wouldn't come clear until later. It was that the raid kept a lot of our supplies from getting ashore where we could get to them. Many of the supply ships quit unloading and got under way. They didn't want to be stationary targets for the Jap bombers, and this interrupted the whole process.

There were tons of stuff already piled up along the beach, but we didn't know where it was or what it was or which part was ours. Even if we had, we didn't have enough manpower to go out and haul it in—not when we needed to work on our defenses at the same time.

That night, I talked with Lieutenant Adams and a few of the other NCOs about what we were going to do the next day. We still didn't have any chow, so we exercised our jaws by talking.

"Where do we go from here?" I asked the lieutenant. "Are we just gonna sit tight and wait for the Nips to come at us or what?"

He shrugged. "Just set up your line and make sure it's solid for tonight. Then we'll talk again in the morning. Captain Patterson's probably waiting to hear from battalion, and battalion's waiting to hear from Colonel Hunt at regiment. Nobody expected the Japs to pull a disappearing act like this. We'll probably send out some patrols tomorrow, but my guess is we won't do much till after the First Marines take the airfield."

The division's first major objective was to grab the airfield that the Japs had been building—but hadn't had time to finish—near the north coast of Guadalcanal. We didn't know it at the time, but that always turned out to be the First Marine Division's first objective on every Jap-held island we hit.

Those Jap airfields worried General "Dugout Doug" MacArthur a lot. He couldn't rest easy at his fancy headquarters in Australia until we converted them to American airfields.

"So should I plan on taking a patrol out tomorrow?" I asked.

"Just sit tight, Mac, and tell your guys to stay on their toes," the lieutenant said. "If I hear anything, I'll let you know."

I want to make it clear right now that Lieutenant Adams was a terrific officer and an all-around good guy. He wasn't the kind of officer to hide out in a command post forty or fifty yards to the rear. He stayed right up there on the front line with the rest of us and even did some of the digging.

He'd picked up that "Scoop" nickname—which became his code name, too—because he'd studied journalism in college and wanted to be a newspaper reporter. There was a good reason that all our officers had code names. If the troops had called them by their rank or used the word "sir" in conversation during combat, it would've been like pasting a big bull's-eye on their backs if the Japs overheard.

Anyway, I've never known an officer who was closer to his men than Lieutenant Adams. He was from a small town named Beacon in upstate New York, and he wasn't a big guy. Only about five-ten and 165 pounds. But there was something athletic about the way he moved, and he was always on the alert. When he walked, he had a habit of glancing over his shoulder to see what was behind him. There was no way in hell you were going to sneak up on him.

I'd admired him ever since I first met him back at New River in North Carolina. Even after he chewed me out good—and rightfully so—for coming back early from a patrol, I still admired him. And I'm not exaggerating when I say I would've followed him anywhere.

So when he told me just to sit tight, I took him at his word.

I GUESS WE SHOULD'VE been thankful the Japs stayed out of our way for a while. If they'd attacked in force that first night, we'd have been in a real pickle with that one precious unit of fire.

K/3/5 and the rest of the Third Battalion, Fifth Marines were strung out along the beach with our backs to Sealark Channel. Our lines ran east to west for about 1,000 yards, then south through a coconut grove and some rugged woods for another 100 yards or so. Then they followed an open ridge that went on farther east. The division headquarters was about 800 yards west of the west end of our line and about 500 yards inland from the sea.

To our right, on the east side of the airfield, we had the First Marines dug in along the Lunga River. There was no way we could fill the long gap between our lines and the perimeters where the First had their three battalions drawn up in circle-the-wagons style, like in the Old West.

I'd estimate it was four or five miles from where our lines ended to where the First's perimeters were set up, and we didn't have nearly enough troops to cover that much distance. When our ships took off that first day to get away from the Jap planes, it didn't help that they took a bunch of Marines with them who were badly needed ashore. We didn't have enough troops to man our defenses adequately, much less pitch in and try to unload and distribute supplies.

From where I sat, that left us uncomfortably close to being up shit creek without a paddle.

I SHARED A FOXHOLE that night with PFC Bill Landrum, an assistant squad leader from Tallahassee, Florida. He was a good Marine who'd been in the Corps a little longer than I had. But even under normal circumstances, he was a quiet guy who never seemed to have much to say. That night, he was quieter than usual.

I was, too. I guess both of us were thinking about people and things that were far, far away. I told him I'd take the first watch and for him to try to get some sleep. Pretty soon, he was snoring, and I was alone, staring into the darkness in front of me.

The longer I stared, the more I started seeing things. Phantom things that weren't really there. And I could tell that other guys up and down the line were doing the same thing.

Now and then, I'd hear some trigger-happy Marine fire a round or two from his '03 at something he thought he saw moving in the brush, and when one guy opened up, others around him tended to follow suit. This wasn't very wise use of our limited ammo supply, but the jitters that caused it were understandable. Several times, I barely kept myself from joining in, but I managed to hold my fire.

My mind was pretty much blank for a while. Then I started thinking about my mother and sister back home in Brooklyn. I could never forget how tough a life my mom had led when I was a kid. In a way, it had been as tough as the lives of any of the Marines around me.

Ever since I'd joined the Corps, I'd been sending almost half of my monthly paycheck home to Mom. It had cramped me a little to do it, especially when I was still stateside and getting weekend liberties. But since shipping out for the Pacific in May of '42, I hadn't had much need for money—not nearly as much as Mom and my sister, Lillian. (Actually, my mother's name was Lillian, too, but to me she was always just Mom.)

For as long as I can remember, my mother always had to struggle financially. She worked long hours and cut every corner she could, but it seemed like there was never enough money to go around. That was one of the things that started me thinking about joining the service.

I'd thought about it for several years, and when I was sixteen, I asked Mom to let me join the Navy. At the time, she said "nothing doing" and refused to sign the papers. But four years later, she agreed to sign for me if I was still determined to enlist. By then, I guess she knew it was only a few weeks till my twenty-first birthday, anyway. Then I'd be old enough to enlist without her permission. I wouldn't have wanted to do it, but I probably would have joined anyway.

That first night on Guadalcanal was one of those times when you start mulling over stuff like that and piecing parts of your past together. Then the next thing you know, you're asking yourself how you ended up in such a dangerous, uncomfortable, foodless hellhole in the first place.

After a while, my thoughts drifted to Charlie Smith, my best friend as a kid back in Brooklyn. Charlie and I had joined the Marines together on the same day, and I started wondering where he might be right now. We wanted to stay together in the same outfit, but we'd gotten separated after boot camp, and Charlie had moved around a lot since then.

The last I'd heard, he was somewhere in the South Pacific with the Second Marines. By now, I thought he might've been on American Samoa. A bunch of Marines had been sent there because the brass thought it might be the Japs' next target.

The actual truth, though, was that Charlie was on one of those islands just across Sealark Channel from where I was sitting on Guadalcanal at that very moment. Of course, I didn't know that at the time.

When we were in our teens, Charlie and I talked for months about joining the Army. Finally, after Mom gave in and agreed to sign for me, we got up enough nerve to take a bus and then a train to the recruiting station on Broadway in downtown Manhattan. I never knew why, but the Army recruiting office was closed that day. So we went up to the Navy Building at 90 Church Street, where a middle-aged Marine sergeant in dress blues talked us into joining the Corps.

Looking back on it, it must've been fate.

The recruiting posters never showed any Marines in sweaty green dungarees with mud up to their ears. They were always dressed to the nines in those snazzy dress blues. Charlie and I could picture ourselves strutting down Broadway in those knocked-out uniforms. That convinced us on the spot that we wanted to be Marines.

When we walked out of the recruiting depot, a bunch of young guys started yelling at us from across the street. I guess they could tell what we'd just done by the looks on our faces.

"You'll be sorr-eee!" they said. "You'll be sorr-eee!"

I had plenty of reasons to remember that on my first night at Guadalcanal.

I didn't have the foggiest idea what was going to happen next. None of us did. By this time tomorrow, we might all be dead. Or we might still be in this same exact spot, wishing for more water and ammo and something to eat.

All I knew for sure was that I was squatting in a foxhole listening to Bill Landrum snore. I'd never had enough money to buy myself a set of dress blues, and I doubted if I ever would. Unless they were bayonet-proof and bulletproof, they wouldn't have done me much good where I was right now. I'd have traded them in a minute for some C rations and another unit of fire.

I squeezed my '03 Springfield with both hands and went on

staring into the darkness. And like a lot of other guys around me were probably doing at that exact moment, I kept hearing the same stupid question repeating itself in my head like a stuck record:

Okay, so how the hell DID I end up in this godforsaken place, anyway?

2

ALWAYS A MARINE AT HEART

I **WAS BORN ON** September 30, 1919, in a hospital at Seventh Avenue and Seventh Street in South Brooklyn, New York.

When I think back over all the years since then, I honestly believe I was always a Marine at heart. Even before I had any idea what a Marine really was—or ever even heard the word "Marine"—I think it was what I wanted to be. I just didn't know what to call it back then.

I'm Irish to the core on both sides of my family. My Grandpa and Grandma McEnery were both born in Ireland, but by the time they got married in 1888, they'd crossed the Atlantic and settled in Brooklyn. Grandma McEnery died in childbirth before I was born, and I didn't see Grandpa McEnery very often when I was a kid because he lived clear over on the other side of Brooklyn from me.

On the other hand, my grandparents on my mother's side were always around. The first place I clearly remember as home was the neighborhood of Gerritsen Beach that began developing on the east side of Brooklyn near Jamaica Bay right after World War I. When I was real small, Mom's parents, Grandpa and Grandma Daniels, lived just a few blocks away from us. But when I was about eleven, my mother and father separated, and she and my sister and I had to move in with Mom's parents in a house at 109 Gain Court in Gerritsen Beach.

If I went back looking for it today, I'd probably have a hard time finding it, but it wouldn't surprise me much if it's still there. Most of the streets have the same names, and many of the old houses are still standing.

The neighborhood—I don't think anybody calls it Gerritsen Beach anymore—was a remote place at that time. It wasn't really like part of the city at all, and it was a long bus and train ride to the older, more established sections of Brooklyn. The neighborhood faced a beach along Jamaica Bay with a swamp on the east side that was eventually filled in by dredging silt from the bay. Then the swamp became a big park with baseball and football fields, playgrounds, and basketball courts.

I spent hundreds of hours playing in that park, and the name they gave it was kind of prophetic where I was concerned. They called it Marine Park.

There was a creek nearby where saltwater from the ocean mingled with freshwater before it emptied into the bay. In the winter, the freshwater would freeze into big chunks of ice that floated in the saltwater. At low tide, there'd be five or six rows of those big ice chunks left grounded at the mouth of the creek, each of them about a foot thick. Then, when the tide started to come back in, the neighborhood kids would make a game out of jumping from one chunk to another as they started to float out into the bay.

We'd walk down the rows of chunks that were on land, but as they started to float, you had to be careful. You had to be fast enough to jump from piece to piece as they moved out toward the main floe where the creek and the bay met. If you stayed on a piece of ice too long, it would sink underneath you. Then you'd find yourself dunked in the ice-cold water. We thought it was fun. We were a little crazy, I guess.

To give you an idea of how far off the beaten path the neighborhood was back in the 1920s, rumrunners would sometimes slip into the creek off Jamaica Bay at night to unload their illegal booze. They'd hire some of the guys from the neighborhood to help them put the stuff in hospital ambulances, which was how they delivered it to their customers' warehouses. Those were Prohibition times, and rum-running was big business.

It was a violent business, too. One time when I was about eight or nine, the cops tried to intercept a boatload of bootleg hooch down at the creek, and a big gun battle broke out. I don't know how many cops and rumrunners got shot, but I remember it scared the pants off one of my girl classmates and her family who lived close by. The girl's mother made the kid lie down on the floor and put a mattress over her to protect her from stray bullets.

On the west side of Gerritsen Beach was a housing development that had been built in three sections. Gerritsen Avenue was the main street and the only way into the neighborhood by land. Knapp Street and Avenue U were other major streets that led down to the water.

In the early spring, all us boys would sneak down Knapp Street, climb over a fence, shed our clothes and hide them, and jump in the creek. We almost froze our butts off. All of us would turn blue from the cold, but we didn't care as long as we could claim the honor of being the first ones to take a dip that year.

THE HOUSE WHERE I lived with my mother and father and sister before we moved in with my grandparents was a small, single-story frame with barely enough room for the four of us. We were poor as a bunch of church mice, as the saying goes, but Gerritsen Beach was far from being a wealthy neighborhood. Most of the people who lived there were first- or second-generation immigrants from Europe, and most of them were just as poor as we were.

It was what you'd call a blue-collar neighborhood. Most families struggled to make ends meet, even in the 1920s when times were pretty good. When the Depression set in, times got a whole lot harder.

ONE DAY WHEN I was about seven years old, I saw something that left a deep impression on me. It must've been Armistice Day of 1926. Everybody celebrated Armistice Day back then, much more than they do Veterans Day now. They wore poppies and held parades and sang songs like "Over There" and "It's a Long Way to Tipperary."

There was a parade that day that ended with some kind of ceremony on the grounds of the Lutheran church in Gerritsen Beach. That was where I saw my first military uniform.

The man who was wearing it was really old, and somebody said he was a veteran of the Civil War. But he stood up straight and erect when he saluted the American flag, and I could tell he was proud of the uniform he wore. It was a lighter color than the dark blue uniforms most Union soldiers wore in the Civil War, and it had to be at least sixty years old, but it still looked good. I really admired that uniform, and I thought how great it would be to have one like it.

I never saw that old soldier again, but I thought about him a lot after that day, and I never forgot him. Seeing him in that uniform started me thinking about what it would be like to be a soldier.

I could picture myself marching in parades where crowds would be cheering and waving flags. I could see medals being pinned on me by some big-shot general, and I thought how much fun that would be. But the best part would be getting to wear a uniform like that old soldier's every day.

I want a uniform just like that, I said to myself, *and one of these days, I'm gonna get me one.*

I guess maybe every boy feels that way at some point. The difference for me was I never got over it. As a seven-year-old kid, I didn't stop to think that soldiering would be dangerous work, much less that you could get killed doing it. All I thought about was the glamour and excitement. I was what you'd call gung ho before that term was even invented.

And when I look back on that Armistice Day, I'm pretty sure that's where it all started. I think I was destined to be in the military from the first minute I saw that old soldier until I actually joined the Marines thirteen years later.

•   •   •

FOR AS FAR back as I can remember, I was a scrappy kind of kid. I never went around looking for trouble, but I never dodged a challenge or ducked a fight, either.

One fight I especially remember was when I was in the fifth grade at good old P.S. 194. There was this other kid in my class who was kind of pushy and a show-off. He seemed to think he was better than all the rest of us, and he liked to boss other kids around. One day, he started smarting off at me until he really got on my nerves bad, and we ended up slugging it out in a vacant lot. I gave him a pretty good licking, and he didn't act so high and mighty after that.

I enjoyed the bumps and bruises of competitive sports, too. I got a kick out of testing my strength and skill against other guys my age, maybe even older. I liked soccer and baseball just fine, but football was always my biggest favorite.

When I was about ten, I got invited to join a kid football team called the Dragons. After that, I played every season, either with the Dragons or another team called the Huskies, until the year before I joined the Marine Corps. They weren't school teams, just groups of neighborhood guys who got together and challenged anybody we could find to play us. We had some fierce rivalries, and sometimes over a hundred people would come out to watch our games.

We didn't have much in the way of equipment, just a few well-worn leather helmets and shoulder pads, but I truly believe the caliber of football we played was comparable to what small colleges played at the time. I played until I was twenty years old, and I figured anything was better than having to sit on the sidelines for part of a game. My goal was to play every down—the whole sixty minutes. I never hesitated to try to tackle a guy twice my size, and sometimes

I succeeded. I guess I was lucky I never got hurt. Banged up a little, but never really hurt.

At first, I switched positions quite a bit. Sometimes I played in the backfield, sometimes on the line, and always on both offense and defense. There was no such thing as two-platoon football in Gerritsen Beach.

Later on, I settled in at right end and played that same position for several years. By then, I was almost six feet tall, but I was still kind of skinny—only 155 pounds dripping wet. I got to where I liked defense best because I got a real kick out of rushing the quarterback. I'd just lower my head and run straight at him as hard as I could go. I usually didn't get there, but sometimes I did, and it gave me a good feeling.

ON SOME DAYS in the hot part of the summer, I stayed on the beach from sunup till dark. Lots of the other kids did, too. The beach ran for a mile or more from north to south. It was a great place to swim, or dig for clams, or just lie in the sun. And sometimes we'd find really interesting stuff that drifted up on the shore. Even during the cooler part of the year, I spent lots of time fishing—not just for sport but to help put food on the family table—and I hardly ever came home without a pretty good catch.

In July and August, bluefish came into the bay by the thousands, and even at other times there were plenty of fish called flukes. They were flat like flounder, but some of them got huge—up to three feet long. When they got that big, we called them doormats. A whole family could eat off one of them for two or three days.

Much as I loved that beach on Jamaica Bay, I didn't feel the same about any of the beaches I landed on in the Pacific. On the contrary, I wanted to get the hell away from them as fast as I could.

I WOULDN'T SAY I was the "churchy" type as a kid, but I did go to church almost every Sunday. My mom had to work on Sundays if she wanted to keep her job, so she hardly ever got to go to mass herself. But she was a devout Irish Catholic mother who wouldn't take excuses for my sister and me not going. She always made sure we had clean clothes to wear and a dime or two for the collection plate, and we knew better than to skip. If we did, Mom was bound to find out.

As somebody who maybe got into more than my share of scrapes, I got acquainted with the confessional booth at an early age. But the priest at Resurrection Catholic Church usually let me off fairly easy when it came to doing penance.

"Just do one 'Our Father,'" he'd say, "and that should take care of it."

That meant repeating the Lord's Prayer all the way through one time. It was the lowest penance there was for committing a minor sin like punching some other guy on the football field.

That was something else I thought a lot about at Guadalcanal. I must've said the Lord's Prayer a couple thousand times while I was there. I started that very first night.

WHEN I WAS about twelve years old, my father, Thomas McEnery, died of pneumonia. He was only thirty-four, but he'd led a hard life. A hard-drinking life, I'm sad to say. It was probably the booze as much as the pneumonia that killed him.

By the time Dad died, my mom had left him because of his heavy drinking. It was during Prohibition, but he never had a problem keeping himself supplied with alcohol. He made his own whiskey in a still in the back room of our house. He was a mechanic by trade, and he made fairly good money when he was sober enough to work, but that was less and less often as time went by.

My mom was commuting up to an hour and a half a day by bus and train to a job as a clerk in a candy store at Prospect Park in Brooklyn. But the paychecks she brought home weren't nearly enough to cover the bills. Before she left Dad, we were forced to move several times because we couldn't pay the rent. We lived on Knapp Street for a while, then on Gerritsen Avenue. Honest to God, I lost count of the places we lived before Mom finally took my sister and me and moved in with her parents.

By that time, we were so broke we didn't know where our next meal was coming from. I had really mixed-up feelings about Dad when we moved off and left him. I was mad at him for being such a drunk and making life so hard for Mom, but I worried about him, too. Of course, there was nothing I could do to help him. By then, nobody could help him.

A little over a year after Dad died, I graduated from the eighth grade at P.S. 194. By then, times were about as bad as they could get. It was the spring of 1932—rock bottom of the Depression—and the only thing that kept us afloat was Mom's piddling little salary and my grandparents' generosity.

Instead of going on to a regular high school, I decided to enroll in a trade school that promised the students good-paying jobs in the aviation industry after graduation. I stuck it out there for six terms, picking up a few dollars here and there at little part-time jobs like delivering messages for Western Union in what spare time I had. But I still lacked two terms to graduate when we couldn't come up with the rest of the tuition money. Then I had to drop out and look for a full-time job.

By this time, my mother had gotten married again to a Polish guy named Peter Paul Muroski, who lived just a few blocks away, and we'd moved in with him. Mom was a fine woman, but she sure didn't have much luck when it came to picking a husband. My stepfather was an even worse drunk than Dad had been—and a mean one at that. Dad was never abusive. He'd just pass out peacefully after he got a snootful, whereas Peter would get really ugly.

But Peter did have a nice little son named Peter Jr. Bad as his father acted, I always loved the kid. I called my brother "Junior" and tried to treat him the way a brother should. If he'd been my full brother, I couldn't have loved him more.

Dad was the kind of guy who wouldn't hurt a fly, but Peter Sr. could lose his temper over anything. On Tuesday nights after he got his weekly paycheck, he'd mix up some kind of drink with alcohol he bought from under the counter at a drugstore. Within an hour, he'd be skunk-drunk, and he'd think up some reason to get mad at Mom. He'd start threatening to knock her around, and more than once he actually did.

One evening when I was fifteen, I came home from trade school to find Peter chasing Mom through the house and threatening to kill her. He sounded like he really meant it, and it scared the hell out of me. My sister was jumping around in the background and screaming bloody murder, and Peter Jr. was hiding someplace.

As I ran through the kitchen after Peter Sr. and Mom, I threw down a cup of milk I was carrying and grabbed up the first thing I could get my hands on to conk him with. It was an electric coffeepot made out of crockery that Mom had gotten with some coupons she'd saved up, and it must've weighed three or four pounds.

"You leave my mom alone," I yelled at Peter, "or I'll bust you with this thing!"

"Like hell you will, you little shit," he said and started toward me.

I swung the coffeepot and smacked him pretty good with it. I wasn't sure exactly where I hit him, but I knew I hit him hard.

He let out a groan and fell on the floor with blood spurting all over the place. I couldn't believe how fast the blood ran down his neck and onto his shirt, and I was afraid for a second that I'd cut his jugular vein.

Oh my God! I thought. *Maybe I've killed the son of a bitch, and they'll send me to the electric chair!*

Then I heard Peter cussing and saw him trying to get up, so I knew he wasn't dead. But he wasn't in real great shape, either, and the next thing I thought about was trying to get an ambulance.

We couldn't afford a telephone, and the nearest one was two blocks down the street at a neighbor's house. By the time I ran all the way there as hard as I could go and called for an ambulance, I was shaking all over. When the ambulance showed up a few minutes later, a cop was following along behind it. I shook even worse when my mother told the cop what happened.

"Is he gonna die?" I asked the cop.

"Nah, he'll be okay," the cop said. "He's bound to have one helluva headache, though. You sure put a dent in his hard head."

"Are you gonna take me to jail?" I asked.

The cop laughed and shook his head. "No, son. All you were doing was trying to protect your mother. From what she tells me, it was self-defense all the way."

Peter ended up with a J-shaped scar right in the middle of his forehead. From then on, he stayed out of my way, and I stayed out of his. And as far as I know, he never threatened Mom or chased her through the house again.

I thought a lot about that stuff with Mom and Peter and Dad and Peter Jr. on that first night at Guadalcanal. I knew I still had some anger toward my dad bottled up inside me for all the misery he caused Mom, but I felt sad about what happened to him, too.

I made a pledge to myself that, if I ever had a wife, I'd never treat her the way Mom was treated, and I believe I've kept that pledge. If any good came out of me busting Peter with that coffeepot, I guess that was it. Plus it taught me later on to keep strict limits on my own drinking. A beer or two was okay, but I always seemed to have a sixth sense that warned me when to stop.

The way I figured it, having two drunks in the family was more than enough.

AFTER I DROPPED OUT of trade school, I wanted to join the Navy. But I was still a few months shy of my seventeenth birthday, and Mom refused to sign for me. I fussed and pleaded, but she wouldn't change her mind.

Maybe she really thought I was too young, or maybe she just wanted to keep me around for a while longer to keep Peter in line. Whichever it was, Mom's refusal turned out to be a lucky break for our whole family. After many months of searching for work, I finally landed a great job as a shipping clerk for a company that manufactured ink pens.

I had to pinch myself to make sure I wasn't dreaming when they told me the salary was fifteen dollars a week. It was like a miracle. There were plenty of guys twice my age who weren't making that much, and it was a godsend for me and Mom and my sister. I was so happy about the job that I almost quit thinking about joining the service for a while. But after the fall of 1939, when the war started in Europe, my friend Charlie Smith and I started talking about enlisting again, this time in the Army.

A private's pay in the Army was only twenty-one dollars a month, which was just about a third of what I was making at the pen company. But all my food, clothes, and housing would be paid, and I could send part of my paycheck home to Mom every month. Every time I saw Charlie, he brought it up, and the more we talked, the more I wanted to do it.

Finally, we did.

LIKE I SAID, I think it was sheer fate that the Army recruiting office was closed the day we went to enlist. I never could figure out why it was closed; it just was. It wasn't a holiday of any kind, and there was a steady stream of guys trying to join up. I think it happened because I was meant to be a Marine—even if I did have some second thoughts about it later.

The Marines didn't give me and Charlie much time to wind up our affairs as civilians before they shipped us off to boot camp. In Europe, World War II had been going on for over a year. Hitler's troops had marched into Paris and taken over France. Now they were bombing the hell out of London. Everybody in New York was talking about it and wondering when the Nazis were going to invade England. From the way they talked, it could happen any day.

"You think they'll send us over to fight with the Limeys?" I asked Charlie.

He shook his head. "I think we'll end up in the Pacific," he said.

That Charlie! He was some kind of prophet!

We enlisted on the Friday before the Labor Day weekend in 1940. They gave us the weekend and the holiday off, but they told us to be back Tuesday morning to be sworn in. Right after we took the oath, a sergeant took us to the nearest subway station and we rode over to the Hudson River, where a civilian passenger liner was docked, and we went aboard. As I remember, there were seventeen of us in the group, all from New York or northern New Jersey.

We were on the ship for three days, heading south in the Atlantic. The weather was perfect the whole time, and so was the way we were treated while we were aboard. Charlie and I had our own private stateroom, and the meals were great. We had the run of the ship just like the civilian passengers. We were allowed to dance and buy drinks and even play the slot machines in the casino. The problem was, none of us had any money.

I'd never been much for getting up early. In fact, I'd always hated it before, but on that trip, I got up every morning at daybreak to look out at the ocean. Sometimes I saw whales and porpoises playing around. That fascinated me.

Our pleasure cruise ended when the ship docked at Savannah, Georgia. It was the first time I'd ever set foot in a southern state. Then they put us on a bus and took us to Parris Island, South

Carolina, over a new road that had just been built through the biggest swamp I ever saw.

Unfortunately, though, there was plenty of swamp left, and I think we slogged through every foot of it during the two months we were there.

It rained just about every day at Parris Island, and there were millions of mosquitoes. I'd never seen such big, bloodthirsty mosquitoes in my life. There was a joke that made the rounds about these two giant mosquitoes who picked up a Marine recruit and looked him over as they got ready to drain his blood.

"Maybe we should carry this one down to the swamp and save him for later," one mosquito said.

"Oh, no," said the other mosquito. "If we do that, the big ones will take him away from us."

ALTHOUGH I BELIEVE I was destined to be a Marine, I didn't know anything about the Corps and its traditions when I first joined. The first time I heard somebody say "Semper Fidelis," which is the Marine motto, I thought they said "seventy-five dollars," and I said, "I'll take it!" No kidding.

I got away with that without getting slugged, but I probably shouldn't have. "Semper Fidelis" is Latin for "Always Faithful." That's what Marines are expected to be, and they take it serious. Even when they shorten it to "Semper Fi," as they usually do, the meaning's still the same. It's a beautiful meaning, and it's no joking matter.

In fact, hardly anything in boot camp was a joking matter—and if it was, the joke was on you. There were all kinds of rules that had to be followed. Most of us "boots" broke at least a few of them, and when we did, we ended up in deep shit. But the important thing was, we learned to live by rules and not make the same mistakes again.

Charlie and I were now officially members of the First Recruit Battalion, Platoon 102, and we were about to learn a whole new language. The Marine NCO (noncommissioned officer) in charge of us was called a DI (for drill instructor). We were all a bunch of "boots" or "shitbirds," depending on the DI's mood at any given moment. He told us we'd damn well better learn to "listen up" so he didn't have to repeat an order. After getting our first "chow" (meal), we were each issued a uniform and a "bucket" (a pail containing a toothbrush, razor, soap, etc.). We also received a rifle (or "'03"), and heaven help any boot who ever called it a "gun."

Two favorite punishments for not following the rules were duck waddling and the belt line. In duck waddling, you squatted with your rifle held over your head and waddled around the marching platoon until the DI told you to stop. As for the belt line, the platoon lined up in two ranks with their belts in hand, and the boot who was being punished ran between them as fast as he could while they swatted at him with their belts.

There were other penalties that the DIs dreamed up as they went along. One day a boot passed wind while standing in formation, and the DI made him fall out of ranks, dig a hole with his bayonet in front of the whole platoon, and bury the fart. Once they'd been singled out for this kind of embarrassment, most guys would've rather exploded than pass gas while they were in formation.

One day at the rifle range, Charlie got in a mess of trouble for leaving the firing line with his rifle bolt closed. This was a definite no-no because the only way the rifle was completely safe to carry was with the bolt open. A gunnery sergeant (gunny) grabbed the rifle, jerked the bolt out, and threw it as far as he could down the rifle range. It took Charlie a good half-hour to track it down and clean all the dirt and debris off it.

To the average boot, stuff like this seemed like nitpicking or just plain meanness, at least at first. But there was a point to having so many rules and penalties. Everybody makes mistakes, but when you repeat a mistake in a combat situation, the penalty can be sudden death—yours or one of your buddies'. In a lot of cases on Guadalcanal, it was exactly that.

Boot camp was made up of two main parts—drilling and maneuvers. First, we'd march for God knows how many miles with rifles and full field gear. Then we'd crawl on our bellies while some guys fired streams of machine gun bullets a few inches above our heads.

Taking target practice at the rifle range was also part of our routine, and most of us were really terrible at it. Out of seventy-six men in Platoon 102, we didn't have a single one who qualified as expert, which was the highest rating. Only three qualified as sharpshooter, the second-highest rating, and only six others qualified at all. Part of the problem was the weather—lots of rain and wind—but even when we came back a second day, we still stunk up the joint.

I was kind of surprised that I managed to make marksman, the lowest qualifying rating, because I'd never fired anything bigger than a BB gun before joining the Marines.

•   •   •

ONE GOOD THING about boot camp is that you make some really good friends there. I was luckier than most guys because Charlie was there with me from the start, but another guy that I got to be really good friends with at Parris Island was Remi Balduck from Detroit, Michigan.

I spotted Remi right off the bat as a guy to watch. There were lots of clowns in boot camp, but Remi wasn't one of them. He was a year and a half older than me, and he acted a lot more mature than most of the rest of us. He was always careful not to do anything to get himself in trouble with a DI or any other NCO.

It wasn't that he was stiff-necked or didn't have a sense of humor. One day in the barracks, Charlie and I were horsing around, and I'd just busted a pillow wide open over Charlie's head. Feathers flew everywhere right before a lieutenant walked in for an inspection. Remi was usually pretty quiet, but that day he was laughing so hard at us he had to cover his face and turn the other way. Luckily, the lieutenant didn't even seem to notice the feathers.

After we finished boot camp, I was really glad when Remi and I were among just five guys from our recruit platoon assigned to guard duty at the Naval Operating Base in Norfolk, Virginia. Charlie was sent someplace else, but Remi and I pulled a bunch of liberties together at Norfolk. Sometimes we'd go with some other guys, but mostly it was just the two of us. We didn't do anything all that special, just went to the movies or out to eat or someplace for a couple of beers. I remember one night we went to see *Gone With the Wind* at the Grand Theatre. I never had much money to spend, but I always had fun with Remi.

He was one of the neatest, cleanest, soberest guys I ever knew. His uniform buttons were always perfectly buttoned. His boondocker shoes were always shined and properly tied. His bed was always made up just so, and when we were marching, he was never out of step. Everything about him was just plain sharp.

Remember those dress blue uniforms I told you about earlier? Well, not only did I never own a set of blues in my life, I only wore them one time. Remi was nice enough to let me borrow some blues he'd bought at Norfolk when I went home on leave to Brooklyn.

Then, God help me, I went to a dance one Saturday night and ended up getting in a fight with a civilian guy who kept spilling drinks on this girl I was dancing with. I decked the guy pretty good, but while I was doing it I ripped a seam out of that beautiful blue tunic of Remi's.

I really felt awful about it, so I took it to a tailor shop and got it fixed the best I could before I went back to the base. I don't think Remi ever noticed anything wrong. At least, he never said anything. But after that I decided one experience with dress blues was enough to last me a lifetime. Remi was the kind of guy who deserved a fancy uniform. I was better off in muddy-green dungarees.

Remi's family had come from Belgium originally, and he talked a lot about some of his uncles who'd been heroes fighting the Germans in World War I. I really enjoyed listening to the stories he told about them. I guess maybe heroism ran in Remi's family. He'd become a hero, too—a big enough hero to have a Navy ship named after him.

I'll tell you more about that later.

MOSTLY, IT WAS good duty at Norfolk, especially compared to what it was at Parris Island. Remi and I spent four hours on duty guarding the Naval Operating Base there and eight hours off when we were on our own. We spent a good bit of our off time sleeping, but the base had once been a summer resort, so there was a lot to do there and plenty of places for swimming, boating, picnicking, and otherwise enjoying the water.

Navy big shots were always showing up at the motor gate to the base where we manned a guard station. One day, a car pulled up with a Navy commander in the backseat. I went over and saluted him like I was supposed to do, and when he saluted me back, I saw it was the former world heavyweight boxing champion Gene Tunney.

Our commanding officer, Captain Saunders, organized a company baseball team, and I was on it. I alternated between playing second base and shortstop. We had a game about once a week against teams from other Army and Navy outfits.

All kinds of traffic came onto the base, including boxcars loaded with high-explosive ammo. It was clear to anybody on the base that we were sending war matériel to the British and tooling up for war ourselves. Meanwhile, according to the newspapers, the situation in Europe kept getting darker and darker.

IN JUNE 1941, the good duty at Norfolk came to an end for Remi and me. I was transferred to the Marine base at Quantico, Virginia, and Remi went somewhere else. Quantico was the home of the legendary Fifth Marines, who'd sailed from there to France in 1917 to become the American unit that was "first to fight" in World War I.

I was assigned to K Company, Third Battalion, Fifth Marines— K/3/5. It would be my home for the next two years and six months. On too many occasions to count, it would also come close to being the death of me.

At Quantico, I was reunited with my Brooklyn buddy Charlie Smith, but Charlie wasn't in K Company or even in the Third Battalion. He was in the First Battalion, Fifth, along with some other guys from old Platoon 102 at Parris Island. So I didn't see Charlie all that much, but it was still good to know he was around.

I hadn't really had any serious field training in boot camp, but now I started making up for it in a hurry. After a short stay at Quantico, we shipped out for amphibious maneuvers and made dozens of practice landings on beaches at New River, North Carolina. That was where Camp Lejeune would be built later to serve as the home of the First Marine Division, but it was nothing but a swampy wilderness then.

Sometimes we were the assault troops, and sometimes we were the defenders. In one landing, we hit the beach and stormed the defenders, and I discovered I was running straight at Charlie Smith, who was laughing like a damned hyena.

After we "killed" each other with our blank ammo, my assault team regrouped and moved inland, where we "attacked and seized" imaginary objectives. We ended the maneuvers with a simulated forced march that was much too real for comfort.

The landing areas at New River covered over 111,700 acres of shoreline, swamps, snakes, chiggers, and mosquitoes, and I think we covered them all. The biggest timber rattlesnake I ever saw was there.

Between landings, they sent me back up to Quantico for a few days to learn to fire the Thompson submachine gun. The first tommy gun I was assigned to was a 1928 Navy model, and it was a piece of junk. I had to aim it at the ground to have any hope of hitting the target.

Later, I was issued an Army model of the same 1928 weapon, and it was terrific. The difference between it and the Navy version was in the bolt, which was heavier in the Army model. It was a million times easier to handle under combat conditions, too. You could drop it in the water or roll it in the sand, then pick it up, and it would fire like nothing had happened.

I made sharpshooter with that Army model, and knowing how to use a tommy gun to maximum advantage would save my life more than once in the months to come.

Another good thing that happened when I went back to Quantico was that I met up again with Remi Balduck, my buddy from Parris Island and Norfolk. He was working on the same firing range where I was firing the tommy guns, and we had a chance to catch up on old times. But our reunion didn't last long, and then we shook hands and went our separate ways.

The following April, I got word that Remi had been shipped to American Samoa with the Seventh Marines, the first of the division's infantry regiments to reach full strength. As it turned out, those few days at Quantico would be the last time I ever saw him.

I made private first class before we left New River. I also survived epidemics of scarlet fever and meningitis that broke out among the troops while we were there.

But K/3/5 was headed for places and problems that would make what we went through at New River look like a Sunday School picnic.

Places like Guadalcanal.

IN THAT SUMMER of 1941, the newly created First Marine Division was just taking shape. It really was the first division ever organized in the history of the Marine Corps, and it was only five months old. It was born on February 1, 1941, at Guantánamo Bay, Cuba. Until then, throughout 166 years of Corps history, the largest Marine unit had been a regiment.

Besides the Fifth, there were only two other active regiments in the Corps at this time. One was the Sixth, based on the West Coast and sometimes called the "Hollywood Marines" because of the bit parts they played in some movies. The other was the Fourth, which was based in China and ended up fighting in the Philippines when the war started. Most other Marines were in small units scattered around the world.

But now the situation was changing fast. One new regiment, the Seventh, was split off from the Fifth, and another one, the First Marines, was activated about that same time. The division's artillery regiment, the Eleventh, was beefed up with new 105-millimeter field pieces to go with their old 75-millimeter pack howitzers.

The division was sure as hell in no shape to actually fight anybody at this point. All the companies were shorthanded, and none of them had functioning machine gun or mortar sections. We were short of everything, and what equipment we did have was left over from World War I. Those of us in the Fifth were called the "raggedy-ass Marines," and we lived up to—or down to—that description.

By the time the Japs hit Pearl Harbor on December 7, 1941, the Corps was growing at a frenzied pace, and the raid on Pearl kicked it into an even higher gear. On April 10, 1942, the Seventh Marines— with Remi Balduck among them—sailed for American Samoa to defend it against an expected attack by the Jap "supermen," who couldn't seem to be stopped anywhere.

Just a day before the Seventh Marines left the States, our forces on Bataan—over 70,000 American and Filipino troops—had surrendered to the Japs. This left only our guys on Corregidor still holding out, and in less than month, they'd have to surrender, too.

I can't tell you how much I admired those guys for the stand they put up. But my biggest heroes were the few hundred Marines on Wake Island who held out against a huge Jap force for sixteen days. They fought off a whole enemy invasion fleet and sank or damaged a bunch of enemy ships. I swore right then that I'd do everything I could to uphold the high standards they'd set for the rest of us in the Corps.

The British were catching it even worse in the Pacific than the Americans were. After they lost 180,000 troops at Singapore, Prime Minister Winston Churchill told President Franklin Roosevelt that "Fighting the Japanese soldier on land is like jumping into a pool full of sharks."

THE FIFTH MARINES were about to be next to take that jump.

On May 17, 1942, we went aboard the USS *Wakefield*, a refitted passenger liner formerly called the SS *Manhattan*. Three days later, we sailed out of Norfolk with a cruiser and four destroyers shielding us from German U-boats. We headed south through the Atlantic and the Caribbean, then took a hard right at the Panama Canal.

As we steamed southwest across the endless expanse of the Pacific, our cruiser and destroyers were nowhere in sight. We had six PT boats as an escort for three days. Then they disappeared, too. We were on our own.

Major General Alexander A. Vandegrift, commander of the First

Marine Division, and his whole division headquarters battalion were aboard the *Wakefield*. So we got the idea that—escort or no escort—wherever we were going was pretty damn important.

On June 14, after riding out a fierce storm in mid-Pacific, we docked at Wellington, New Zealand, where, it was announced, we were to train for six months.

Twelve days later, on June 26, the division received its orders: "Occupy and defend Tulagi and adjacent positions on Guadalcanal, Florida, and Santa Cruz Islands."

Our debarkation date was initially set for August 1. Then it was grudgingly moved back to August 7.

So, instead of having six months to get ready for the first U.S. offensive ground action of the Pacific war, we were actually getting just six weeks—including travel time.

And that, in so many words, is how I happened to be in that godforsaken place called Guadalcanal.

Along with the rest of K/3/5, I'd be there for a little over four months. They were four months that seemed more like four years.

When they were over, a lot of the guys I'd shared foxholes and swapped stories with were dead, and those of us who managed to leave Guadalcanal alive would never be the same again.

If there was any kid left in me, I lost him right there.

3

DISASTER AT SEA, SLAUGHTER ASHORE

AT FIRST LIGHT on August 8 (D-Day-plus-1), Lieutenant Adams got the word from K Company headquarters and passed it along to everybody in the First Platoon. "The whole company's going on a recon patrol as a unit," he said. "We'll check out the area to our immediate front. If everything looks okay, we may form a new line farther west."

The first thought that popped into my head was: *Oh crap, sounds like we're in for more digging!*

About 9 AM, we moved out and proceeded very cautiously to the southwest. Despite the fact that our mission was supposed to be strictly reconnaissance and not combat, we were all on high alert. But we still didn't see or hear any sign of enemy ground activity.

We advanced maybe 1,500 yards, using the undergrowth and coconut palms for cover and staying within sight of the beach. After that, we stopped for a break, then started retracing our path back toward our original defense line.

We were nearly there when a formation of Jap Zeros and Betty bombers suddenly showed up.

It was about 12:30 PM, almost exactly the same time as the first Nip air raid the day before. The Zeros were flying real low, and this time we had enough sense to either take cover or hit the deck where we were. But just like on the first raid, these planes didn't have the slightest interest in us. They were looking for bigger game out in Sealark Channel.

They never slowed down or gave us a second look, but one of the Zeros flew directly over me, and I swear he wasn't over fifteen or twenty feet above the tops of some of the coconut palms.

For a second, I could see the pilot as clear as if he was sitting across a table from me. He was the first Jap I'd ever gotten a close look at. He was wearing goggles, so I couldn't see his eyes, but the grin on his face looked like it was a foot wide.

So this is what a Jap looks like, I thought. *I wonder if the ones on the ground look the same way.*

The bombers did a little better job this time around than they had on their first raid. They brought the unloading of our supply ships to a standstill and scored a major hit on the USS *George Elliott*, a transport carrying most of the supplies intended for the Second Battalion, First Marines. They left the *Elliott* blazing from stem to stern. It was damaged too bad to be saved and finally had to be scuttled.

Except for that, nothing much happened on our patrol that

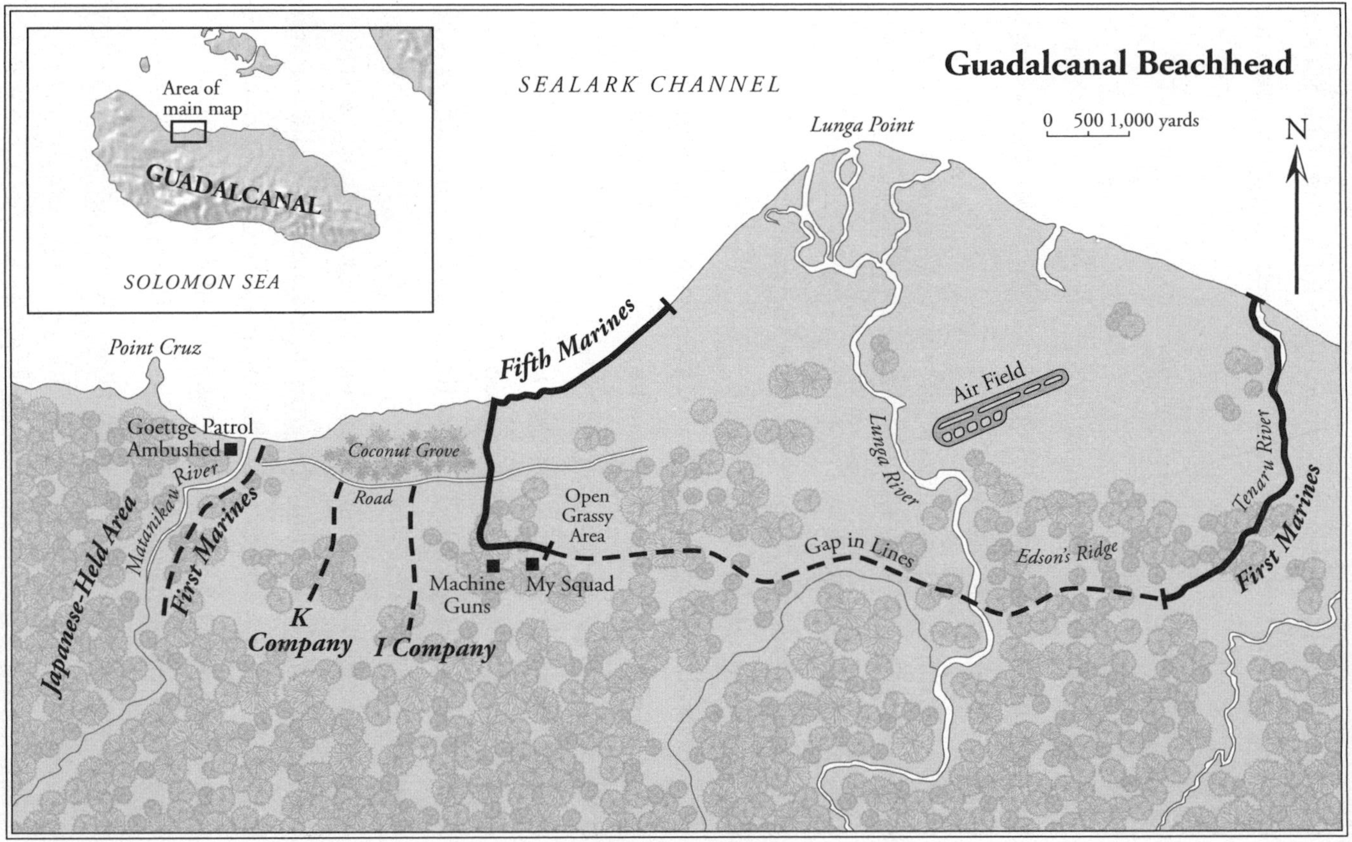
Guadalcanal Beachhead
SEALARK CHANNEL
0 500 1,000 yards
N
Area of
main map
GUADALCANAL
SOLOMON SEA
Lunga Point
Point Cruz
Fifth Marines
Air Field
Lunga River
Tenaru River
First Marines
Goettge Patrol
Ambushed
Matanikau River
Coconut Grove
Road
Open
Grassy
Area
Gap in Lines
Edson's Ridge
Machine
Guns
My Squad
K
Company
I Company
First Marines
Japanese-Held Area

second morning. We did manage to pick up a few supplies off the beach, but otherwise it was a dry run. By 1 PM, we were back at our original line and still waiting to see something happen on the ground.

WHILE WE WERE patrolling the beach, the First Marines were moving toward the airfield. Along the way, they made a couple of very important discoveries.

For one thing, the jungle undergrowth was almost impenetrable in some places. You could chop at it for hours and never seem to make any headway. There were giant trees in it with trunks as tough as steel and as wide as a tank was long with vines as thick as a man's thigh wrapped around them.

For another thing, the maps we'd been given were all fouled up. They weren't worth a damn for anything, except maybe toilet paper. If you tried to follow them, you were sure to get lost.

The First Marines' mission that day of seizing the airfield was a lot more critical than ours was in K/3/5. But because of the thick jungle and bad maps, the First got seriously bogged down on the way to their objective. That "Grassy Knoll" they were supposed to use as a landmark was actually a mountain named Mount Austen. It was four or five miles from where the maps showed it, and the area they were trying to march through was crisscrossed with rivers and streams that didn't show up on the maps at all.

Because of the delays, it was 4 PM by the time the First got the airfield secured, but what they found when they got there was real encouraging. The work the Japs had been doing on the field was almost finished. That meant our planes might be able to start flying missions from it in about a week, which was good news. The Marines also captured a lot of heavy equipment and supplies the Japs had left behind. They even took some prisoners, but most of them turned out to be Korean construction workers, not actual Nip combat troops.

The Koreans didn't have any great love for the Japs because they'd been brought to Guadalcanal by force and then had to work their butts off carving that airfield out of the jungle. So the Koreans didn't mind a bit telling our intelligence people everything they knew about how many Japs were on the island and where they'd gone. As a result, we got some very interesting information before the day was over.

According to the Koreans, there was nowhere near the 5,000 Nip troops—including a regiment of 2,100 infantry—we'd been told to expect on Guadalcanal. Except for two naval construction battalions with a total of around 1,800 men, there were actually fewer than 500 enemy combat soldiers there. And when our planes and ships started blasting the island, those had panicked and hauled ass to the west as fast as they could go.

What it added up to was the Marines' first victory on Guadalcanal. But we knew it was way too early to celebrate, and we didn't have time to do much of that, anyway.

After the news about the small number of Japs on the island reached Fifth Marines headquarters, Colonel Hunt got orders to contract our beachhead and advance west toward where the Japs were supposed to be. There was a road near the beach we could follow, and we were supposed to leave early the next morning, D-plus-2. En route, we were told to check out a village called Kukum and flush out any Japs that might be hiding there.

Suddenly, everything started looking a lot simpler—and easier—than it had that morning. We felt like we'd gotten a big break. All we had to do now to finish our job on Guadalcanal was find and take care of those few hundred Jap combat troops and get the airfield into operation. Then we could kiss this damn island goodbye and turn it over to the Army.

Boy, it looks like we've got this one made! we thought.

We never stopped to consider what might happen if the Japs launched an all-out naval attack on our ships in Sealark Channel. In two major air raids, they'd only put one of our ships out of commission, and we heard they'd lost twenty-five or thirty planes in the bargain. So with all the firepower our task force had available, we just assumed it wouldn't have much problem holding the Nip navy at bay.

But, my God, were we ever wrong!

On the night of August 8–9—before K/3/5 and the rest of the Third Battalion, Fifth, even got started on our new assignment—a powerful strike force of enemy ships left the Jap base at Rabaul and slipped down a sea lane through the Solomon Islands called the Slot. An hour or so before midnight, they attacked the task force of Allied cruisers and destroyers supporting our landings. Then all hell broke loose.

Those of us ashore thought at first it was a great American victory. That's how out of touch we were. We cheered like crazy when we saw the big guns flashing and heard the explosions far out in the channel. We were convinced our Navy brothers were giving the Japs an ass-kicking they'd never forget.

Instead, what we were watching was the worst American naval defeat since Pearl Harbor.

• • •

By LATE AFTERNOON on August 9, D-plus-2, we found out what really happened. As I remember hearing it, it went like this:

After the Jap air raid on August 8, Admiral Frank J. Fletcher, commander of the carrier task force providing air cover for the Guadalcanal operation, received some news that got him seriously worried. Reliable reports from Navy reconnaissance pilots to the northwest warned Fletcher about that large, mean-looking Jap strike force that was headed our way.

Fletcher notified Admiral Richmond K. Turner, the man in charge of the landings on Guadalcanal and the other islands, and told him that all U.S. aircraft carriers supporting the landings were going to be withdrawn that night. Fletcher said the carriers had to leave because they'd lost a bunch of planes and their supply of gasoline was running low.

But the main reason Fletcher was pulling his carriers out was this new threat from the approaching Jap strike force. Plus, there were other reports that a flock of Jap submarines was heading into the area.

Admiral Turner wasn't happy at all when he found out what was about to happen. In effect, he told Fletcher, "Hey, I'm not leaving my transports here as sitting ducks if you bug out and take away all our air cover."

Unless Fletcher changed his mind by 6 AM on August 9, Turner said he was ordering all his supply ships to safer waters, and they wouldn't be back till they were guaranteed to have air support. Whatever hadn't been unloaded by the time they left would just have to go with the ships.

At this point, close to half of the First Marine Division's total supplies and equipment were still aboard those ships in the channel. So you can imagine how upset General Vandegrift, our division commander, was when Turner broke the news to him at a meeting that night on Turner's flagship, the attack transport USS *McCauley*.

Vandegrift stayed aboard the *McCauley* arguing with Turner till almost midnight. The general said later he was "most alarmed" by Turner's decision. He said he did everything he could to make Turner realize what a disaster it would be for the Marines ashore if the transports pulled out half-unloaded and with several Marine units still aboard. But Turner refused to budge. He wouldn't change his mind.

Vandegrift felt like the Marines were being sold out—and rightly so—but Turner did have a point. If he hung around long enough to finish the job, he could lose every transport in the convoy. But his decision to pull out sure played hell with our hopes of making short work of the Guadalcanal campaign.

Fletcher took a lot of flak later on for not keeping his air cover in place, but maybe he had a point, too. The Navy had already lost one carrier at Midway and another one in the Battle of the Coral Sea, and Fletcher was scared shitless of losing a third one. If he had, it would've left only three U.S. carriers in the whole Pacific and given the Japs a big edge in naval airpower.

Still, it was pretty damn obvious that Fletcher thought more of his carriers than he did of the Marines he was leaving marooned in the middle of enemy territory.

As it happened, it was our fighting ships, not our transports, that took a battering from the Japs on the night of August 8–9 in what came to be called the Battle of Savo Island. Savo is a round chunk of land near the west end of Sealark Channel and about ten miles off the northwestern tip of Guadalcanal.

The Japs sank three of our heavy cruisers, the *Vincennes, Astoria,* and *Quincy,* and one Australian heavy cruiser, the *Canberra,* that night. A fourth U.S. heavy cruiser, the *Chicago,* was badly damaged, along with two of our destroyers, the *Patterson* and *Ralph Talbot.* A total of 1,077 American and Allied sailors and Marines were killed, and another 700 were wounded.

For some unknown reason, another damaged U.S. destroyer, the *Jarvis,* limped away alone from the Savo Island battle that night. I guess the *Jarvis's* captain had lost radio contact with the rest of the ships and was just trying to get the hell out of there.

Anyway, early on the afternoon of August 9, the *Jarvis* was spotted and sunk by Jap planes 130 miles southwest of Savo. None of her 160-man crew lived to tell about it, and nobody ever knew what happened to her until after the war.

Only three enemy ships—all cruisers—were even hit during the battle, and the damage they suffered was strictly the easy-to-repair kind. Jap casualties were just fifty-eight killed and seventy wounded.

After that terrible night, the brass changed the name of Sealark Channel to Iron Bottom Sound—for obvious reasons. Its floor was now paved with the wreckage of our ships.

THE ONLY THING that didn't go the Japs' way that night was that, by some good maneuvering and maybe a small miracle, Admiral Turner's transports, which were most likely the Jap strike force's main target, got away clean.

I found out later that as soon as Turner heard gunfire that night he ordered his ships to quit unloading and weigh anchor, and within five minutes they were all under way. To Turner's credit, though, his ships stayed in the area the rest of the night and part of the next day while he begged Admiral Fletcher again for air support that never came.

Visibility in the channel was close to zero that night, and Turner managed to stay out of harm's way by keeping his ships circling in the dense fog. The next morning, after the Jap strike force withdrew, his crews were able to unload quite a few supplies on Tulagi.

But any hope Turner had of unloading more stuff on Guadalcanal ended late on the afternoon of August 9, when he got reports of a huge flight of Jap bombers headed his way. About sunset, he gathered up his transports and sailed south as fast as he could go. He didn't stop till he got to the port of Noumea on the island of New Caledonia.

In case you're not too familiar with the geography of the South Pacific, New Caledonia lies off the east coast of Australia and more than 1,100 miles southeast of Guadalcanal.

There was no way we were going to see anything else of Turner's ships and the supplies they carried for a long, long time. We were being left high and dry, like they say.

In *The Old Breed*, author George McMillan's classic history of the First Marine Division, he put it this way: "The only sign of the American Navy the men of the First Division got on the morning of August 9 was the sight of burning and damaged ships. And this was more than they were to get for many mornings after that."

That report on the Jap bombers turned out to be a false alarm, by the way. They never showed up.

• • •

ONCE WE FOUND out what had really happened in the big navy battle, our confidence sank down to about the same depth as those sunken hulks in Iron Bottom Sound. Less than a day before, we'd thought we were almost home free. Now we knew we were in trouble up to our eyeballs.

The ships and planes of our Navy had disappeared and left us stranded on Guadalcanal with barely enough supplies to survive on. The Japs were in full control of the air and the sea around us. There was nothing to stop them from sending in as many supplies and reinforcements as they needed to pin us down and bleed us to death.

What it boiled down to was that the First Marine Division was surrounded by the enemy. Beyond our perimeters, the Jap troops already on the island could move freely wherever they wanted to go and hit us whenever and wherever they chose. And we didn't have anywhere near enough fortifications and fixed defenses to hold off a Jap amphibious landing, even if it was right under our noses.

For the time being, though, there was nothing for K/3/5 to do but follow orders and move west in a hurry. We still didn't have but one unit of fire per man for our '03 Springfields. We heard there might be some additional ammo at the Third Battalion command post, but that was a good half-mile away. So we just marched with what we had.

In my case, that was five clips that held five rounds apiece on each side of my belt. That came to fifty-five rounds total, including the clip in my rifle. Some of the guys who'd been shooting at phantoms those first two nights ashore had considerably less.

"Conserve your ammo," Lieutenant Adams told us as we started out along the beach road. "When we make contact with the enemy, don't waste a single round. Make every shot count. Use your bayonets whenever you can."

By now, almost everybody in the company was down in the mouth and moping. Some guys started talking about Bataan and Corregidor in the Philippines and comparing our sorry situation to the one those poor devils had faced three or four months ago.

A private in the K/3/5 mortar section was walking beside me when we moved out that morning. He had an expression on his face that looked like somebody had just kicked him in the nuts. "Oh Jesus, Mac," he said, "you think we'll ever get off this damn island?"

He must've asked me that same question at least a hundred times over the next four months. I always tried to give him a positive answer, even though sometimes I wasn't sure I believed it myself.

This was definitely one of those times.

"Yeah, yeah," I told him. "We'll be fine."

Roughly an hour into the march, the road along the beach led us just north of the airfield, which was to our left, and still within sight of the water to our right. It had been quiet all the way so far with no sign of enemy activity.

Then, all at once, we saw a submarine surface out in the channel maybe a hundred yards from shore.

"That's a Jap sub!" somebody yelled. "Hit the deck!"

We did exactly that, but like the Zeros that had flown over us twice before, the sub paid no attention to us. It opened fire toward the airfield with its one deck gun, and we could hear the shells whizzing over our heads. We could also hear the explosions as the shells hit off to the south. The sub kept firing for two or three minutes. Then it moved away and slipped out of sight under the waves.

I almost felt like laughing. Here I was in an infantry rifle platoon, and the first and only Jap I'd seen was flying over me in a Zero at treetop level. Now I'd just come under fire—well, sort of—from a Jap submarine. But I still hadn't seen a single enemy soldier on the ground. It all seemed nutty as hell to me, and I couldn't help wondering what the odds were of something like that happening.

"Okay, the sub's gone," Lieutenant Adams said. "Show's over. Let's move out."

We brushed ourselves off and started marching west again. We continued on for a couple of miles until we were ordered to stop and start setting up a new defensive perimeter near an outcropping of land called Lunga Point, where the Lunga River emptied into the sea.

From there, our Fifth Marines perimeter would be tied in a lot more securely with the lines of the First Marines. The Fifth's lines ran along a ridge and through some coconut plantations, but the First's were mostly in the jungle. At least we were both in better positions now to protect the airfield and hold our ground if the Japs decided to attack us with something bigger than a submarine.

And, sure enough, they did.

Their planes came first, and since there weren't any American ships left to target, they concentrated on the airfield they'd given up and our troop concentrations. It hadn't taken them long to realize a couple of things. First, our carriers were long gone. Second, until the airport was finished, we wouldn't have any planes of our own to fight back with.

At the moment, all we had to protect the airfield were a few outdated 90-millimeter antiaircraft guns and a couple of searchlights.

Our .30-caliber machine guns in K/3/5 and the other infantry companies were about as effective as peashooters against enemy bombers. What few 50-calibers we had were with the Third Battalion weapons company a considerable distance away.

The number of Jap planes in the formations that targeted the airfield ranged from five or six to a couple of dozen. They'd aim a few bombs at our positions in passing, but they saved most of what they had for the airfield. We were well dug-in and had pretty good cover from the coconut palms, so we hardly had any casualties to speak of.

But the bombings jangled our nerves and kept us on edge. Especially the ones at night. After dark, they'd send over just one plane at a time. The pilot would come in slow and leisurely, like he didn't have a care in the world. He must've known we didn't have a damn thing bigger than a .30-caliber or a BAR to fire at him. He'd circle around for a while, then drop one bomb and fly away. A couple of minutes later, another plane would show up and go through the same routine.

The thing that hurt worst was they kept us awake most of the night. Plus they were such arrogant, infuriating sons of bitches. They knew there was nothing we could do against them. It was like they were just toying with us and getting a big kick out of it. We called all the Jap pilots by the same name—"washing-machine Charlie."

About 1 AM one morning, I heard a frustrated Marine cussing the third or fourth low-flying "Charlie" of the night from a couple of foxholes away.

"Damn you, you asshole!" he yelled. "I'd give a hundred-dollar bill for thirty seconds with a .50-caliber machine gun right now!"

I knew exactly how he felt.

• • •

IN BETWEEN AIR raids, we did finally get something to eat.

As far as I remember, the first time we had what you'd consider a full meal was late on the afternoon of August 10 (D-plus-3). Up to that point, the only chow I'd had was a few captured Nip candy bars. But that evening, I got a mess kit full of boiled rice with some dried fish mixed in and a can of tangerines. Naturally, it was all Japanese.

The rice was okay, and it was filling, but the tangerines were really great. I don't think I ever ate anything before or since that tasted so good. Of course, the fact that I'd gone over three and a half days with almost no food probably had a lot to do with how much I enjoyed them.

With the small amount of edible stuff—mainly just coffee—that had been unloaded from the ships, plus the large supply of Jap rice our guys had found stored near the airfield, we supposedly had enough food to last us about fourteen days. That was only figuring on two meals a day, though. Like I said earlier, our breakfasts were at least 90 percent black coffee—no cream, no sugar—and there was no such thing as lunch.

By this time, some of our guys were getting fairly adept at busting open coconuts. And God knows, there were enough of those. According to the rumors we heard, the Japs were living almost totally on coconuts, now that they'd lost their rice supplies. I can tell you for sure we didn't feel sorry for them.

The one big break we got in the food situation during those first couple of weeks came in the form of a steer that wandered into our area. For several days, we watched it grazing in a grassy open space down below the ridge where we were set up. None of us had had a bite of real meat since we'd left the troopship.

"Look at all that beef on the hoof," one of the guys in my platoon finally said. "Every time I see that beast, my imagination runs wild, and I think I smell steaks cooking."

"Well, hell, let's shoot the son of a bitch and have a barbecue," somebody else said. "I bet I can drop him from here."

As far as I remember, we didn't take a vote of any kind on this suggestion, but a few seconds later three or four of my platoon mates raised their '03s and started taking pot shots at the steer, more or less in unison. At least one of them hit the steer, and it fell over in its tracks without making a sound. It was still kicking a little when a half-dozen of us ran down and grabbed it and dragged it back to our lines.

We had to cook the steer in daylight because there was a strict ban on fires at night, and instead of barbecuing it, we cut it up in chunks and boiled it in some twenty-gallon GI cans. The Marines who'd done the killing, skinning, and butchering were surprisingly generous with the meat. I think everybody in K Company got a chunk or two, and we even let some of the guys in I Company have a taste.

To me, no prime filet mignon in a fancy restaurant ever tasted as good.

WITH FOOD BEING so scarce, a lot of the guys in the Third Battalion, Fifth, started feasting on rumors—and there were some wild ones going around. One story that made the rounds was about a patrol that came in after half a day in the woods and told an intelligence officer they'd found a batch of cosmetics and toilet articles belonging to women being held by the Japs.

The officer immediately got on the phone to division headquarters and asked for permission to organize a rescue mission to free the women.

"A fat lot of good freeing them would do an old fart like you," division told him. "Forget it and stay where you are."

But after what took place on the evening of August 12 (D-plus-5), a Marine would've had to be totally crazy to go chasing off into the no-man's-land to the west to check out a rumor.

What happened on that date to a twenty-five-man Marine patrol led by Lieutenant Colonel Frank Goettge also didn't leave us much time—or stomach—for thinking about food.

Those invisible Japs we'd been looking for behind every bush for the past five days were about to get all too real.

ON THE AFTERNOON of D-plus-5, word reached our regimental headquarters by way of a captured Jap sailor that a group of enemy soldiers was willing to surrender if the Marines would send out some troops to liberate them and guide them back to our lines.

As I understand it, Colonel Goettge's patrol included quite a few guys in intelligence, and they'd already been planning a reconnaissance mission into the area west of our Lunga Point perimeter, where most of the Japs on the island were allegedly concentrated.

Since Geottge and his guys were going into the same area where these Japs that claimed they wanted to surrender were, the brass told him to try to make contact with them.

I've heard that some of our officers—including Geottge himself—fell for this surrender story hook, line, and sinker. Geottge really believed his men were on some kind of humanitarian mission because the Japs were supposed to be starving and some of them badly injured. Somebody even claimed to have seen a white flag fly-ing above one of the Jap positions.

Anyway, Goettge took along the assistant First Division surgeon, Lieutenant Commander Malcolm Pratt, to help those that were hurt. He also took one of a handful of language officers in the division to serve as a translator.

The patrol started out just as it was getting dark. This was a silly thing to do in itself because they couldn't see what they were head-ing into. It was black as pitch out there. Lots of clouds and no moon. All the guys were packed into a single Higgins boat for the short trip along the coast, which was another dumb move. An enemy machine gun or a couple of well-placed grenades could've wiped out the whole lot of them before you could bat your eyes.

I guess because they were so convinced the Nips were going to welcome them with open arms, the only weapons the Marines had were rifles and pistols. There wasn't a single BAR or machine gun among them. They didn't even take along any grenades.

The Goettge patrol was nothing but one big, terrible series of mistakes. All of us were naive as hell at that point, but as green as some of our officers were, they should've known better.

As time went on, we'd learn the hard way in the Pacific that Japs *never* surrendered. To them, surrender was the worst thing they could imagine, and they'd a whole lot rather die than disgrace their family by doing it. In fact, thousands of them committed suicide when they were surrounded and trapped just to keep from surren-dering.

But we didn't know anything about that in those first days of combat. We didn't know how sneaky and bloodthirsty the bastards were, either.

The whole thing with the Goettge patrol was a ruse—a carefully laid trap.

Goettge and his men walked straight into an ambush. Only three of the twenty-five Marines escaped alive. The rest were slaughtered before they could get off the beach where they landed. Then the Japs entertained themselves by chopping up the bodies into little pieces.

One of the guys who survived said the last thing he saw early the next morning, when he glanced back at the beach where the massacre took place and swam for his life, was "swords flashing in the sunlight."

TWO MORNINGS LATER, after the three survivors dragged themselves back to our lines and the story of what happened got around, Third Battalion headquarters sent a bunch of patrols into the area where the ambush had taken place. As soon as it was good daylight, Lieutenant Adams called me over and assigned my eight-man rifle squad to one of the sectors to be checked out by these patrols.

We were also supposed to look for an F4F Wildcat fighter that had gone down and bring out the pilot if he was still alive. We never found a trace of the plane or pilot, and after what we *did* find, we forgot all about them.

"Be damn careful out there, Mac," the lieutenant said. "Don't take any unnecessary chances." Then he paused, looked me straight in the eye, and added, "Don't take any prisoners, either."

"No chance of that," I said. "We don't need no extra mouths to feed."

Every guy in my squad was mad as hell about what had

happened, and so was I. We were itching for some kind of payback. By now, it was the sixth day since we'd landed, and so far we hadn't even *seen* a Jap on the ground, much less had a chance to take a shot at one. I think most of us hoped this would be the day we did.

We knew one thing for sure. If we found the murdering bastards, they wouldn't have any luck pretending to surrender this time.

Moving in single file, we waded across a knee-deep stream and climbed the three-foot-high mud bank on the other side. Then we made our way through dense undergrowth and a thick grove of coconut palms. Our feet squished in our boots. Before long, we'd get used to that feeling.

Over the next twenty minutes or so, we covered several hundred yards, gradually circling back toward the beach. That's when we spotted the bodies—or what was left of them—scattered in pieces near the water's edge.

We'd stumbled across the exact spot where the Goettge patrol had been ambushed by the Japs and where they'd been butchered afterward like a bunch of pigs.

The first thing I saw was the severed head of a Marine. I almost let out a yell because the head was moving back and forth in the water and looked like it was alive. Then I realized it was just bobbing in the small waves lapping at the shore. They would wash it up onto the sand a few inches, then it would float back out again when the waves receded.

The next thing I noticed was a leg that had been hacked off at the knee. It was still wearing its dead owner's boondocker shoe with its laces neatly tied. A few feet away was part of a bloody sleeve from a Marine first sergeant's shirt with the chevrons still attached. Other chunks of rotting flesh that had once been human body parts were floating in the water and lying on the sand. The smell was overpowering.

"Holy shit!" I heard a guy behind me groan. "I think I'm gonna puke!"

He stumbled over to a clump of brush and I heard him gag. I almost gagged myself. None of us had ever seen anything like this before. If I'd had something besides black coffee in my stomach, I probably would've been as sick as a dog.

It still kind of surprises me that none of the guys in my squad started screaming or cussing or otherwise going hysterical. Mostly, they just stood there frozen in their tracks, like their brains couldn't process what they were seeing. When I think back on it, I figure they were all thinking something similar to what I was thinking.

I won't ever forget this—not ever! I told myself. *I'll never see a Jap in my life without thinking about it.*

Over the next two-plus years, I saw a lot of gruesome sights in the Pacific, but I can't remember anything worse than what we saw that morning.

As best we could tell, there were pieces of at least four bodies scattered along the beach, and there may have been several others in some bushes a few yards in from the water. We didn't bother making a detailed search. It was totally obvious what had happened to Goettge and his men.

When I got hold of myself and looked around, the first member of my squad I saw was PFC Kenneth Blakesley, a skinny blond kid not quite eighteen years old. He was standing a couple of feet from me and staring wide-eyed at the bodies and shaking his head. When he tried to talk, it sounded like he was choking on his own words.

"For God's sake, Mac," he said, "why would anybody do this?

Wasn't killing 'em enough? Did they have to make mincemeat out of 'em, too?"

I put my hand on Blakesley's shoulder. The kid was a good Marine who was always willing to go out on a work detail when I needed somebody. But right now, he looked like he was about ten years old.

"They just want to scare us, Kenny," I said. "They want to show us how tough and mean they are so we'll think they're a bunch of damn supermen. But we're gonna show them a few things, too, before this shit's all said and done."

A minute or two later, Lieutenant Adams showed up with the rest of the platoon. They'd been moving parallel to my squad on our left, and they'd come across some dead Marines, too.

"What should we do with these bodies, Scoop?" I asked him. "You want us to try and bury them?"

He shook his head, and there was a look of pure misery on his face. "Just leave 'em where they are, Mac," he said. "There's no time for it right now. Maybe we can send back a burial detail later, but frankly I'd hate to risk it."

I got my squad together and the whole platoon moved out. Later on, First Marine Division headquarters refused to confirm that the slaughter of the Goettge patrol had ever actually happened. But I never really understood why. Any man who'd seen what we saw that morning knew better.

Patrols from two other companies—L/3/5 and I/3/5—also reported finding mutilated body parts. But the bodies of Goettge himself and other members of his party were never recovered or officially identified. As a result, as far as I know, all of the dead Marines are still listed as "missing in action."

The fact that all three of the survivors, Platoon Sergeant Frank

L. Few, Sergeant Charles C. "Monk" Arndt, and Corporal Joseph A. Spaulding, described the slaughter in detail in interviews, magazine articles, and official reports didn't seem to make any difference.

Sometimes I think the brass were just too embarrassed by the whole thing to admit the truth because Goettge and his men were naive and gullible enough to walk right into a trap. I guess United States Marines were supposed to be too smart and tough to make mistakes like that.

Maybe the brass just wished everybody would forget it, but I knew I wouldn't. And I don't think any of the other guys who were there that morning ever forgot it, either. We still had an awful lot to learn about the Japs—but we *were* learning.

As we marched away that morning, I could hear a voice inside my head repeating the same words over and over: *I won't forget! I won't forget! I won't forget!*

That afternoon, mostly just to take my mind off the things I'd seen that day, I took a few sheets of Jap paper I'd found out of my pack and wrote my mom a letter.

Even if the censors had let me get away with it, I wouldn't have mentioned anything about what happened to Colonel Goettge and his party or anything else about the situation on Guadalcanal because it would've worried Mom and my sister, Lil, too much. Instead, I tried to make it sound as cheerful as I could.

At the time, I really had my doubts that they'd ever get to read what I was writing, anyway. Our mail service wasn't too reliable, to say the least.

But after all these years, I still remember how I started the letter.

"Well, here we are on this beautiful tropical island," I wrote, "and everything's just fine . . ."

4

BUSHIDO TAKES A BEATING

VERY FEW MARINES had ever heard the Japanese word "Bushido" at the time we landed on Guadalcanal. But no word in any language was more important to Japanese soldiers, from the highest-ranking officer on down to the lowliest private. It was a whole lot more than just a word. It was a way of life—and death.

Bushido was an ancient warrior's code that the Japs believed gave them greater physical power and spiritual strength than the "soft, spoiled" Americans they were fighting. It was based on the idea that the Japanese were a superior race. They called themselves the "sons of heaven" and thought they were divinely favored by the Sun God, whose symbol was splashed across their "flaming asshole" battle flags.

In the Imperial Japanese Army, Bushido was the foundation for a military caste system based on sheer brutality, one that was practiced like a religion. Privates in that army were beaten and abused unmercifully by soldiers who outranked them. Then, after they were promoted to a higher rank, those former privates handed out the same cruel punishment they'd gotten to other new privates.

In combat, Bushido emphasized using bayonets and swords instead of bullets whenever possible, especially when the Jap attacks came in the dark of night. The theory was that slashing blades were even scarier to their enemies than gunfire. Up until Guadalcanal, the Japs were always on the attack, and they'd had great success with their fanatic banzai charges, where hundreds of screaming troops threw themselves at enemy positions with swords and fixed bayonets.

In the early going, these charges worked like a charm against Allied troops all over the Pacific. They scared the hell out of defenders and paralyzed them to the point they couldn't fight back. When they saw the Japs coming at them that way, they usually either broke and ran or just gave up. This is how 80,000 British, Australian, and Indian troops ended up as prisoners of war after the fall of the "impregnable fortress" of Singapore.

But on Guadalcanal, the Japs started finding out those banzai charges were like a double-edged sword. They could cut either way. If the troops they were attacking held their ground and kept firing, a charge like that could end up being mass suicide for the attackers.

That's one thing the Marines taught the Bushido bastards in August and September of 1942.

•   •   •

WHOEVER CAME UP with that old saying about how it's "always darkest before the dawn" could've been talking about what happened on Guadalcanal during the four weeks between August 20 and September 14.

That's when two of the bloodiest battles in Marine Corps history were fought on the island and our situation in general was looking bleak as hell.

It just so happened that I wrote another letter to the folks at home on August 20. Mom saved it, and I still have it, as a matter of fact. In it, I was still trying hard not to let on how grim our situation was.

"How are you all?" I wrote. "I'm fine myself, and I hope you are all the same. I'm on Guadalcanal Island now and in the best of health and feel fine as far as morale is concerned."

At the time, we actually felt like we had our backs to the wall, and it was hard to see any way out. Jap planes were bombing us around the clock, and their destroyers were pulling in close to shore to shell the airfield and our positions around it. Our Navy was still somewhere else far away, so the Nips were landing reinforcements just about every night with no opposition, and until we got some naval or air support, there was nothing we could do about it.

But when the second of those two major battles ended in mid-September, over 1,700 banzai-charging Nips were dead, and our fighter planes and bombers were flying missions out of the former Jap airfield. The Marines renamed it Henderson Field in honor of Major Lofton Henderson, a Marine pilot killed at the Battle of Midway.

Things got a little brighter after that, and we could finally feel the tide beginning to turn our way. But they couldn't have looked much lousier than they did at the time I was writing that letter.

Now don't get me wrong. We still had a long way to go. But when the Marines won those two big fights—the history books call them the Battle of the Tenaru River and the Battle of Edson's Ridge—we began to see a few glimmers of light at the end of the long, dark tunnel we were in.

THERE'S NO CANAL on Guadalcanal in spite of what a lot of people seem to think. But there's a shallow little river there that I'll never forget. It was more like a creek than any of the rivers I ever saw in America. I mean, in most places you could wade all the way across it without ever getting wet much above your shins.

It's called the Matanikau, and I couldn't even pronounce its name for a long time. I thought it was "Makanakow" or something like that. But this puny excuse for a river turned out to be what the brass called the "most strategically important natural geographic feature" on the whole damn island.

It was more important than other streams we fought along, like the Tenaru or the Lunga or Alligator Creek, for one simple reason. Everything west of it was owned by the Japs, while Henderson Field and the territory on the east side of the Matanikau were held by the Marines. And like I said before, the Japs wanted that airfield really bad.

Beginning in late August, the First Marine Division had set up its main defensive perimeter in a big semicircle that followed the Tenaru River inland from the sea, then curved to the west south of the airfield until it reached the sea again about two miles from the Matanikau. After making several moves to the west, K/3/5 and the rest of the Fifth Marines were dug in along a low ridge that faced the Matanikau from the east. From there, the lines swung north through a coconut grove to the waters of Iron Bottom Sound.

Things started getting hot and heavy on August 18. That's when three companies from the First and Third Battalions, Fifth Marines, were sent across the Matanikau for the first time to strike at enemy forces on the west side of the river, where the Japs were strongly in control.

When word filtered down that General Vandegrift was planning this attack, a lot of us in K/3/5 hoped our company would be one of the ones picked to go, but it didn't turn out that way. Instead, the outfits assigned to this mission were Company B of the First Battalion, Fifth Marines, and our sister companies, I and L, of the Third Battalion.

Company L, commanded by Captain Lyman Spurlock, kicked off the action by advancing to a river crossing about 1,000 yards inland, killing ten Japs along the way. Late on the afternoon of the 18th, they set up their defenses on the west side of the river.

But the next morning, August 19, the going got tougher. Company L had a hard time hacking its way through the jungle, and the men came under heavy fire from a ridge several hundred yards to the west. One of the platoon leaders was killed, and when Lieutenant George Mead, the company executive officer, took over the platoon, he was killed, too.

Still, the company made slow but steady progress until about two o'clock that afternoon, when they encircled Matanikau Village, near the mouth of the river, and heard Jap voices jabbering and yelling "Banzai!" This alerted Captain Spurlock that an enemy attack was forming up, and he quickly alerted his troops to get ready.

A few minutes later, when the Japs charged with fixed bayonets, his Marines met them with volleys of hot lead.

After a firefight that lasted close to two hours, the Japs bugged out, and when Spurlock's men went into the village, they found sixty-five enemy bodies there. Their own losses were four dead and eleven wounded.

All three Marine companies pulled back across the river after that, so the attack didn't really gain any permanent ground for us. But the best thing that came out of it for the men of L Company was bloody, positive proof that banzais don't win battles.

Bullets do.

And L Company's experience was just a small sample of what happened next.

Action along the Matanikau continued later in the day on August 19, when a company-size patrol from the First Marines also crossed the river looking for a Jap force reported on the west side. They surprised an enemy patrol in another small village, and another firefight broke out. When it ended about an hour later, thirty-one of the thirty-four Japs in the patrol were dead, and only a handful of Marines were wounded.

This was good, but when the Marines took a close look at the bodies, they could tell by the Japs' uniforms that a lot of the dead ones were officers. Division headquarters decided this was a strong indication that enemy reinforcements were being landed on Guadalcanal. Actually, there hadn't been much doubt about it before, but this evidence pretty well convinced the brass that the Japs were steadily increasing their strength.

This *wasn't* good news, but before word about it spread to the grunts in the foxholes, we all had another reason to celebrate.

The next day, August 20, we watched our first two Marine air squadrons circle over Henderson Field and come in for a landing. VMF-223 arrived with nineteen F4F Grumman Wildcat fighters, and VMSB-232 showed up with twelve SBD-3 Douglas Dauntless scout bombers.

Boy, were they a sight for sore eyes! In K/3/5's sector of our defensive perimeter about a mile southwest of the airfield, everybody started cheering and waving their arms and throwing their helmets up in the air. Some of the guys actually got all teary-eyed at the sight of those planes. As for me, I didn't shed any tears, but the planes gave me a better feeling in my gut than I'd had since we landed.

The first thing I did when I saw them was get down on my knees and say, "Thank you, Lord."

The planes and pilots based at Henderson Field immediately became known as the Cactus Air Force because "Cactus" was the military code name for Guadalcanal. But it was a really appropriate nickname for other reasons, too, because they sure turned out to be a thorn in the Japs' side.

It meant an awful lot to us just to know they were there and that we had air support again. Now maybe those "washing machine Charlies" wouldn't act so damn comfortable on their raids anymore.

NATURALLY, THE PRESENCE of the Cactus Air Force drew a lot of attention from the Japs, too, because it meant a lot of trouble for them. To tell the truth, I think the idea of having to deal with our planes drove the Nips a little nuts, judging from the bone-head moves they made over the next thirty-six hours.

With a few hundred enemy reinforcements slipping in almost

every night and no U.S. fighting ships in the area to stop them, the Nip commanders had figured on kicking us off the island in short order. When our planes showed up, though, that whole picture changed, and as long as Henderson Field stayed operational and in our hands, it was going to stay changed.

That's not to say the Japs weren't still plenty cocky. They were cocky enough to do some really dumb things. They'd been having their way in the Pacific for so long they didn't think anybody could stop them. They were hell-bent and determined to grab that airfield back, and that's where they made one of their biggest mistakes.

The first thing they did was try to bomb Henderson Field and its new crop of planes out of existence. All our troop movements in the vicinity of the airfield had to be suspended for a while because of constant dogfights, antiaircraft barrages, and Jap bombing runs.

Our fliers got some valuable help in fighting off the Jap air attacks from a network of coast watchers at points all through the string of islands between Guadalcanal and the Jap bases at Rabaul and Truk. The watchers were mostly civilian natives hired by the Australian navy. When they spotted enemy planes headed in our direction, they radioed warnings that gave our slower, less agile F4Fs time to get off the ground and high above the altitude of the Jap raiders before their Zeros and Betty bombers reached the airfield.

The results were amazing—five Jap planes shot down for every one we lost, even though ours were usually outnumbered by four or five to one.

According to a commendation given to Marine fliers by General Vandegrift, their toll on enemy aircraft and shipping between August 21 and August 30 included twenty-one double- and single-engine bombers and thirty-nine Zero fighters shot down and three destroyers sunk. Five other enemy ships—a cruiser, two destroyers, and two transports—were listed as "probably destroyed."

But the Japs made their biggest screwups on the ground. One of the first—and worst—of these was made by Colonel Kiyoano Ichiki, commander of the so-called Ichiki Detachment, an elite unit of the 17th Japanese Army.

Using the standard Bushido tactic of screaming night attacks with swords and bayonets, the Ichiki Detachment had already overrun Allied defenders in a series of amphibious assaults in the Pacific. Because of the reputation they'd built, no one in Japan's high command had any doubt they could do the same thing with ease at Guadalcanal.

When Ichiki and his 2,100 shock troops were rushed from Guam to the Japanese base at Truk in mid-August, six destroyers stood ready to take them the rest of the way to Guadalcanal. Their orders were simple and straight to the point: Recapture the island's airfield and destroy any upstart Americans who tried to stand in their way.

Ichiki split his force into two echelons and sent the first one as an advance unit. But he didn't actually think he'd even need the second, and larger, group to complete his mission.

"Colonel Ichiki . . . was so confident when he arrived at Guadalcanal on the night of August 17 with his advance echelon," wrote First Marine Division historian George McMillan, "he did not feel it necessary to wait for the second echelon of the detachment, some 1,200 more men, which was [traveling] in slower-moving transports. He was going right ahead. He was going to take Henderson Field with 900 men."

Yeah, like hell he was.

What Ichiki actually did on the morning of August 21 was destroy half his detachment—and himself. He did it with blind, impatient overconfidence—but he got a helluva lot of help from the First and Second Battalions, First Marines.

ACCORDING TO SOME EXPERTS, the bloodbath identified in history books as the Battle of the Tenaru River didn't actually take place at the Tenaru River at all. Author Richard Frank, who wrote the longest book I ever saw on Guadalcanal, claimed it took place on Alligator Creek, which wasn't really a creek at all. It was a muddy, sluggish tidal lagoon that only flowed after heavy rains.

And by the way, there weren't any alligators in Alligator Creek, either, but there *were* a good many crocodiles.

If you think all this sounds confusing, you're right. But it was the kind of confusion we had to put up with every day on Guadalcanal. On the maps we were given, almost none of the stream names were accurate. Some rivers were just creeks and some creeks were just mud holes. In reality, the points where the Tenaru and Alligator Creek empty into the sea are more than a mile apart, and their wandering courses never take them much less than 1,000 yards from one another.

What's more important, though, is what happened in the area between the Tenaru and the Alligator on the night of August 20–21, 1942.

During the day on August 20, Lieutenant Colonel Edwin Pollock's Second Battalion, First Marines set up on the west bank of Alligator Creek. Their lines ran north from about 1,000 yards inland to a large sandspit where Alligator met the sea.

The Marines had put together a strong defensive position with well-dug-in machine guns covering the sandspit and a point of land beyond it on the east bank. They had a 37-millimeter gun loaded with canister shot that could rip closely packed infantry troops to shreds, and it was positioned to rake the same area. They also strung a barbed wire barrier across the sandspit near the west bank.

After dark that evening, the Marines farthest to the east got reports of Japanese patrols and gunfire on the east side of the stream, and they started falling back toward the sandspit. The reports worried Colonel Pollock, and he went east on his own to investigate. But a runner caught him before he got to the scene of the trouble and told him about a badly wounded native who'd stumbled into Marine lines claiming he'd seen "maybe 500 Japs" off to the east.

"By this time, I knew something was up," Pollock said. He called division headquarters to get help for the wounded native, and while he was on the phone, firing broke out along the Alligator. A few minutes later, at about 1:30 AM on August 21, a green flare lit the sky above the east bank of the stream, and about 200 Japs came charging across the sandspit.

Colonel Ichiki didn't seem the least bit concerned about the Marines' well-prepared defenses. I guess he expected his charging troops to slash through the American lines like a hot knife through butter—just like they'd always done before.

Man, was he ever wrong!

When the Japs reached the barbed wire, they stopped, just as machine gun, small-arms, and 37-millimeter canister fire from the Marines tore into them. Dozens of Nips were killed before they could cut their way through the wire.

A Marine lieutenant later described the scene like this: "They waved their arms wildly and shrieked and jabbered like monkeys, but they kept coming."

A few Japs got through and jumped into the Marines' foxholes, where our guys rose up to meet them in hand-to-hand fighting. This was the first organized, large-scale enemy assault on Guadalcanal. It was also the Marines' first chance for some real payback—for Pearl Harbor, Wake Island, Bataan, Corregidor, the Goettge patrol, and all the rest. What happened over the next few minutes answered forever the question of whether the Japs were invincible supermen and whether American troops could stand up to them toe-to-toe.

One young Marine, Corporal Dean Wilson, mowed down Japs with his BAR until the weapon jammed. Then he grabbed a machete and hacked three more onrushing enemy soldiers to pieces.

Just as Corporal John Shea jumped into an adjacent foxhole to try to clear his tommy gun, he was jabbed twice in the leg by an enemy soldier's bayonet. His response was to jam his right foot into the Jap's belly, throw him against the wall of the foxhole, and give him five shots in the chest with the tommy.

Private John Rivers, a machine gunner, poured hundreds of rounds into the closely packed enemy ranks until he was fatally wounded by a bullet that struck him square in the face. Even then, according to eyewitnesses, his dying fingers squeezed off another 200 rounds to keep killing Japs.

Private Al Schmid took over Rivers's machine gun and kept it firing until fragments from an exploding grenade blinded him in both eyes and hurled him away from the gun. Then he drew his pistol and emptied it at the shrieking Japs around him.

Ichiki tried desperately to reassemble his shattered forces, but

Colonel Clifton Cates, a future Marine Corps commandant, delivered a deadly blow to the remnants of Ichiki's detachment. Cates managed to reach the command post of the Third Battalion, 11th Marines, and call for artillery support. In less than a minute, 75-millimeter shells were raining down on the main body of Jap survivors.

Some of them tried to regroup for a new attack by running along the beach beyond the sandspit and through the surf to hit the Marines' flank. But our guys saw them coming and raked them with machine gun fire. Then they finished them off with more artillery and a platoon of light tanks.

War correspondent Richard Tregaskis, author of the famous book *Guadalcanal Diary*, wrote this description of the carnage when the tanks chased the last remaining Japs through a coconut grove: "It was . . . something unbelievable to see them knocking over palm trees which fell slowly, flushing the running figures of men from underneath their treads, following and firing at the fugitives."

When the tankers came back to the Marine lines on the east bank of the stream, General Vandegrift noticed that the tanks' treads and rear ends "looked like meat grinders."

The "meat" was definitely Japanese.

At least 777 of Ichiki's men were killed in the battle. Only fifteen enemy soldiers—thirteen of them wounded—were taken prisoner. Marine casualties totaled forty-four dead and seventy-one wounded.

There would've been quite a few more prisoners taken alive if so many of the Jap wounded hadn't done their damnedest to kill any Americans who tried to treat their wounds. In several cases, dying Japs discharged grenades when Marines or Navy corpsmen came close, killing themselves and the guys attempting to help them.

General Vandegrift was shocked when he found out about this. "I've never heard of this kind of fighting," he told a friend. "These people refuse to surrender. The wounded wait until men come up to examine them and blow themselves and the other fellow to pieces with a hand grenade."

For us in the ranks, it just drove home a realization that would be pretty much universal by the time we left Guadalcanal. We learned that "the only good Jap is a dead Jap," as the saying goes, and we made sure that all the wounded ones left on the field after a firefight got to be "good Japs" just as quick as we could shoot them.

When Colonel Ichiki realized how bad his men had been defeated, he made himself a "good Jap" by burning his regimental flags and shooting himself in the head. My sentiments when I heard about it can be summed up in two words: Thanks, asshole!

General Harukichi Hyakutake, commander of Japan's 17th Army, sent the following message to Tokyo after he learned how the battle ended: "The attack of the Ichiki Detachment was not entirely successful."

This had to be one of the biggest understatements of the war.

BY EARLY SEPTEMBER, my platoon still hadn't seen any live Japs near enough to shoot at with small arms, and some of the guys in K/3/5 were starting to feel kind of left out and neglected. When it came to combat, we never seemed to be where the main action was.

That's not to say I hadn't already been pretty close to some major fireworks a time or two. On August 30, I'd decided to take my first real bath since I'd been on Guadalcanal, and since there was no fresh water where K/3/5 was set up, I went down to Iron Bottom Sound to dunk myself in the surf. I piled all my gear on the beach and jumped in, but I'd barely gotten wet when I heard about six Jap dive-bombers coming in low and fast.

I jumped out of the water again, grabbed up my stuff, and ran like hell for cover. Then I crouched there in some bushes and watched those Jap planes zero in on one of our destroyer transports, the USS *Colhoun*. They must've caught the ship just as she tried to slip away after delivering some much needed supplies ashore.

I saw the bombs hit the *Colhoun* in a series of bright orange explosions. In a matter of seconds, the whole ship was blazing like a torch. Then the stern of it went down, and the bow stood straight up in the air. In the space of about three minutes, it slid under the water and disappeared.

Watching it made me sick all over. I never felt so damn helpless in my life. I heard later that about fifty members of the *Colhoun*'s crew went down with her.

Things like that ate at me while K/3/5 marked time and waited.

It wasn't that we were a bunch of eager beavers just itching to get in the big middle of a shootout like the Tenaru battle. So far, though, about all we'd done except for finding those bodies from the Goettge ambush was make a few uneventful patrols and stay hunkered down when the bombs and shells started falling.

In my personal case, it didn't help that I'd just been promoted to buck sergeant and assigned as reconnaissance NCO for the company. Sometimes I had the feeling I didn't deserve the promotion because I hadn't done anything to earn it yet.

It may sound stupid, and maybe it was, but we were an infantry company in the United States Marines, and we'd come to this shitty place to fight Japs, not sit around and scratch mosquito bites and watch our socks rot on our feet.

We knew our turn on the hot seat had to come sooner or later, but all this waiting was getting on our nerves. It was like until we got our baptism of fire, as they call it, all we could do was mark time and wonder about how we'd do when it finally happened.

About eleven o'clock on the morning of September 7, we found out.

THE SECOND PLATOON of K/3/5 was already on the line and drawing heavy fire when our First Platoon was ordered to go in and give them some help.

Captain Lawrence V. Patterson, our company commander, called me to his command post and told me to collect two men from each of the four squads in the First Platoon and hustle them up to the line as fast as I could.

After I picked two guys from my own old squad, I checked with the three other squad leaders and let them pick the guys they wanted to send until I had my eight-man quota.

"Come on," I told them then, "let's move out."

I don't remember much about any of the eight guys I picked, except for Private Kenny Blakesley, the kid from my old squad who'd been so upset when we stumbled onto the cut-up bodies from the Goettge patrol. I picked him because I knew he was steady and dependable, even though he was still just seventeen years old.

We tried to move as fast as we could, staying low to the ground, but it took us four or five minutes to cover the seventy-five yards to where the Second Platoon was pinned down. Just as we eased up to the top of a slight ridge, I glanced ahead at Blakesley's rear end about two yards ahead of me and slightly to my left.

The firing was sporadic except for a Marine lying flat on the ground in some grass about ten yards to my left and blazing away with a BAR. I didn't recognize the guy, but I thought he'd probably come from the company CP. Anyway, he was big and burly, and he handled that nineteen-pound weapon like it was a water pistol. He was giving the Japs pure hell, and the barrel of the BAR must've been red-hot. I could see the slugs from it chewing so hard into a bunch of Japs running toward him that their blood was spraying into the air.

I emptied one five-round clip of my own from my '03 Springfield, but I'm not sure if I hit anything. I'd just glanced toward where Blakesley was hugging the ground and easing forward when I heard the pop of a Jap rifle. I saw the kid grab at his chest and flop over on his back with dark red blood staining the left side of his dungaree shirt.

I yelled, "Hit the deck!" as the other Marines scrambled for cover. Even in the shock of the moment, I realized this was the first time I'd come directly under hostile fire on Guadalcanal. It was something I'd been expecting since that day in the Higgins boat exactly a month ago, but it hadn't happened until now.

When I crawled up next to Blakesley, he was groaning and his face was pale.

"No use bothering about me, Mac," he mumbled. "I think he got me in the lung. I'm probably done for."

I lifted the kid's arm and tore open his shirt for a better look. "Nah, I think it's between your arm and shoulder, Kenny," I said. "Just take it easy. You'll be okay."

"Don't let the bastards chop me up if I die out here," he whispered. "Promise me you won't, Mac."

"Don't worry, we're gonna get you outta here," I said. "Nobody's gonna chop you up." I wadded up his torn shirtsleeve and pushed it against the wound to slow the bleeding.

"Corpsman!" one of the guys behind me screamed. "We got a man down here!"

Within a few seconds, I was surprised as hell to see Corpsman William Hughes come from somewhere to my left and squat down beside Blakesley. But before he could even start treating the wound, there was another shot. It looked like the bullet went straight through Hughes's chest, and you could tell by the way he fell across Blakesley's body that he was dead before he hit the ground.

"Stretcher-bearer!" somebody yelled. "Now we got two guys hit!"

Then damned if another corpsman named Raymond Scott didn't come running up, but the Jap snipers killed him, too, just as he was trying to lift Blakesley in his arms. A bullet drilled Scott right through the head, and he died instantly.

Seeing all this made my stomach churn and my head spin, and the next few minutes were just one big blur for me. I jammed another clip in my '03, but I felt for a second like I was going to pass out, and I didn't know if I dared try to raise the rifle and fire. Those snipers really had a bead on this particular spot.

We need to get the hell out of here, I remember thinking, *before they pick us all off one at a time.*

But I forced myself to stay down and keep still a little longer. While I tried to make myself invisible, I grieved for those two dead corpsmen.

The medics assigned to Marine rifle companies were some of the bravest guys in the world. It tore me up to think that two of them had been killed a few feet from me within about thirty seconds of each other.

All our corpsmen wanted to do was help people that were hurt. I figured out later that was why the Japs liked to target them so much. I think they actually got a bigger kick out of killing corpsmen—who were mostly Navy pharmacist mates second class—more than high-ranking officers. This was because they thought the more corpsmen they killed, the more of our wounded would die from lack of treatment.

And the saddest part about it was they were right.

When firing slacked off a little, I managed to get Blakesley on a stretcher and move him a few yards to a spot with better cover than the one where he and the medics had been hit. Then a couple of the guys that had come up to the line with me carried him back to the rear. They had to drop the stretcher and take cover three or four times to keep from getting hit themselves.

The firefight we were in that day lasted for two or three hours, and before it was over, the whole company was involved. But some Marine Raiders and guys from the Marine Parachute Battalion were sent up to bolster our line, and the 11th Marines came through with some artillery support. Finally, the Japs that were left withdrew back to the west side of the Matanikau.

Our fight wasn't nearly as big as the one on the Tenaru, but the Japs' goal had been exactly the same—to take back the airfield—and we knew they weren't about to give up trying anytime soon.

I found out later that day that PFC Blakesley was still alive when they got him to a field hospital. That night, I couldn't get the kid off my mind. I kept remembering the day we went on patrol and he lost the bolt out of his rifle. He'd had a round in the chamber, and the bolt was up. It must've caught in a bush while we were moving through some heavy undergrowth and just pulled out.

We'd probably gone a quarter-mile before he realized the bolt was gone, and by then there was no way to ever find it. The rifle was basically useless without it, and we had to get Blakesley a new weapon when we got back to camp.

I especially remembered how I chewed his ass out over it, up one side and down the other. I did it mainly in hopes that giving him a hard time might help save his life someday. He just kept saying, "I'm sorry, Mac, I'm sorry. It'll never happen again, I promise."

Later on, he brought me a piece of chocolate as a kind of peace offering. He was that kind of kid, and I knew I was going to miss him.

As time went by, I often wondered what became of him and if he'd ever completely recovered from his wound.

After the war, I had a chance to go through a complete list of Marines who were killed in action or died of wounds on Guadalcanal, and I felt relieved when I didn't find Kenny's name there.

But I never saw him or heard from him again, and sometimes at night I still wake up and wonder whatever happened to him.

SOUTH AND SLIGHTLY east of Henderson Field there's a twisting snake of a ridge that runs from northwest to southeast for about 1,000 yards. I'm not sure if it even had a name before September 12–14, 1942. But ever since then, it's been called Edson's Ridge— and for damn good reasons.

The ridge is named for Colonel Merritt A. Edson, commander of the First Marine Raider Battalion. This was the outfit that had given the Japs one helluva beating on the islands of Tulagi, Gavutu, and Tanambogo across Iron Bottom Sound from Guadalcanal back in August.

In early September, they'd landed on Savo Island and secured it, then raided a village called Tasimboko near the Lunga River east of our defensive perimeter, where natives reported seeing about 400 Japs. After they flushed a small party of enemy soldiers out of the village, the Raiders found large stores of food, ammo, and weapons, including machine guns and 75-millimeter howitzers.

On September 10, after all the fighting and traveling Edson's men had done, General Vandegrift thought the Raiders deserved at least a few days' rest, so he decided to send them down to a bivouac area inland from the airfield that seemed fairly quiet and safe.

But "Red Mike" Edson, as he was known to his troops because of his carrot-colored hair, wasn't so sure any place on Guadalcanal was really going to stay quiet and safe for long. Because of what his men had discovered at Tasimboko, he was sure a much larger enemy force was lurking somewhere in the area.

"That bunch at Tasimboko was no motley [group] of 400 Japs but 2,000 to 3,000 well-organized soldiers," Edson said later. "When they sent us out toward the ridge, I was firmly convinced we were in the path of the next Jap attack."

He decided this was no time for a routine bivouac. So without even giving his men time to read the first letters from home they'd gotten in the Solomons, Edson ordered them to dig in along this unnamed ridge and send out patrols just as if they were still on the front lines.

As it turned out, they were.

The first patrols went out on September 11 and poked around in the jungle without finding anything. But on the 12th, Red Mike sent them out again, and this time they made a contact.

It was nothing big or serious. Just a brief skirmish with a small party of Nips that seemed to be right at home in the area. But it convinced Edson he'd better act fast. He put his men on full alert and ordered them to set up no-bullshit lines of defense for that night.

"Put them as far forward as you can get," he told them.

It was a good defensive setup. Any attackers trying to approach the ridge faced deep ravines on both sides, and some of them were so heavily wooded that the Japs would have to cut their way through. Several rugged spurs that stuck out on either side of the ridgeline offered good visibility of the countryside and great vantage points for Marine machine gunners.

The downside was that Edson didn't have enough men to form a continuous line, so he ordered small strongpoints to be set up, hoping the combination of heavy fire from them, plus the tough terrain, would keep the Nips from penetrating the line in strength.

Some of the men grumbled about the new orders. Marines do that sometimes, even Marine Raiders. I know from talking to some of them that they would've followed Red Mike over the edge of a cliff if he'd led the way. Still, they'd been through a lot. They were tired. They wanted to open their packages from home and read their letters. They'd been promised a rest break—and they deserved one if any outfit in the Corps ever did.

But there'd be no rest for the Raiders on the night ahead. No rest for the First Parachute Battalion, which was sent down by division headquarters to fill gaps in the line after Edson told the brass what he suspected. No rest on the night of the 12th. Or the 13th. Or the 14th, either.

On those three nights, only the dead found rest on Edson's Ridge.

Aᴛ ᴀʙᴏᴜᴛ 9 ᴘᴍ on September 12, the sky was lit up by a flare from a Jap float plane. Half an hour later, the enemy cruisers out in Iron Bottom Sound opened up with their eight-inch guns and pounded the ridge area for twenty minutes or so.

As soon as the echo of the last Jap shell faded away, the troops on the ground attacked immediately. They aimed their main thrust at the right flank of C Company of the Raiders, who were spread out for 300 yards down the right side of the ridge, from the top of a spur all the way to the bank of the Lunga River.

Fortunately, C Company had just gotten back its commander, Captain Kenneth Bailey, that morning. Bailey had been evacuated with serious wounds he'd gotten at Tulagi, and he'd been in a hospital at Noumea, New Caledonia, for two or three weeks.

Actually, he'd skipped out of the hospital without being discharged by the medics and caught a ride on a plane back to Henderson Field. The guys in C Company worshipped Bailey, and they loved him even more because he'd been the one who brought along several bags of their mail that had piled up in Noumea. They fought their guts out for him that night.

One platoon of C was forced to fall back along the riverbank, and B Company, behind them, was pushed back, too. But the Japs couldn't score any kind of breakthrough, and they weren't able to hold any of their gains. There was a lot of confusion in the jungle while the Japs milled around and tried to cut fire lanes through the heavy foliage. By daylight, the Raiders had reclaimed some of their lost positions, and the Japs were still basically back where they'd started.

Edson was confident his men could hold, but division headquarters wasn't so sure, and they had good reason for pessimism. After their losses of the night before, the Raiders were down to about 400 men, and although nobody knows to this day how many Japs were out there, some reliable estimates put the number at 4,000. In other words, Edson's guys were outnumbered ten to one.

Division tried to send the Second Battalion, Fifth Marines in to help, but like those of us in the Third Battalion, they were way out on the west end of our lines. It was a long march, and they had to cross the airfield to get there, which was impossible because the field was under constant heavy bombardment by the Nips. They did their best, but most of them didn't get there until sometime on September 14.

On the afternoon of the 13th, Edson called together as many troops as he could get within hearing distance and gave them a speech, although his voice was notoriously soft and whispery, and it probably didn't carry more than a few yards.

"Okay, this is it," he said. "There's nothing left between the Japs and Henderson Field but us. If we don't hold, the field will be lost, and the whole Guadalcanal campaign will be a flop. I think we can hold the line because you're the finest bunch of fighters I've ever known—but it's up to you."

Edson's audience was small, but the quiet sincerity in his voice must've deeply impressed the guys who heard it. "The men really turned to," said one listener. "There was no more grumbling."

Instead, the Raiders got ready quietly and seriously for the second night. Edson chose the high point in the center of the ridge as the main line of resistance, and he shortened the perimeter by 1,800 yards, still a lot of distance to cover for 400 guys.

As the light began to fade, the Raiders and Parachutists could hear the chattering from the Japs getting louder and louder. Some of the Marines later swore they heard the Japs yelling, "Gas attack! Gas attack!" There wasn't actually any gas, just a series of smoky flares.

At about 6:30 PM, the Japs charged. They hit the area held by B Company of the Raiders out on the right flank the hardest, and drove them back toward the top of the ridge. The Japs also surrounded one of B Company's platoons, forcing them to retreat and leaving a sizable gap in the line.

The situation was looking bad when Red Mike himself jumped in and took control of it. Around dusk, he'd already moved his CP forward to the nose of the ridge, where he was less than ten yards from the front-line machine guns. The area around him was under constant heavy enemy fire, and Edson had to lie flat on his belly to direct return fire from his gunners with a hand phone.

Now and then, he jumped up and ran at a crouch to rally men who seemed too scared and confused to fight back. When he found some Marines milling around dangerously on top of the ridge, he gave them an ass-chewing they'd never forget.

"Listen, you guys," he yelled, and for once they could've heard him from a hundred yards away. "The only thing those Japs have got that you don't have is guts! Now get the hell over there and get to firing!"

Then he grabbed them and pulled them behind him until he had them back in firing positions.

Meanwhile, Captain Bailey, the CO of C Company, gave Edson

plenty of support. Even though Bailey was still pale from his wounds, he seemed to recover every bit of his strength and then some.

"He was the big guy that was all over the place," said one of his Marines. "He kept running around that night and grabbing guys by their sleeves and yelling in their faces. 'What the hell you wanta do?' he'd say. 'Live forever?'"

At one point that night, the Marines on the ridge were down to one box of grenades for the whole bunch. But Bailey made it his business to see they got more. He made about a dozen trips down to a small supply dump at the foot of the ridge to get fresh supplies of grenades and haul them up.

Edson gave Captain Harry Torgerson, the Parachute Battalion's executive officer, credit for getting his depleted companies back on the line when some of them were down to just thirty or forty men still able to fight. He called them by name and challenged them individually to move forward and stand their ground.

"He instilled the will to fight into a lot of men who didn't want to fight anymore," Edson said after the war. "He did it with his voice. He started with two or three, and it just spread."

At 10 PM on the 13th, Edson sent word to division that his force on the ridge was down to 300 live and unwounded Marines, but he still thought he could hold. Division wasn't nearly so confident. Occasional Jap sniper fire was already hitting the division CP.

Thirty minutes later, the Japs launched a new charge with fresh troops at what was left of the beat-up Parachute Battalion. The strength of this new attack was too great for the Parachute guys to withstand, and they had to give ground—quite a bit of ground.

And that turned out to be a blessing in disguise.

The artillery men of the 11th Marines had been standing help-lessly by their guns for hours, but they hadn't been able to fire a sin-gle round because the Jap and Marine lines were so close together.

Now, with the Parachute guys pulling their whole line back and re-forming it higher on the ridge, it gave the artillery the opening they'd been waiting for. Our 105s opened up with the heaviest bar-rage anybody on Guadalcanal had ever seen, and the Japs helped out by stupidly firing off red rockets before each of their assaults so the 11th's gunners knew right where they were.

It was a total slaughter. Only a few Japs got onto the ridge itself, and they pulled the bonehead stunt of using more flares to light up our lines as they came. Big mistake. Our machine guns and BARs finished them off.

About 2:30 AM on September 14, the worst of the Jap attacks had been beaten off, and Edson told division his men could hold. By daylight, the attacks had fizzled out altogether.

By some reliable estimates, the Nips lost at least half their 4,000-man force to death or wounds. They left over 600 bodies for the Ma-rines to count on the slopes around the ridge alone. Several hundred more were killed in mopping-up operations by Edson's men and the First and Fifth Marines. Even my Third Battalion, Fifth, got in a few licks as the retreating Japs passed our way. Others died from wounds or disease when they tried to claw their way to the coast through the dense jungle beyond our perimeter.

Total Marine casualties for September 12–14 were amazingly low, all things considered—31 dead, 104 wounded, and 9 missing.

Red Mike Edson and Captain Bailey were both awarded the Medal of Honor. As far as I'm concerned, no two American officers ever deserved it more.

•   •   •

IN HIS BOOK *The Old Breed*, George McMillan called Edson's Ridge "the most critical and desperate battle in the entire Guadalcanal campaign."

I think he was right.

The largest Jap offensive on Guadalcanal so far had turned out to be a big fat failure. Of course, we knew damn well there'd be others, and none of us was dumb enough to think the Japs would just go away and leave us alone. We knew they'd try again. And again. And no telling how many times more.

But when I look back today on what happened on that island between August 20–21 and September 12–14, 1942, I honestly think the most important turning point of the whole Pacific war may have come right there in that twenty-four-day period.

Much bigger battles with much bigger enemy body counts would be fought later on in the Pacific. But those of us who were there on the 'Canal know how important the Battles of Edson's Ridge and the Tenaru River were. It goes way beyond the number of Japs killed.

Before those battles, our mental state hadn't been too good. We didn't know if we could trust ourselves or not. But what happened at the Tenaru and the Ridge gave us a hefty shot of self-confidence— even for guys like me who weren't directly involved.

After those battles, the Japs knew they couldn't make us break and run with their banzai charges in the middle of the night. At first, the arrogant bastards didn't think we'd stand and fight. They thought we were a bunch of pushovers.

Now they knew better—and so did we.

5

JAPAN'S OFFENSIVE HITS A WALL

AT 7 AM ON SEPTEMBER 18, we got our first reinforcements on Guadalcanal since D-Day. A five-ship Navy convoy delivered the three infantry battalions of the Seventh Marines that morning, giving us a total of ten on the island. A second Raider battalion, another artillery battalion, and other small units were also landed, plus about two dozen more tanks.

The convoy brought a total of 4,157 more Marines to our garrison along with 137 vehicles, 4,300 barrels of fuel, and some much-needed food supplies. The transports also evacuated 160 badly wounded men along with the survivors of the beat-up First Parachute Battalion.

For those of us who'd already spent forty-plus days on the island, it was a terrific morale boost to know we were getting this much help. But I also got a big personal lift out of the news because I was almost sure my old friend Remi Balduck was among those Seventh Marines reinforcements.

I thought it'd be great if I could get together with Remi, even for just a few minutes, but I figured the odds against it were pretty long. Where the guys from the Seventh were setting up was quite a distance from our sector, and none of us was likely to have much time for visiting.

Mostly, the First and Fifth Marines were still concentrating on defending the airfield at this point, and all these fresh bodies gave us a chance to put new muscle in our perimeter protecting the field and plug a lot of gaps that were still in our lines.

But, as it always seemed to happen, this good news came with plenty of bad news mixed in. Just three days before the reinforcements arrived, the aircraft carrier *Wasp*, part of a task force that had come back into our area for the first time since early August to give the convoy air support, was sunk by torpedoes from a Jap submarine. With the *Enterprise* at Pearl Harbor undergoing repairs to heavy damage suffered in the Battle of the Eastern Solomons, this left us with only one active carrier, the *Hornet*, to face six Jap carriers in the South Pacific. Not very favorable odds, to say the least.

The destroyer *O'Brien* was fatally hit by torpedoes, too. It sank a couple of days later, and one of our new fast battleships, the *North Carolina*, was so badly damaged it had to limp back to a stateside shipyard to have a thirty-two-foot hole in its side repaired.

Thanks to our Navy, things were starting to look brighter on the island itself, but the Japs still held the upper hand in the seas around us. Just to drive the point home, the Nips shelled the airfield and our defensive positions almost every night. Their destroyers and cruisers did most of the firing, but I remember one particular night when a Jap battleship opened up on us with fourteen-inch shells. One of them hit just a few yards from where I was holed up. Thank God it was an armor-piercing shell and not the high-explosive kind. Otherwise, I wouldn't be here.

Most of the Jap gunners aimed at the airfield, but when they finished shelling it, they'd switch their sights to the west and shoot at our defenses. Since the ridge we were on ran east–west, sometimes we'd move over the top of the ridgeline and get on the south side of it, where we were shielded from the enemy fire. We'd hunker down there and watch their shells land out in the woods. Sometimes the whole jungle looked like it was jumping, but nearly all their stuff was falling in uninhabited territory.

In the meantime, off to the west of us, the Jap destroyers took turns landing more troops. When they finished unloading, they'd head off to the northwest as fast as they could go to get out of range of the Cactus Air Force. Some of them weren't fast enough, though. Lieutenant Colonel Richard Mangrum's squadron of Dauntless scout bombers was credited with sinking a Jap cruiser and destroyer and damaging four other destroyers.

When it came to aerial victories, Captain Joe Foss of VMF-121 was Marine aviation's all-time leader. Foss's twenty-six kills tied the U.S. record set in World War I by the legendary Captain Eddie Rickenbacker and earned Joe both a Medal of Honor and a Navy Cross.

Several other Cactus fighter pilots also became aces at the 'Canal. Major John L. Smith was murder in his Grumman F4F Wildcat. He shot down nineteen Jap planes, and Captain Marion Carl was close behind with sixteen confirmed kills.

I'll never forget Major Smith. He was a real morale builder to us grunts on the ground. Sometimes when he came back from a mission, he'd fly right over our positions at low altitude and do some barrel rolls. The troops loved that.

One day, an F4F flew directly above me while he was right on the tail of a Zero. About the time the Zero got over open water, the 'Cat started blazing away with its wing guns, and smoke started pouring out of the Zero.

"Oh good, he got him!" I said.

But then the smoke stopped, and I said, "Oh shit, he must've missed, after all!"

But a second or two later, the Zero just broke all to pieces and came floating down like big sheets of paper. The whole bunch of us on the ground punched the air and cheered.

The next day, being as we were set up so close to the airfield, I had a chance to go down and talk to a couple of the fighter pilots. I told them I really admired their guts for locking horns with those Zeros, and I described what I'd seen the day before.

"Oh, hell, that was General Geiger himself flying that 'Cat," one of them said. "That old man's fifty-seven years old, but he still flies like he was twenty-five."

Maybe he was pulling my leg, but he sounded serious. He was talking about Brigadier General Roy S. Geiger, commander of the First Marine Air Wing, who'd come to the 'Canal on September 3 to take personal charge of the Cactus Air Force.

Geiger had flown every kind of military aircraft, from British Spads in World War I to the latest U.S. fighters, and "he commanded from the cockpit, not a desk," as one writer put it. But the best thing about him from an infantryman's point of view was his firm belief that Marine air was in business mainly to support the riflemen on the ground.

Geiger realized the Cactus Air Force pilots had several important advantages over the Japs who came to bomb Henderson Field, and he was quick to capitalize on them.

For one thing, most of the enemy planes flying bombing missions against us were based at Rabaul, which was a hard four-hour flight away. That meant the pilots were less than fresh when they got to the 'Canal. For another thing, unless they wanted to take off or land in the dark, their flying time always put them over Henderson between about 11:30 AM and 2:30 PM, so the timing of their bombing runs was usually easy to predict.

The third advantage we had was those coast watchers I mentioned earlier. They kept Geiger's staff so well informed of the Jap pilots' progress that our Marine fliers usually knew at least forty-five minutes in advance when a raid was due. This gave the F4Fs time to climb up to interception altitude, and our other planes had time to take off and fly east to avoid the Jap bombs.

AS FAR AS I know, no man in K/3/5 ever killed another Marine by accident on Guadalcanal, but we did have some friendly fire casualties in our outfit caused by guys in other companies.

The worst case of friendly and fatal small-arms fire I remember was right after the Battle of Edson's Ridge. K and I Companies were moving together along the coast road trying to head off the Jap retreat. When K Company cut into the woods to get in position between I Company and the Matanikau River, some of our scouts came under fire from I Company.

One bullet went right through the heart of PFC Jimmy Snodgrass, a damn good Marine, and killed him instantly. Then the same bullet continued on and hit Private Dick Tweedie, but he survived. (Later on, Tweedie got hit again at Cape Gloucester, this time by a Jap, but he lived through that shooting, too.)

AT 7 AM on October 7, the whole Third Battalion, Fifth Marines, moved out for a new strike across the Matanikau. We were assigned to lead the advance in the biggest American offensive operation yet on Guadalcanal. All told, our force included six infantry battalions out of the Fifth, Seventh, and Second Marines with 3/5 out in front and 2/5 close behind.

The first objective for our battalion was to gain a permanent foothold on the east bank of the Matanikau. We were told to set up our machine guns, mortars, and rifle squads when we got there, while some of our guys would pretend to be building a bridge. This was supposed to be a trick to draw the enemy to the river, but we never got a chance to do the part about the phony bridge because the Japs came along too soon.

We'd been on the march for about three hours and were still east of the Matanikau, with K Company on the left and I Company abreast of us on the right, when we ran into what looked like a full company of Nips.

Very quickly, we set up a line running east and west to try to keep the Nips from getting past us to the south, and within a few minutes we had a pretty hot firefight going. As K/3/5's reconnaissance sergeant, I was spending most of my time as a runner out of the company CP taking messages back and forth between Captain

Lawrence Patterson, K Company's commander, and the leaders of our three rifle platoons.

On one of my running trips, I'd just been given a message to deliver to the platoons by Red Mike Edson, who was sending a company of his Raiders in to help us. I was pounding along when I caught the attention of a group of four or five Japs, and one of them threw a grenade right at me.

It was the first time this had ever happened to me—although it wouldn't be the last—and I've got to admit it was pretty scary. The damn thing might've gotten me, too, only it hit a tree and bounced slightly off course. I ran the other way as hard as I could go and managed to get fifteen or twenty yards away from the grenade before it went off.

I breathed a big sigh of relief when I was sure it had missed me, and I just kept on running. I could hear bullets slapping the leaves on the bushes around me—probably from the same bunch of Japs— but I wasn't about to slow down long enough to fire back at them with my '03 Springfield.

At that point, all I wanted to do was deliver my message and get the hell out of there.

WITH THE HELP of the Raiders and the First and Second Battalions of the Seventh Marines, we were able to encircle some of the Japs and keep them from moving around us to the south.

That night, the Marines of 3/5 and 2/5 intentionally made a lot of noise with amphibious tractors. We called them amtracks. The idea was to make the Nips think we were getting ready to make a major river crossing into enemy-held territory. I don't know if we fooled them or not, but they stayed remarkably quiet all night long.

A heavy rain started falling the next morning and stalled the biggest part of our operation. Except for a scouting unit commanded by Colonel William J. Whaling, which slipped across the river and made a hard march into the hills beyond, most of us sat where we were and tried to wait out the weather. Unfortunately, though, the rain kept pouring down all day, and our main force hardly moved at all.

About dusk that evening, the Japs east of the Matanikau tried to break out of the loop we'd closed around them. There was a nasty hand-to-hand fight between about a platoon of Raiders and a much larger enemy force. Most of the Raiders were killed, but they made the Japs pay a heavy price for breaking out of the loop. Sixty-seven Jap bodies were found the next morning tangled in a barbed wire barricade the Raiders had thrown up across a sandbar in the river.

Out on our right flank where I was running messages, there were dead Marines from I and K Companies and the Raiders scattered all over the place. I found the body of Private Emil Student, a Marine I knew fairly well, leaning up against a tree. He almost looked like he was asleep. There were about thirty Jap bodies out there, too, along with maybe a dozen other Marines.

By this time, two full months into the fighting on Guadalcanal, I'd gotten fairly used to being around dead Japs. Usually, I could just step over them and go on about my business. But it still upset me when the bodies belonged to Marines.

I mean, I could sit down and eat my C rations around dead Japs without even thinking about it. But I totally lost my appetite when dead Marines were lying there a few feet away.

That day, I couldn't choke down a single mouthful of food.

•   •   •

THE NEXT MORNING, October 9, the Fifth Marines' assignment was to hold the line on the east side of the Matanikau. Meanwhile, Whaling's men and the Seventh Marines were supposed to
cross the river and carry out a previously planned flanking maneu-
ver to slip past the main enemy force. Once they got west of the Japs,
they were to make a sharp turn north toward the sea to cut them off.

But while everything had been put on hold until the rain let up,
a coast watcher near Rabaul radioed a warning to division headquarters that drastically changed the plan. According to the watcher,
the Japs were getting ready to ship out a major new invasion force
for Guadalcanal.

This news caused division headquarters to scale back the attack by the Whaling group and the First and Second Battalions
of the Seventh. Instead of driving on into the heart of enemy territory, they were told to halt their attack at a certain point and
return to the Matanikau perimeter, even if they were successful.
The Fifth Marines would hold at the Matanikau until Whaling's
men and the two battalions of the Seventh got back to the east
bank of the river.

But before he led his men back to the east, Lieutenant Colonel
Lewis B. Puller, commander of 1/7, wrote the first chapter in what
was destined to become a Marine Corps legend.

Colonel Puller was known to his troops as "Chesty," partly because of his barrel chest and jutting chin and partly because of the
hard-driving way he had about him. Two years later, when he was
commanding the First Marines on Peleliu, Puller damn near got his
whole regiment wiped out because he kept throwing his men against

Japs holed up in deep caves. But on that day at Guadalcanal, it was the Japs who got slaughtered.

Puller brought his battalion to the top of a dominant ridge, where he set up his mortars and machine guns with a fine view of the coast and the surrounding countryside. And for reasons that are hard to understand, 1,000 or more Japs from the Imperial Army's Fourth Infantry Regiment were ordered to attack head-on and up-hill against Puller's men in this strong position. It was pure Bushido bullshit. You'd think the Nips would've learned by now.

Only a handful of the attackers lived to regret it.

After their first costly attempt to climb to the top of the ridge, the Japs fell back to a narrow ravine at its base, where they were sitting ducks for the 1/7 mortar section. They tried to come up a second time and suffered even more ghastly losses. Then they retreated back to the death trap of the ravine, and the mortars chewed them up again. Finally, they tried to escape by climbing the opposite side of the ridge and ran straight into massed 1/7 machine guns.

"The diary of a Japanese field officer said 640 of his men were killed in this engagement," wrote George McMillan in *The Old Breed*. "Our losses for the entire three-day period were 65 killed and 125 wounded, while total Japanese losses were estimated at above 900."

Even more important than the enemy casualty figures was the fact that the Marines now held a well-fortified battle position along the Matanikau. But that's not to say the Japs had given up trying to regain control of the river. They kept punching and probing at our Matanikau lines again and again during the rest of October, trying to find a weak spot, and we kept punching back at theirs.

All these attacks and counterattacks ended in pretty much of a stalemate with the Japs still holding on to the west bank and us still holding the east bank.

One main reason we were able to do this was because the mouth of the Matanikau was too wide and deep to be forded from either side. So as long as we could keep the Japs from getting past us to the south, where the river was so shallow you could walk across, we managed to hold them at bay.

The tragic thing is, a lot of good Marines were killed or wounded in this back-and-forth fighting. But the days when the Japs were sole owners of the Matanikau and everything west of it were over for good.

WE HAD A MIXTURE of good luck and extremely bad luck on October 13. We got word that day that our second large batch of reinforcements would be landing in a few hours. It was the 164th Infantry Regiment of the Army's Americal Division. They were National Guard troops—and the first Army outfit we'd seen—so the Marines took their arrival as a sign that somebody in the U.S. command structure finally thought we were actually going to hold on to the island.

"Hell, they don't send in the Army guys until the tough fighting's over, and the Marines have the situation well in hand," cracked one of the guys in the K Company CP. Some Marines never missed a chance to poke fun at the Army, but a lot of us were damn glad these new troops were coming to help us.

Most members of the 164th were from farming and ranching country in North and South Dakota, and none of them had ever come under enemy fire before, much less in a steamy shithole like Guadalcanal.

As the ships carrying the 164th approached the island, the Japs launched one of their heaviest air-artillery attacks of the war. It was the start of thirty hours of pure hell. No American who lived through what happened on Guadalcanal between noon on October 13 and the night of October 14 will ever forget it. I guarantee you I won't.

By then, we Marines had been shelled so many times in the sixty-seven days we'd been there that we thought we'd seen everything the Nips could possibly throw at us. We'd seen the jungle look like it was dancing under Jap barrages, and I've already mentioned that fourteen-inch shell that almost landed in my lap.

Under the circumstances, we figured, *what else can they possibly do for an encore?*

Well, they showed us.

The bombardment by the Nip navy and air force started about noon on the 13th, and it didn't let up for more than a few minutes at a time until early evening on the 14th.

This time, they blasted away with not one, but two, battleships— the *Haruna* and the *Kongo*—accompanied by a supporting cast of cruisers and destroyers out in Iron Bottom Sound. The whole island shook under the pounding.

At almost the same time the naval bombardment started, twenty-four twin-engine Betty bombers, shadowed by a flock of Zeros, showed up over the airfield and dumped full loads of bombs. Somehow, these planes had slipped past the network of coast watchers, and for once, they caught the Cactus Air Force with its pants down.

Two hours later, fifteen more Bettys bombed the field again. They blew up a huge storage tank of aviation gasoline and sent flames spewing in all directions. The damage from the explosion and fire wasn't nearly as serious as the loss of the fuel itself. It left our pilots on short rations at one of the most critical points in the Guadalcanal campaign.

And right in the midst of all this, the little eight-ship convoy carrying the fresh-faced, clean-uniformed troops of the 164th Infantry came steaming in. Fortunately, the Jap planes were too busy blasting the airfield to notice the convoy until the new troops were disembarking. But once they did, those Army guys started getting their first casualties almost as soon as they set foot on dry land.

Then, about dusk, the 150-millimeter guns the Japs had brought onto the island three days earlier joined the bombardment. It was the first time that shells from enemy land-based artillery had reached Henderson Field.

A little later, the 150s turned their sights on the Navy's operating base on the coast near the village of Kukum. Then they dropped hundreds of rounds along our defensive perimeter before finally shifting toward the transports that had just unloaded the 164th.

At this point, we were dug in as deep as it was humanly possible to get, so we suffered only a few casualties out on the line. But the constant explosions tore our nerves to shreds and made us ache for some way to fight back.

There wasn't any, of course. All we could do was lie there and take it.

At 1:30 AM on October 14, a series of star shells lit up the whole sky, and the Japs cut loose with everything they had. Every gun on every ship in the sound and every land-based battery started firing at once. You couldn't hear any individual explosions. It was just one constant, rumbling roar.

The ground trembled under us and around us as we huddled face-down in the deepest parts of our foxholes. It was the beginning of the heaviest artillery barrage the U.S. Marines would ever face during World War II.

It lasted for eighty minutes that seemed like forever. I lay there face-down in the deepest part of my foxhole, hugging my arms around my head. At times, I prayed. At other times, I tried to think about home and visualize my mother's face. Eventually, I just went so numb all over that I couldn't think about anything.

When one incoming round miraculously missed us, there wasn't even time for a sigh of relief before we had to brace ourselves all over again for the next one. I saw guys crying like babies and beating their fists against the ground, but it was more out of frustration than actual fear.

"Just shoot me, goddamn it!" I heard one Marine yell out above the shell bursts. "I can't stand this shit any longer!"

We lost a good two-thirds of our Cactus Air Force that night. It was later reported that those two Jap battleships hit Henderson Field and the surrounding area with close to 1,000 fourteen-inch shells. That, plus all the other heavy stuff dumped on the field by other enemy ships, planes, and land-based artillery, destroyed every last one of our Avenger torpedo bombers at Henderson. We also lost a dozen of our forty-two F4F fighters and all but seven of our thirty-nine Dauntless dive-bombers. And with all that aviation fuel now gone up in smoke, there was barely enough to keep what planes we had left in the air.

It was probably just as well that those of us on the ground didn't realize just how bad the situation was at Guadalcanal after that horrible night.

Finally, around 3 AM, the firing tailed off, but at 5:30, it started again, and Jap planes continued their bombing runs until daylight. Then it was over.

In the silence that followed, we crawled out of our foxholes like drunks after an all-night binge. We shook our heads to try to clear them and stared at each other like a bunch of total strangers. For a while, my ears were ringing so bad I couldn't hear anything else.

Then that private from K/3/5—the one who was always asking the same stupid question every time I saw him—came wandering up.

"Oh God, Mac," he said. "You think we're ever gonna get off this damn island?"

I just stared back at him for a second while I fought off the urge to punch him in the face.

"Damn right," I said. "I'll get off this son of a bitch, and you can make book on it—but I ain't so sure about you."

IN LATE OCTOBER, my old First Platoon lost one of the best front-line leaders I ever knew when Lieutenant Scoop Adams was transferred to the K/3/5 command post to become the company exec. He actually just swapped jobs with Lieutenant Rex McIlvaine, the former K Company exec, who took over for Adams as leader of the First Platoon.

At the time, I was assigned to the CP myself as company reconnaissance sergeant, so the change didn't have much direct effect on me. I still saw Scoop every day, but the rest of the First Platoon was bound to have missed him.

McIlvaine, who was from someplace in Ohio, was a good officer and a regular guy, but he was also on the quiet side, and the guys in the platoon didn't feel the same kind of closeness with him as they had with Adams.

The word was that Adams was stressed out from nearly three months of constant combat conditions and just needed to get off the line for a while. But I think he was physically sick at the time, too.

As anybody who's been in combat can tell you, a platoon leader's job is the toughest one any commissioned officer can have, and the casualty rate's also the highest. The reason for this is that most other commissioned officers spend their days and nights in a company or battalion or regimental CP that's located anywhere from a hundred yards to a mile or more behind the front lines and better constructed than an ordinary foxhole.

Platoon leaders, on the other hand, are never much more than a grenade toss from enemy troops in combat situations.

Unfortunately, in Lieutenant Adams's case, he came down with a really bad strain of malaria within a few days after his transfer. It affected his brain somehow, and he had to be evacuated to one of the big military hospitals. He was gone before I knew what happened, and I never saw him again until after the war.

Malaria was almost as widespread on Guadalcanal as trench foot and jungle rot. They fed us bunches of quinine tablets to try to keep us from getting it—I remember swallowing up to five tablets a day at one point—but most of us were hit with it sooner or later, anyway. In fact, the only Guadalcanal Marine I knew of that never got malaria at all was Sergeant T. I. Miller, who served as platoon guide for the First Platoon.

For most people, symptoms of the disease come and go. You'll be burning up with fever or shaking with chills one day and up playing Ping-Pong the next. But in some people, it can turn into a potential killer, and that seemed to be how it was with Scoop Adams.

FOR THE REST of October, we slugged it out with the Japs along the Matanikau again and again. Practically the whole First Marine Division, as well as the Army's 164th Infantry, saw action in a series of tough fights.

On the night of October 21, it was the Third Battalion, First Marines, that came under heavy fire from Jap artillery, then faced a tank-supported infantry attack across the sandbar at the river's mouth. This attack was beaten off, and an answering artillery barrage by some of our huge 155-millimeter howitzers that had just been delivered killed an estimated 600 bunched-up Japs.

Division headquarters was well aware by this time that at least a full division of enemy troops was now operating on the 'Canal, and our brass couldn't understand why they kept hitting us in fairly small-scale attacks instead of throwing one big knockout punch at us. The brass also played a constant guessing game about where the Japs would attack next.

Since the flank of our advanced position along the Matanikau seemed the likeliest target for a major Nip assault, General Vandegrift ordered two battalions of the Seventh Marines to leave their position on a ridge south of the airfield to reinforce the Matanikau flank. The problem was, this left only Colonel Chesty Puller's 1/7 to man our defenses on the ridge.

A reserve battalion of the 164th Infantry was ordered into the line to support Puller's men, but the Army troops were held up by the kind of torrential rainstorm the 'Canal was notorious for.

And, sure enough, just after midnight on October 25, as the guys from the 164th were being fed into the line piecemeal, the Japs threw one of their biggest attacks yet at Puller's outnumbered Marines. They were still hell-bent on recapturing that airfield.

This was the fight where Sergeant John Basilone of 1/7 earned fame and the Medal of Honor for the steel nerves and sheer guts he showed in turning back the Japs that night.

Later, I read an interview where Basilone told how he did what seemed impossible against the charging Japs—not once but over and over again—with three machine guns and a pistol.

"We kept firing and drove them back, but our ammunition was getting low," he said, "so I left the guns and started running to the next outfit to get some more. Soon after I got back, a runner came in and told me that at the emplacements on the right, Japs had broken through . . . and the guns were jammed.

"I took off up the trail to see what happened. . . . After that I came back to my own guns, grabbed one of them, and told the crew to follow me. Up the trail we went. I was carrying the machine gun by the tripod. We left six dead Japs on the trail.

"While I fixed the jams on the other two guns up there, we started to set up. We were really pinned down. Bullets were smacking into the sandbags.

"The Japs were still coming at us, and I rolled over from one gun to the other, firing them as fast as they could be loaded. . . . We all thought our end had come.

"Some Japs would sneak through the lines and behind us. It got

Private First Class Jim McEnery shows off his new PFC stripes during training camp at New River, North Carolina, in October 1941.

With his 1903 Springfield in hand, McEnery pauses en route to the rifle range at New River to talk to a buddy, Private Shirley Keith, who is working a cleanup detail.

Lou Gargano (friend) and Jim McEnery in Australia, 1943.

Men wade across the Lunga
to begin a patrol on Guadalcanal.

Jim McEnery.

Colonel Merritt "Red Mike" Edson, one of Jim's most-admired officers, whose troops turned the tide at Guadalcanal by repelling fierce Japanese attacks against Henderson Field.

A machine gunner at Cape Gloucester comes off the hill after the battle has been won.

U.S. Armed Forces Cemetery at Cape Gloucester.

Tex Goodwin.

Jim's Marine Corps ID card
(note that he was in
for the "duration").

Parris Island, South Carolina
(Jim McEnery and friends).

Marines crossing the Matanikau on Guadalcanal.

Jim (in white cap) poses for a Marine Corps photographer with other battle-weary members of K/3/5 after their hard-won victory at Peleliu.

Sergeant McEnery (second from right) stands on the beach at Peleliu with the only other four senior noncommissioned officers of K/3/5 still alive and unwounded after the battle. From the left, his companions are Sergeants Dick Higgins, David Bailey, Donald Shifla, and John Marmet.

Men of the Fifth Marines begin to cross the Peleliu airfield under intense enemy fire.

Captain Andrew Haldane, beloved commander of K/3/5 on Peleliu, killed in action near the end of the fighting.

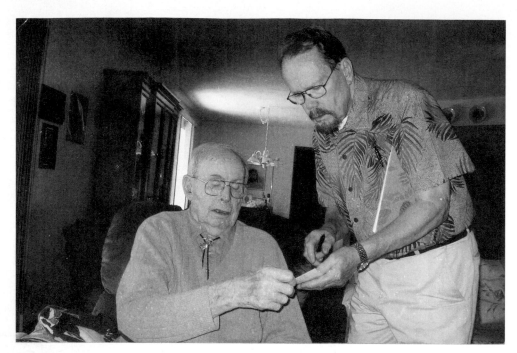

Jim McEnery and coauthor Bill Sloan.

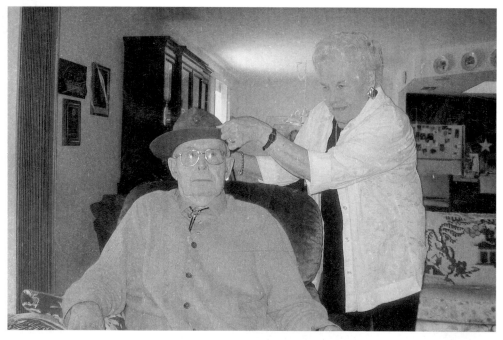

Gertrude McEnery, Jim's wife of 65 years, prepares for a photo at home in Ocala, Florida, in May 2011, adjusting the 72-year-old campaign hat her husband was issued in boot camp in 1940.

pretty bad because I'd have to stop firing every once in a while and shoot behind me with my pistol.

"At dawn, our guns were just burnt out. Altogether we got rid of 26,000 rounds."

More of the same continued through the day on the 25th and all that night, until early on the 26th, when the Seventh Marines broke the back of the Jap attack.

At the same time, other attacks were hitting our positions along the Matanikau. All of them were repulsed with heavy losses.

During the period of October 21–26, the Marines and the Army's 164th Infantry killed an estimated 2,200 enemy troops, and many experts believe that estimate is way low.

Total Marine losses for the period were 86 dead and 192 wounded. The 164th reported 19 killed or missing and 50 wounded.

For the Japs, it was the beginning of the end on Guadalcanal— but only the beginning.

ON THE MORNING of November 2, all three infantry battalions of the Fifth Marines were sent on an operation across the Matanikau that ended up changing the whole course of the Guadalcanal campaign.

The First Battalion moved out on the right—or north—side of our advance across flat land that ran through a coconut grove west of the native village of Matanikau. Their assignment was to attack another small village called Kokumbona, which was supposed to be the headquarters of the 17th Japanese Army.

Meanwhile, the Second Battalion was advancing on the left—or south—side of our front and following a ridge that ran west from the river. Our battalion, the Third, was in support of the other two and following in the tracks of the Second.

Before they'd gone far, the First Battalion was stopped cold in the coconut grove by a Jap defensive line anchored by at least two 75-millimeter field pieces and about a dozen machine guns. There were also hundreds of Jap riflemen firing from a natural ditch that ran inland from the coast for 100 yards or more.

The First took a god-awful bunch of casualties before they knew what hit them. Then, when they tried to take cover in the coconut grove, those 75s opened up and blasted most of the trees into stumps, pinning the First down not far from the mouth of the river and near an outcropping on the coast called Point Cruz.

A first-aid station was set up just west of the river's mouth where Higgins boats could pull in to pick up the First's wounded and take them back to sick bay.

Meanwhile, our Third Battalion was sent in to form a skirmish line behind the First so they could send their casualties through us, and we could cover them while they withdrew to a more secure position. Our setup was K Company on the left and I Company on the right, with L Company in support.

One of the jobs I had as company recon sergeant was meeting the walking wounded from the First and helping them get to the area where the boats were. I must've walked eight or ten guys back along the same route through the trees when I spotted what looked like a path, and on my return trip to pick up another wounded guy, I decided to take it.

In all the time I'd been assigned to the job of running messages back and forth and guiding wounded, I'd never been given a compass to help me keep my bearings and find my way. So I was basically just operating on instinct when I turned down this path. I was hoping it led toward Matanikau Village and was a shortcut to where the boats were.

Bad idea. Bad decision. Bad move.

I hadn't gone five steps when I heard a shot and felt a bullet whiz past my head. Then I heard a Marine yell from behind a clump of brush where he was hiding.

"Get down! For Chrissake, get down! You're in a Nip fire lane!"

I didn't lose any time doing what the man said, and it was a good thing I did. Seconds later, an unsuspecting lieutenant came trotting along with a runner of his own, and another shot rang out.

The lieutenant's runner wasn't nearly as lucky as I was. The bullet caught him squarely in the throat, and he went down hard, gushing blood. The wound looked really bad, but I never knew if the guy lived or died. I didn't recognize either the lieutenant or the runner, and I thought they must be from the First Battalion.

I crawled on my belly till I was maybe fifteen yards away from the Nip fire lane. Then I got up and ran like hell through the trees and brush. That's what runners are supposed to do.

Anyway, getting the First and Third Battalions realigned took most of the rest of the afternoon, but it doubled the size of our force facing that ditch.

THIS WAS THE START of K/3/5's toughest battle on Guadalcanal—one that played a big part in finally breaking the Japs' grip on the island. We won it by beating the Bushido bastards at their own game and mounting two bayonet charges of our own. That surprised the hell out of them. They didn't think Americans could do stuff like that.

I saw a lot of incredible things in my nearly two and a half years in the Pacific. But I think the action I witnessed—and took part in— on November 3, 1942, on Guadalcanal was the most unforgettable one of all.

As the sun rose that morning, the temperature started shooting up toward 100 degrees, and a lot of guys in the First Battalion, Fifth Marines were still stuck out in the open where that coconut grove used to be before the Japs blew it away. Not only were they frying out there in the blistering sun with hardly any place to take cover, but one of those Jap 75s started zeroing in on them again.

Lieutenant Charles J. Kimmel of I Company was crouched in the middle of a bunch of Marines from I and K Companies and staring down into the coconut grove, when he jumped up all of a sudden and yelled: "Those guys are getting murdered by that 75 out there," he said. "We got to give 'em some relief. Who wants to help me knock out that damn gun?"

The first man to step forward was Corporal Weldon Delong, a husky Marine just under six feet tall who was from somewhere close to Boston.

"Sure," he said. "Let's hit 'em!"

Delong was from Nova Scotia originally, but he'd moved to the States as a young boy and joined the Marines about the same time I did. I'd known him since boot camp, and he was a born leader who'd taken over my squad of the First Platoon when I was assigned as company recon sergeant. He was also a crack shot with either a rifle or a pistol and one of the gutsiest Marines I ever knew—exactly the type of guy you wanted with you when the chips were down.

Corporal John Teskevich, a coal miner from Pennsylvania, stepped forward next. "Sure, count me in," he said. "It'll give my old man another shot at collecting my GI insurance."

Teskevich was notorious for his hot temper, but he was also known for being cool as a cucumber under fire. He'd been in so many brawls since he joined the Corps that his squad mates started calling him "the mad Russian."

Never to his face, though.

"Yeah, I'll go along, too," said PFC Charles "Slim" Somerville, a short, skinny West Virginian who talked with a slow drawl but was the fastest man with a BAR in all of K Company.

After that, dozens of guys in K and I Companies started jumping up and hollering, "Me too! Me too!" Captain Wells, the CO of I Company, was there, too. He jammed his fist in the air to show his approval.

"Okay, fix bayonets!" Kimmel said. "And when I say 'Charge,' just run at the bastards like your pants are on fire."

A few seconds later, close to a hundred Marines formed up in a ragged line. Then they yelled like a bunch of lunatics and took off like crazy toward that Jap-held ditch forty or fifty yards away.

I'd just delivered a message to the K/3/5 CP when another runner came in and told Captain Patterson, the CO, that something strange was going on out on the line.

"Hey, Mac," Patterson said, "get back out there and see what's happening. Then report back to me."

I thought at the time if Patterson was the same kind of officer as

Lieutenant Kimmel and Captain Wells of I Company, he'd be out on the line himself in a case like this. But I didn't say anything. I just did what I was told.

When I got back to the line, a second wave of the charge was forming up with Captain Wells leading it, and I got caught up in the excitement and joined it.

There were at least another hundred guys in this second wave, and I was squarely in the middle. I noticed that PFC Bill Landrum, the assistant leader of my old squad, who'd shared a foxhole with me on our first night on Guadalcanal, was just three or four guys to my right.

Right before we jumped off, I'd heard Landrum tell the Marine next to him, "Just give your soul to the Lord, and let's go!"

We went right through the ditch where the main Jap line had been, but it had already fallen to pieces. The first wave of the charge had completely ruptured the enemy line. I saw Japs blowing themselves up with grenades and others running like so many scared rabbits.

I remember thinking they didn't look much like supermen now.

I emptied one five-round clip from my '03, and a couple of Japs sprawled on the ground in front of me. When I lowered my bayonet and jabbed at them, they didn't move, so I jabbed them again.

I saw two or three Marines I knew get hit and fall, but that wasn't nearly enough to slow down the momentum of the charge. I recognized one of them as Bill Landrum, and I tried to block it out of my mind. Another guy I knew, Private Paul Gunter, was killed about the same time, although I didn't see it happen. Gunter was another one of those kid Marines, maybe eighteen years old.

Over the years, people have asked me what I thought and how

I felt when we were charging those Japs and saw buddies like that cut down. I've always had to tell them I don't distinctly remember, that everything was just a big blur, and it was all happening so fast I didn't have time to feel much of anything.

In situations like that, you can't focus on anything but the job you're trying to do. That's just the way your mind has to work if you want to get through it alive. Everything else gets blanked out.

It's later on, when the excitement fades away, that you start thinking. That's when the knots come up in your insides, and you feel sad and sick about the guys you knew that died. You may even shed a tear or two, or say a prayer like the "Our Father" I said that night for Bill Landrum. But along with your sorrow, you also feel relief that you weren't one of those who went down. You know damn well you could've been, just as easy as not.

Anyway, within a minute or two, we'd chased all the Japs that were still able to move out of the ditch. They left their howitzers behind in a wild scramble to find some other cover. They also left about 400 bodies behind. They were scattered all over, in and out of the ditch.

Now there was only some mopping up to do, but it turned out to be almost as dangerous as the charge had been. Jap survivors were scattered over a wide area singly and in small groups. Some were wounded, but they all had weapons of some kind, and they were more than willing to use them.

After the ditch was clear of live Japs, Weldon Delong started running back and forth with nothing but a pistol and firing whenever he saw a downed Jap make a move. I guess he'd dropped his rifle in the heat of the charge instead of trying to reload.

Delong had put several enemy wounded out of their misery

when Slim Somerville spotted three or four Japs hiding in some water behind a log. They thought we couldn't see them, but Somerville noticed their reflections in the water.

The first thing Slim did was try to warn Delong, who was out in the open and unprotected.

"Get down! Get down!" Slim yelled.

I'd always liked going on patrols with Delong because he was always so alert to everything around us. Always looking up in the trees and behind the bushes. Always checking out anything that looked suspicious. Other guys in my squad were good, too; they just weren't as good as Weldon Delong.

But on this particular afternoon, he was too intent on looking for Japs to hear Somerville's warning. One of the Japs in the water fired, and the bullet slammed into Delong's chest. He went down without a sound, and never moved again.

After some other Marines took care of the Japs behind the log, I ran over to Delong. He was lying in a puddle of blood with his eyes wide open and his pistol still in his hand. The bullet had gone straight through his heart. He was as dead as a man could get.

By now, the adrenaline that had kept me going was drying up, and I felt like somebody had kicked me in the gut. Delong's death left me shaken as bad as I've ever been. I considered him the best Marine in my former squad and maybe the best in the whole platoon. I could trust him with any job, no matter how tough it was. But now, one moment of carelessness had cost him his life.

He was posthumously awarded a Navy Cross for outstanding valor that day in leading the charge against one of those Jap field pieces and then wrecking the gun. He also had a ship named in his honor.

But even more important than that, he was my friend.

"Don't beat yourself up about it, Mac," said Private Lou Bors, another member of the squad I'd led. "If you hadn't warned me to keep my head down, I wouldn't be alive now, either."

I nodded numbly. I didn't even remember warning him.

"Yeah, God knows every one of us damn nearly bought it right here," said John Teskevich. Then he laughed. "I almost made my old man $20,000 richer today, but I guess he'll have to wait a while."

I felt like total crap, but I tried to stay busy to keep from thinking.

Sergeant John Kelly, our third in command as platoon guide in the First Platoon, had just made lieutenant the day before. Now he was unconscious on the ground, shot through the body and bleeding like a stuck hog.

A corpsman did his best to stop the bleeding and patch up Kelly's wound, and I went over to see about him.

"Is he gonna make it?" I asked.

"Hard to tell," the corpsman said. "He don't look too good, but I'd say he's got a chance."

I stayed with Kelly (who I learned years later did survive his wound, by the way) until the stretcher-bearers came to pick him up. By then, it was after dark, and a day I knew I'd never forget was almost over.

In one way, it was the worst day of my life so far. I was sick at heart about the friends I'd lost, and I spent a long time that night with their faces floating through my mind, thinking about them and praying for them. But buried somewhere underneath my grief for Delong and Landrum and the others was the feeling we'd really accomplished something that day.

The Japs never advanced east of the Matanikau again, and after a few more halfhearted attempts, they quit trying.

Their three-month offensive to drive us off Guadalcanal had hit a wall, and now they were running out of gas.

As it turned out, I was, too.

6

"WE'VE GOT THE BASTARDS LICKED"

IT WASN'T MORE THAN a week after that last big fight along the Matanikau when I came down with a sudden, nasty case of malaria. And when I say "came down," I mean that literally.

I didn't even know I was sick until it hit me out of the blue; I thought I was just tired and weak from hunger. I was walking along in the K/3/5 bivouac area on my way back to the CP one morning when I passed out cold and fell flat on the ground.

The next thing I knew, I was in sick bay burning up with fever, and the medics were cramming quinine down me. I had a lot of company in that field hospital, too. The place was running over with malaria patients.

When the malaria outbreak on the 'Canal first got serious, the medical officers had made a standing rule that guys with the disease should be hospitalized for at least ten days. But after a few weeks, there were so many cases they had to scrap that rule and start discharging malaria patients a lot sooner.

After three or four days in the field hospital, they gave me a handful of quinine tablets and sent me back to the company. I felt okay for a while, but the malaria bug kept coming back on me from time to time for as long as I was in the Pacific. Actually, I even had a few flare-ups with it after I got back to the States.

Following the action of November 2–3, K/3/5 was pulled off the line and sent to a rest area in the rear, and as it turned out we never went back on the line on Guadalcanal again. Our company hadn't been in the thick of the action as much as we'd expected when we landed in August, but we'd had a baptism of fire on the 'Canal that would serve as a useful dress rehearsal for what lay ahead of us on New Britain and Peleliu.

Along about this same time, beginning the second week in November, we started hearing a lot of scuttlebutt about the whole First Marine Division being relieved and shipped to Australia. The Japs were still sending platoon-size patrols to probe our lines along the Matanikau, but it seemed like they'd lost interest in any more all-out fights.

What we didn't know was that a large Jap convoy, accompanied by an escort force of cruisers and destroyers, was heading our way with thousands of fresh troops and plans to launch a whole new invasion of Guadalcanal. The Nips who'd been taking it on the chin from us during October and early November may have been ready to call it quits, but Imperial Army headquarters obviously had other ideas.

Before he got word about this new threat, Admiral William F. "Bull" Halsey, commander of the Navy's South Pacific Area—a man I truly admired and still do—had also sent a major force of U.S. warships and transports toward Guadalcanal. There were four transports carrying the Army's 182nd Infantry Regiment to reinforce our garrison on the 'Canal, and they were escorted by six cruisers and fourteen destroyers. There were also three cargo ships loaded with all kinds of equipment and supplies.

Halsey had a second, even bigger task force standing by down at Noumea, New Caledonia, including the battleships *Washington* and *South Dakota*. The aircraft carrier *Enterprise* was there, too, but she was still undergoing repairs by a crew of eighty-five Seabees for heavy damage inflicted by the Japs.

(The "Big E," as she was known, was now the only U.S. flattop afloat in the South Pacific. The gallant old carrier *Hornet*, which had launched Colonel Jimmy Doolittle's bombing raid on Tokyo the previous April, had joined her sister ship, the *Wasp*, at the bottom of the ocean on October 26 after being hit by Jap torpedo planes during the Battle of Santa Cruz Island.)

Meanwhile, the Japs had two battleships of their own, the *Hiei* and the *Kirishima*, in the southern Solomons, and the two opposing forces were on a collision course as they steamed toward Guadalcanal.

The U.S. Navy's main goal was to get our new troops onto the 'Canal ahead of the Japs and then get our transports and cargo ships out safely. Once that was done, Halsey's fighting ships were ready to take on the enemy force jaw-to-jaw.

Far out to sea, one of the most furious sea battles ever fought was rapidly taking shape. None of us ashore had any idea what was about to happen, but the fate of every sick, battle-worn, half-starved Marine already on Guadalcanal was hanging on that battle's outcome.

AS LUCK WOULD have it, the first group of U.S. ships did beat the Japs to the island—but not by much. They anchored at Lunga Point at 5:30 AM on November 11. Just four hours later, while they were still unloading, they came under their first attack by enemy planes, and the transport *Zeilin* was damaged. A second air attack soon followed, but the unloading was completed that afternoon.

The second group of transports came in on the morning of the 12th and their escorts fought off another Jap air raid while they unloaded. But the only damage was to the cruiser *San Francisco*, caused when an enemy plane dived on her kamikaze-style. (Suicide attacks were rare by Jap pilots at that time, but within a couple of years they'd be crashing into our ships by the hundreds.)

So far, our side was doing okay, but it wasn't over yet. Far from it. As the cruisers and destroyers escorting the transports started withdrawing from the area early on the morning of November 13, inadequate radar caused them to move directly into the path of the approaching enemy naval force.

It was only when some of the Jap ships turned on their searchlights that the Americans realized what they'd stumbled into. Then, in the confusion, several of the American ships may have actually opened fire on each other.

It turned into one helluva bloody mess. Our cruisers *Atlanta* and *Juneau* were sunk along with four of our destroyers. Two other U.S. cruisers and three other destroyers were damaged.

Still, we got in some good licks, too. We sent the Jap battleship *Hiei* to the bottom with over eighty shell holes in her, and we also sank two Jap destroyers and damaged four others.

But our Navy's biggest challenge was still ahead. Those enemy transports carrying an estimated 15,000 reinforcements—roughly a whole division—had to be stopped before they could land those troops. Otherwise, the Marines on Guadalcanal would be in deep shit, and everything we'd gained over three-plus months of hard fighting could go down the drain overnight.

To Halsey, the stakes couldn't have been any higher, but he didn't admit publicly how desperate he considered the situation to be until he wrote his memoirs in 1947.

"If our ships and planes had been routed in this battle," he said then, "our troops on Guadalcanal would have been trapped as were our troops on Bataan. We could not have reinforced them or relieved them. . . . Unobstructed, the enemy would have driven south, cut our lines to New Zealand and Australia, and enveloped them."

Halsey knew the ships he'd lost were much less important than keeping those 15,000 fresh Jap troops from joining the fight for the 'Canal, and he pulled out all the stops. He ordered his battleships and the Big E north from New Caledonia at top speed. In the meantime, he sent every available plane aboard the *Enterprise* and at Henderson Field, along with a squadron of PT boats already in our area, to attack the Jap shipping.

At 11 AM on November 14, our search planes found the enemy transports, and what became known as the Naval Battle of Guadalcanal finally exploded full force. As Halsey remembered it later: "We threw in every plane that could take the air—planes from the *Enterprise*, Marine planes from Henderson, B-17s . . . fighters, dive bombers, and torpedo planes. They would strike, return to base, rearm and refuel, and strike again."

Six of the ten Jap transports were sunk outright. The other four were destroyed by Marine artillery and planes after they ran aground on Guadalcanal. Most of the troops aboard them were killed.

In a duel with the *South Dakota* and *Washington*, that other Jap battleship, the *Kirishima*, was also sunk, along with one enemy destroyer. We lost three destroyers, while the *South Dakota* and another destroyer were damaged.

After the remnants of the Jap invasion armada struck out for safer waters, Halsey summed up the situation in a five-word dispatch to Pacific Fleet headquarters in Hawaii.

"We've got the bastards licked!" it said.

BAD AS I hate to admit it, the First Marine Division itself was pretty well whipped by this time, too. Not by the Japs but by a combination of exhaustion, stress, malnutrition, hard labor, and those damn malaria mosquitoes. We'd lived with almost constant rain and mud for close to three and a half months. Our socks had long since rotted and fallen to pieces in our shoes.

During the Fifth Marines' fight along the Matanikau, our manpower losses from malaria got so bad that the medics were giving every man on the line twenty grains of quinine per day—and they were still dropping like flies.

At the middle of November, General Vandegrift reluctantly declared the division "no longer capable of offensive operations," and by the end of the month more than 3,200 Marines had been hospitalized with malaria. If misery loves company, I guess I should've been happy as a pig in shit. Only I wasn't. I was totally miserable.

There seemed to be a widespread feeling about this time among the brass at division headquarters that the Fifth Marines needed some "new blood" among its officers. So after we were pulled off the line, a series of big changes started taking place in the regiment's command structure.

At the very top, Colonel Red Mike Edson was named the new regimental commander of the Fifth Marines, replacing Colonel LeRoy Hunt. As weak and tired as I was, I was overjoyed when I heard the news. It wasn't that I didn't admire and respect Colonel Hunt. How could you *not* admire a guy who earned a Distinguished Service Cross, a Navy Cross, and a Silver Star as Hunt did in France in 1918? And, anyway, it wasn't like the Marine Corps was giving Hunt a demotion. He went on to become the commanding general of the Second Marine Division.

But if the Fifth Marines was looking for the kind of young, aggressive, hands-on commander who could inspire men in battle by his example, they couldn't have found a better man than Red Mike Edson. Like Hunt, he'd served in France in World War I, but he was only a boyish second lieutenant then, and now he was still in his mid-forties. He was the kind of leader who got right out there with his troops and fought with them shoulder to shoulder. He'd proved himself plenty of times on the front lines on Guadalcanal and had been awarded a Medal of Honor for it.

With this change at the top of the regimental command structure, there was a kind of ripple effect that ran all the way down through the battalion and company levels.

For instance, I don't think the brass was very happy with the job Captain Patterson had done with K/3/5 in the three months we'd been in combat, and I can't really say I blame them. Patterson almost never left his command post during a fight, and nobody in the company was more aware of that than I was. After all, I was the guy who ran back and forth with messages from his CP to the platoon leaders out on the line. A lot of them were messages Patterson could've—and I think should've—been close enough to his men to deliver himself.

To me, there's something wrong when a company commander has to send a runner like me to find out where his own damn company is. On the other hand, there's nothing that revs up a Marine's fighting spirit more than seeing his CO alongside him when the going gets rough.

At any rate, we got a new company commander named Captain Murray. In the short time I knew him, he struck me as being a really good, competent guy, but I never had a chance to see how he'd do in combat, because we never went back on the line at the 'Canal.

For reasons none of us really understood, Murray was replaced before long by Captain Charles Cobb. He was only with K/3/5 for a few weeks, and then he was also gone. The only thing I remember about him is that he didn't seem to like me much—I never knew why—and the feeling was mutual. I never knew what happened to him, and I never really cared. I was just glad I'd never have to go into battle with him in command.

ON DECEMBER 9, 1942—four months and two days after D-Day—the rumors we'd been hearing came true. We Fifth Marines became the third major unit to be relieved on Guadalcanal. The casualty-riddled Marine Raiders and Paratroopers had left several weeks earlier, and within a few days all the rest of the First Marine Division would also be pulling out for Australia.

On that same date, December 9, General Vandegrift turned over command of U.S. forces on Guadalcanal to Army General Alexander Patch, and even as we were leaving, the American troop buildup on the island continued. The Second Marine Division was already there, plus two Army infantry regiments, Army artillery, the Second Marine Raider Battalion, and all kinds of support and supply units.

Before the end of December, we'd have a total of 50,000 U.S. troops on the 'Canal, and the Jap high command finally saw the handwriting on the wall. Halsey had been right. The bastards were licked and they knew it.

We now know that on December 12, top officers of the Jap navy recommended to Imperial General Headquarters in Tokyo that Guadalcanal be abandoned, and two weeks later they started drawing up a secret plan of withdrawal.

If the Japs had any second thoughts about the final outcome of the fight for Guadalcanal, an American offensive that kicked off on December 18 put an end to them. By early January 1943, the offensive had cost the Japs about 3,000 men killed to only 250 KIAs for the Americans.

During the first week of February, virtually all remaining enemy troops on the island were evacuated, leaving behind more than 30,000 dead.

According to official records, total casualties for the First Marine Division were 621 killed in action, 1,517 wounded in action, and 5,601 hospitalized with malaria.

Our battle casualties were incredibly low for a campaign that lasted so long, saw so much hard fighting, and changed the whole complexion of the Pacific war, but the reasons for that were simple: We'd held our ground in well-entrenched defensive positions against troops that threw themselves at us in human-wave attacks.

The Guadalcanal campaign was over, but even then, not many people realized its full importance. General Vandegrift himself described it at the end as only "a modest operation."

But the truth became more and more obvious as time went by. The Jap navy went into hiding and didn't come out again for almost two years. The Americans gained a major airbase and staging area deep in the heart of formerly Japanese territory for our island-hopping drive across the Pacific. Because of its huge losses in ships, planes, and manpower, Japan's whole military machine was weakened so much that it was never able to mount a major offensive action again. Our naval losses were even heavier, but we could afford it because our production capabilities were much higher than Japan's.

And best of all, to those of us who were there when things looked the darkest, we showed the world—and ourselves—that the Nips weren't supermen, after all.

"Never did the enemy succeed in coordinating the attacks of his always-superior forces," wrote Marine historian John Zimmerman. "He under-estimated both the number and quality of the troops who first landed on the island. He committed his troops piecemeal and thereby suffered shocking losses."

Toward the end of the war, Army Chief of Staff General George C. Marshall summed it up very nicely when he said: "The resolute defense of these Marines and the desperate gallantry of our naval task forces marked the turning point in the Pacific."

•   •   •

WHILE WE WERE waiting to go aboard ship, I kind of wished I'd run into that squirrelly little character from our mortar section who'd kept asking me for months if I thought we were ever going to "get off this island." If I had, I'd have laughed in his face and said, "I told you so." But I guess by that time he'd already gotten his question answered once and for all.

Among the last things some of us did before leaving Guadalcanal was pay a visit to the new military cemetery near the airfield. I dragged myself out there, too, and I was glad I did.

The graves were still marked with crude crosses, and many of them had the dead man's mess gear and other possessions attached to the crosses. In some cases, friends of the deceased had written simple inscriptions like "Our buddy" or "To a swell guy."

But there was one in particular that was as straight to the point as it was poetic. It read:

> *And when he gets to Heaven,*
> *To St. Peter he will tell:*
> *"Another Marine reporting, Sir.*
> *I've served my time in hell."*

When we climbed up the cargo nets to board the USS *President Jackson* and sail to Australia, many of us were so weak and exhausted we had to have help from the ship's crew to make it to the top. Personally, I was so tired I wasn't even embarrassed by it. I just thanked the swabbies for giving me a hand and looked for the nearest place to sit down.

After five days at sea, we docked at Brisbane, Australia, and got our first look at the "Land Down Under." I'll never forget that day. I kind of wish I could.

I have to admit I wasn't very impressed with Brisbane. The problem was, it was in northern Australia, where the climate was just as hot and miserable as it was on Guadalcanal. Brisbane was a really tropical city with banana plantations everywhere you looked, and the countryside around it was one big, stinking swamp. You could almost see the steam rising from it. It was the middle of summer in the Southern Hemisphere, and, of course, there were clouds of mosquitoes everywhere.

Besides that, a lot of us were ready to hate the place even before we saw it, because it was Dugout Doug MacArthur's headquarters, and we'd all heard what he'd said about the Marines before he bugged out from the Philippines.

He'd refused to let the Fourth Marines fight on Bataan because he wanted to keep them on Corregidor to protect his own headquarters till he left for Australia. And thanks to Dugout Doug, they were also the only American unit that got left off the presidential unit citation given to the Bataan and Corregidor defenders by President Roosevelt.

When somebody asked MacArthur about it, he said, "The Marines got more than their share of glory in World War I, and they're not getting any in this war."

Then, about three months later, he'd had the gall to send the First Marine Division into a hellhole like Guadalcanal. Now we were under his command, and most of us figured he expected us to defend Australia. The whole idea started us doing quite a bit of cussing under our breath, and what came next was like throwing gasoline on a smoldering fire.

Once all the troops had disembarked, I was put in charge of a

K/3/5 working party assigned to clean up the mess the Fifth Marines had left behind on the *President Jackson*.

Obviously, none of the guys from Guadalcanal wanted to be stuck with this kind of job. You could almost feel their anger and disgust building up and up until it finally exploded like a bomb. The guys were already nettled because they didn't like MacArthur or the look and feel of Brisbane, and getting stuck with cleaning up after about 2,500 Marines only added insult to injury. Then, as the final straw, this turkey of a ship's captain lit into us in a report that described our cleanup job as "the worst" he'd ever seen.

I personally thought we'd done a fairly decent job, all things considered. I mean, what did this guy expect from a bunch of men who'd gone through over four months of fighting Japs and malaria with almost no food, no way to take a bath, only the ground to sleep on, and no fresh clothes until we were aboard his ship?

"Look at this lousy place," some of the guys started yelling. "What kind of a place is this? If this is how it's gonna be, just take us back to the 'Canal, for Chrissake!"

A few of them actually threw their rifles overboard. That was something I never saw Marines do before or since. As it turned out, it didn't matter much, I guess, because we were about to be issued the new semiautomatic M-1 Garand rifles to replace our old '03 Springfields anyway. But the guys' behavior pissed off the ship's captain even more than he already was—not that any of us particularly gave a rat's ass.

When we finally got to go ashore, they loaded us in trucks and drove us out to a campsite that looked more like a city dump than a bivouac area. Some other outfit's trash was all over the place, meaning we had another cleanup job to do. We were housed in moldy pyramidal tents, and a stagnant little corner of a swamp ran right through the middle of mine. If the water rose a few more inches, I'd have needed a life preserver.

Oh, well, I told myself, *what the hell?* I was so tired I could've slept on a bed of nails.

Naturally, mosquitoes were swarming all over the camp, and when our division surgeon had some of them tested, he confirmed that, yes, they were definitely the malaria-carrying kind.

I thought, *Okay, so what? I've already got malaria, so that's nothing to worry about.*

Some of our First Marine Division officers protested to members of MacArthur's staff about the crappy conditions at the camp, but it didn't do any good. "When you talked to these people," one Marine officer said, "you got the feeling they thought our troops were just another supply item that could be stored in a warehouse until they were needed."

FORTUNATELY, WE DIDN'T have to stay at Brisbane very long. I think General Vandegrift was determined to get us out of there ASAP, and he used his influence to put as much space as he could between us and Dugout Doug.

None of us wanted to be MacArthur's palace guard, but it wasn't that we had any bad feelings toward the Australians. On the contrary, the ones I met were good people, and they treated us great the whole time we were there. They knew that what we'd done at Guadalcanal had kept the Japs from invading their country, and they were grateful.

Anyway, when the Army claimed they couldn't find sufficient transport to move us somewhere else, Admiral Halsey stepped in to help. The next thing we knew, the biggest troop transport in the U.S. Navy showed up in Brisbane harbor. It was the USS *West Point*, which had been the passenger liner SS *America* in peacetime. It was so big it couldn't get to the dock, and we had to take a Liberty ship out to where it was anchored before we could get aboard.

We sailed from Brisbane on January 9, 1943, and three days later we arrived at Melbourne and disembarked into a place that seemed like a completely different world from where we'd been.

In the first place, Melbourne is probably the most beautiful city I've ever been in, and after four months on Guadalcanal and three weeks at Brisbane, it looked like heaven on earth to me. It lies at the extreme southeastern tip of Australia, where the climate is mild and pleasant the year round, and there isn't a swamp or a jungle within a thousand miles.

In the second place, the people in Melbourne gave us a welcome that none of us would ever forget. The day we arrived, the newspapers there called us the "Saviors of Australia," and that's exactly the kind of reception we got. Thousands of people opened their homes to us Marines and treated us like royalty.

We were stationed at Camp Balcombe, near a town called Mount Martha and about forty miles by train from Melbourne. K/3/5 was put on a "no duty" schedule because of our worn-out condition, and so we had plenty of free time to take a train ride into the city.

Our first stop was Flinders Street Station, and right across the street was a restaurant and bar called Young & Jackson's Pub, where most of the Marines headed as soon as they got off the train. Right in front of the bar was Melbourne's best known piece of artwork. It was a painting of a nude woman named Chloe by the famous French artist J. J. Lefebvre.

But there were plenty of other places to have fun in Melbourne—beaches, amusement parks, theaters, fancy department stores, soda fountains, ritzy hotels, beautiful parks and flower gardens, and, of course, lots of other bars and restaurants.

And maybe the best thing of all about Melbourne was that, wherever you went in the city, it felt so relaxed and orderly and *normal* after being in a hellhole like Guadalcanal. So after the Marines downed their first couple of Foster's beers at Young & Jackson's, they'd scatter in all directions and head for their favorite hangouts.

One of my own favorites was a restaurant run by an older Russian lady. I used to bring her cigarettes and chocolates, and she'd fix me unforgettable meals. I especially remember how much I liked her borscht, a type of soup made out of beets. I called her "Mom" because she reminded me of my mother. Sometimes, after a long, hard night on the town, she'd let me sleep in a spare bedroom above the restaurant.

I met a girl named Marian Curtis, who lived in a small town outside Melbourne called Marubeni, and I dated her quite a few times. Marian was really a sweet girl, and she had a very nice family. They invited me to stay with them sometimes and fixed up comfortable sleeping quarters for me on their wide front porch.

It was also in Melbourne that I became close friends with Lou Gargano, a Marine I'd first met at New River in North Carolina. Lou had been with K/3/5 ever since then, but he'd been leading a mortar squad on Guadalcanal, and I never saw much of him there. But when we got to Camp Balcombe, he was reassigned to the First Platoon, and we saw each other every day.

We were both buck sergeants and eligible for the same special NCO assignments, so we could've easily become rivals. It's also been said that Italians and Irish don't get along very well, but that wasn't true with Lou and me. Within a couple of weeks, we became best buddies. He was from Bayonne, New Jersey, just across the Hudson River from my hometown of New York City, and we were about the same age. It seemed like we could always find a lot of things to talk about, and we started pulling a few weekend liberties together in Melbourne.

Lou had what you might call movie-star-caliber good looks, with the kind of dark eyes and wavy black hair that women love, and I noticed early on that he got a lot of attention from the girls we encountered in the Melbourne bars. But I also noticed that he never flirted with them or even paid much attention. He was always polite, but that was as far as it went.

On our second or third night on the town, I found out why.

"When I first joined up, I planned to make a career out of the Marine Corps," Lou told me, "but then I got married, and now I've changed my mind. When this stinking war gets over, all I want to do is settle down with my wife and little girl, maybe have another kid or two."

What he said kind of surprised me. I already knew he was married, but I didn't know how serious he was about it, and I hadn't realized he had a kid. Back in those days, lots of guys in the military got married on the spur of the moment right before they shipped out, but as time went by, either the guy or the girl he left behind started having second thoughts.

"Where's your wife now?" I asked him.

"Oh, she's going to school at East Carolina Teachers College," he said. "She's still got about a year to go to get her degree. Then she says she wants to find a job teaching first grade."

Lou reached for his wallet and showed me pictures of his wife and baby daughter. The kid looked pretty much like all babies to me, but I had to admit his wife was a really attractive woman. I gave both pictures an appreciative nod.

"Very pretty lady," I said. "Cute kid, too. How old is she?"

"A little over six months old," he said. "I didn't find out my wife was expecting until I got overseas. She had to drop out of college for a semester to take care of the baby, but she's a smart gal, and she went right back. I may have to go to college myself after the war, just to keep up with her."

As the weeks passed, I saw less and less of Marian Curtis. I knew for sure now that Lou wouldn't have anything to do with the girls in Melbourne—and there were plenty of them, I can tell you—so there was no chance of us double-dating. I also didn't think any of us would be very comfortable if I brought Marian along on my beer-drinking bull sessions with Lou.

But there was another factor involved, too. Marian had let me know more than once that she was in the market for a husband and wouldn't mind at all if it turned out to be a Yank. She sent me a beautiful picture of herself along with a long letter that pretty much summed up her feelings.

Like I said, she was a lovely girl, but I wasn't ready to get married. Not anywhere near ready. I knew this stopover in Melbourne was going to end one day soon. When it did, I'd be going back into battle on some other damn island, and I didn't want to leave any Aussie war widow behind.

After a while, I just quit calling Marian, and that was the end of it. From then on, Lou and I spent our liberties at our favorite "slop chutes," as we called them, or took in one of the American movies that were always playing in Melbourne.

After I stopped seeing Marian, I still thought about her fairly often, and I never forgot her. I've always hoped she had a good life. Matter of fact, I still have that photograph of her somewhere. My wife, Gertrude, the wonderful woman I've been married to for the past sixty-five years, thinks it's funny that I've kept it all this time.

And when I stop to think about it, I guess she's right.

MY SADDEST EXPERIENCE during our time at Camp Balcombe happened one day when I went over to the Seventh Marines' area looking for Remi Balduck, my old friend from Parris Island. I didn't know what company he was in, so I just started asking around, hoping that somebody would recognize his name and steer me to him.

The first few Marines I asked gave me nothing but head shakes and blank stares. But I finally came to this one guy whose expression told me instantly that he knew who I was talking about and what he was going to tell me wasn't good.

"Sure, I knew Corporal Balduck," he said. "Were you a friend of his?"

That past tense he was using gave me a sinking feeling in my gut.

"Yeah, we were in boot camp together," I said. "Then we were both stationed at Norfolk for a while. Do you know where I can find him?"

The guy frowned and looked away. "In a hole in the ground on Guadalcanal," he said. "Remi bought it there last November."

The guy told me how Remi's G Company, Second Battalion, Seventh got into a heavy firefight with the Japs east of the Lunga River. Normally, he was a squad leader, but that day he spearheaded an attack by his whole platoon against a Jap position.

"He was hit just as he threw a grenade," the guy said, "but we wiped out the Japs and took the position. Remi's up for a Navy Cross for what he did."

I learned later that the citation for that Navy Cross praised Remi's "relentless fighting spirit, extraordinary heroism, and utter disregard for his own safety."

That was the Remi I remembered.

The day he was killed was November 9, 1942. At that same time, I was in a field hospital with malaria, and it was strange to think that I'd only been a couple of miles away when it happened.

In 1944, the high-speed transport USS *Balduck* (APD-132) was named in Remi's honor.

NOT LONG AFTER K/3/5 settled in at Camp Balcombe, we got yet another new company commander, this time to replace Captain Cobb. His name was Captain Andrew Allison "Ack-Ack" Haldane, and he'd done a great job leading a machine gun section on the 'Canal.

Haldane was our third CO in about a month, but I guess the third time was the charm, like they say. Ack-Ack was one helluva great guy and an outstanding officer.

He'd been a big football star at some college in New England, but he was a regular guy who got along fine with the enlisted men.

He was firm with the troops but always fair, and he never raised his voice. As a fighting man, I think he was cut out of the same cloth as Red Mike Edson.

(Red Mike, by the way, was destined for bigger things than being CO of the Fifth Marines. In August 1943, he'd become chief of staff of the Second Marine Division and was later promoted to brigadier general and assistant division commander. He was succeeded as Fifth Marines commander by Colonel John T. Selden, who would lead the regiment at Cape Gloucester.)

Haldane's arrival put an end to the game of musical chairs with our K/3/5 COs. He'd be in charge of the company for almost the next two years, and when we got to places like Cape Gloucester and Peleliu, we'd realize how fortunate we were to have him.

I'll be telling you more about him later—a lot more.

ONCE WE RESTED UP, recovered from our malaria and malnutrition, and passed a complete physical, we were put through some of the most rigorous training we'd ever had. Reveille at Camp Balcombe was at 7 AM, and usually it signaled the start of a busy day of simulated combat maneuvers.

During the Australian summer of 1943—wintertime in the U.S.A.—I was sent to an Aussie combat training school for NCOs, and it was terrific. The trainers were Australian sergeant-majors, who taught us boxing, jujitsu, and other self-defense techniques we'd never learned before.

We were split up into groups or wings with one group lying in wait and hiding until another group went by. Then the first group would jump out and attack the second one. What followed was a real brawl with a lot of good, honest, clean fighting. We got plenty of scrapes and bruises, but nobody got seriously hurt.

We also had a bunch of swimming competitions. The Aussies were noted for their excellent swimming, but we Marines outdid them. I won a handful of medals that I was really proud of from the Royal Life Saving Society.

The Aussies were fierce, tough competitors, and when we were on liberty, we got into some pretty wild brawls with them. I'll say this for them, though: They never fought dirty. No sticks or broken bottles or thrown chairs. But if you ever got into it with one of them, you'd have to take on the whole gang. They had kind of a herd mentality in situations like that.

ON JULY 8, 1943, General William Rupertus took over command of the First Marine Division from General Vandegrift, and after that training got considerably more intense at Camp Balcombe. We knew the good, relaxed times were coming to an end. Our next operation was getting close.

By this time, a lot of new replacements had joined the division, and they were being integrated into all three of K/3/5's infantry platoons to serve beside the Guadalcanal veterans and learn from their experiences during field exercises.

The new guys needed an education if they wanted to improve their odds of surviving the next operation, and we were glad to try to give it to them. We filled them in on the tricks Jap snipers used, like tying themselves in the tops of trees and waiting for a column of Marines to pass. And like cutting fire lanes a few feet wide at right angles to the Marines' line of march, then setting up machine guns to mow us down as we crossed the lane.

We warned them that Japs liked to slip up behind the last Marine in a column on patrol and slit his throat before he could make a sound, then do the same thing to the next guy in line. And the next, and the next.

In August, we started making practice landings from rubber boats, and learning how to work closely with tanks. Most of our liberties were canceled, and our leisurely weekends in Melbourne became a thing of the past.

Along with our new M-1 rifles, we were also issued a new piece of equipment to wear in a special sheath on our belts. It was a broad-bladed instrument that could be used either as a sidearm or a utility tool. It closely resembled the famed Bowie knife of the Old West, but it was called a Ka-Bar.

"You can do many different things with this knife," we were told when we received our Ka-Bars. "You can open a can of C rations with it. You can chop up firewood with it. You can clean the mud off your boondockers with it. And, of course, you can slit a Jap's throat with it."

The time for our next battle was getting close, and we all knew it.

ABOUT DUSK ONE evening, Captain Haldane surprised us by telling us to get our gear together and prepare to move out. We hiked all night long with full packs and bedrolls and carrying our M-1s. We'd march for fifty minutes, then get a ten-minute rest break.

The next morning, field cooks met us and served breakfast. Then the same routine started all over again. We hiked all day at the same pace as before, never getting a break longer than ten minutes, and then we kept it up for a second straight night.

The second day was constant maneuvers with tanks, artillery, and machine guns firing live ammo over our heads as we crawled on our bellies and planes bombing and strafing the area immediately in front of us. Finally, about 4 PM, all the firing stopped, and we started hiking back to camp.

On the way, I spotted an apple orchard where the trees were loaded with fruit, and I led my squad into it. We were relaxing in the shade and eating apples when the owner of the orchard came along. I expected him to tell us to get the hell off his property, but he surprised me.

"You Yanks are welcome to anything I have," he said. "I've got a son in America, and everyone treats him marvelously over there. You can bed down here for the night if you want. I'll get you some blankets."

When we got back to Camp Balcombe, considerably later than the rest of the company, Lieutenant Daniel Dykstra, our new platoon leader, wasn't nearly so charitable or understanding.

ON SEPTEMBER 27, the Fifth Marines left Melbourne and sailed north through the Great Barrier Reef and around the broad curve of Australia's east coast. General Rupertus and his staff had expected the division to travel aboard APAs, the Navy's new, specially designed assault transports, but we were in for a big disappointment.

The First Marine Division was now part of the U.S. Sixth Army, and Army brass didn't give a hoot in hell about our comfort or convenience. So we ended up spending two weeks aboard a cramped

Liberty ship named the SS *B. F. Shaw*. It was a Merchant Marine vessel that was never meant to carry troops, and we were crammed into quarters that ranged from primitive to nonexistent.

We shared the cargo hold with hundreds of crates, artillery pieces, trucks, jeeps, deflated rafts, and other equipment. We had two sleeping choices—we could either hang hammocks between steel bulkheads and girders in the hold, or we could bed down on deck under ponchos and the sections of two-man tents we called "shelter halves."

Our makeshift showers, toilets, and galley were located out on the weather decks, which were sure to be awash with garbage, sewage, and seawater in rough weather. Food had to be served and eaten on open decks, regardless of weather conditions.

Of course, we had no idea where we were going or how long it would take to get there. We had no specific information on our ultimate destination, but most of us from Guadalcanal could guess that it was "another damn island with another damn airfield."

We were right on both counts.

On October 11, the Fifth Marines landed at Milne Bay on the eastern tip of New Guinea. Meanwhile, for reasons only the Army knew, the Seventh Marines went on past Milne to Oro Bay, eighty miles away on the northwestern coast of New Guinea, and the First Marines and division headquarters ended up on Goodenough Island, about fifty miles off the eastern tip of New Guinea.

Milne reminded me of Guadalcanal in more ways than one. Our home there was a tent camp that Marine engineers had gouged out of the jungle along with a narrow street composed mostly of shin-deep mud.

The rain poured down in sheets for hours at a time. Then it

rained some more. The legs of our cots sank into the mud until we were practically lying on the ground.

It was a grim, gloomy, depressing place, and we were destined to be there for two and a half months while Army and Marine Corps brass butted heads over the plans for our next invasion.

It was almost Christmas when we finally learned where we were headed. It was a place called Cape Gloucester on the island of New Britain, some 600 miles away.

"The Cape," as we came to call it, would make our interlude at Camp Balcombe seem like a vacation in paradise. By comparison, even Milne Bay would look like the garden spot of the Pacific.

7

RED MUD, RED BLOOD, GREEN HELL

THE FIRST MARINE Division was given the day off on Christmas Day 1943. But the very next morning—December 26— troops of the Seventh and Fifth Marines hit the beaches at Cape Gloucester. Once again, just as we'd expected, taking a Jap airfield was the division's prime objective.

This one was at the southwestern tip of New Britain, a large island east of New Guinea. The big Nip air and naval base at Rabaul was at the extreme eastern tip of New Britain, but it was 300 miles away from our objective and in a separate combat zone where Admiral Bull Halsey was in charge. Our zone was under the jurisdiction of Dugout Doug MacArthur and General Walter Krueger, commander of the U.S. Sixth Army.

The American and Australian navies and air forces pounded the daylights out of our target area for ten days before the Marines went in. This was more than twenty times the advance preparation we'd gotten at Guadalcanal, but I was still thankful that K/3/5 wasn't in the first wave on this landing. Actually, the whole Third Battalion, Fifth, was still at Oro Bay when the invasion started. This may have been because of the logistical mess the Army had created when it broke up our division and scattered the various regiments out in different camps up to eighty miles apart.

This time around, it was men of the Third Battalion, Seventh Marines, that got the "honor" of going ashore first. They landed at 7:46 AM on December 26, and two minutes later they were followed by the First Battalion, Seventh. The First and Second Battalions, Fifth were next in line.

I'm sure all these guys were nervous as hell because they couldn't even see the beach ahead of them for all the smoke raised by the bombardment.

As it turned out, though, Jap opposition to the landing was exactly the same as we'd seen at the 'Canal—meaning it was zero. There was no opposition at all, and the coxswains on the landing craft came back to the LSTs (landing ship, tank) offshore yelling, "Landing unopposed! Landing unopposed!"

The reason for this was that, instead of hitting the beach closest to the airfield, the Marines surprised the Japs by landing a few miles to the southeast, in an area called Beach Yellow near the shores of Borgen Bay. Not a single enemy shot was fired at them that morning.

But just as they did at Guadalcanal, foul-ups by our mapmakers set up some dangerous booby traps for those first guys ashore. The maps were based on aerial photographs made on a cloudy day—which most days were at Cape Gloucester—and the areas covered by clouds were simply left blank on the maps. So there was no way to tell what was there.

Beach Yellow itself was swallowed up in a wild tangle of jungle growth that came almost to the edge of the surf. Then came the big shock. Just a few feet farther inland, an area described on the maps as "damp flats" was actually an impassable swamp.

"Time and again, members of our column would fall into waist-deep sinkholes and have to be pulled out," one Marine said of the swamp. "Any slip could mean a broken leg, a sprained knee, or a twisted ankle."

Despite all this, the Marines advanced west along the coast toward the airfield with surprising ease on the morning of D-plus-1, meeting only scattered opposition. By that night, they were at a position they hadn't expected to reach until D-plus-3, but from that point on, the going got tougher.

About 2 PM on D-plus-2, with Sherman tanks leading the way, men of the Third Battalion, First Marines broke through a Jap defensive line of pillboxes, machine gun bunkers, and 75-millimeter field pieces. None of the Nips' weapons even fazed the heavily armored Shermans.

"We turned a corner and ran right into a Jap 75," said a Marine tanker. "I saw one Jap walk calmly over and pull the lanyard. The shell . . . hardly scratched the tank. They were so astonished they just stood there while we mowed 'em down and smashed the piece."

At almost the same time that afternoon, the Second Battalion, Seventh was repelling a determined Jap charge in a swampy area near the beach. When it was over, our troops counted 466 enemy bodies in the mud. Marine losses in the fight were 25 killed and 75 wounded.

A series of firefights continued over the next couple of days, but at 1 PM on December 30 (D-plus-4), General Rupertus, our division commander, notified General Krueger that the airfield was secure.

"First Marine Division presents to you as an early New Year gift the complete airdrome of Cape Gloucester," Rupertus's message read. "Situation in hand due to fighting spirit of troops, the usual Marine luck, and the help of God."

At that point, a lot of people probably thought the battle for the Cape was as good as over. They were sadly mistaken.

BY THE TIME K/3/5 landed on New Year's Day, Marine engineers had used hundreds of logs to build a road of sorts across the swamp so supplies could be moved inland, and we didn't have it nearly as tough as our first troops had. But it was obvious from our first few minutes ashore that Cape Gloucester was one of the most miserable places on the face of the earth. In the mornings, a heavy blue-green mist rose from the jungle like steam. It shrouded the sun so it looked like twilight until about the middle of the day.

On that first morning, a driving rain began, and once it started, it never seemed to end. By the time we'd been ashore ten minutes, all of us were soaked to the bone, and I don't think we ever dried out completely in the nearly four months we were there.

I'd thought Guadalcanal was bad, but the weather at Cape Gloucester was the worst—and wettest—I ever saw anywhere. Absolutely and without a doubt. The ground—when you could find it for the water—was nothing but squishy red mud. It stuck to everything like glue—to our skin, our rifles, our packs, our uniforms, our boondocker shoes. Within a few minutes after we landed, we were covered in it so thick you could hardly tell a Marine from a Jap.

A pair of socks would turn to mush in your boots in less than a week from the constant moisture, but not many of us noticed because we'd go for days without ever seeing our feet. We had cases of trench foot and jungle rot by the hundreds.

It didn't take us long to get into some heavy action. I heard rifle fire the minute we landed, but it was hard to tell where it was coming from. The Seventh Marines were somewhere up ahead of us, and we were supposed to pass through their right flank and take the lead position in the day's advance.

Late that afternoon, we started to dig in for the night when a dozen or so Japs suddenly charged out of the jungle, waving their bayonets and yelling. Our riflemen killed most of them, but a few melted back into the undergrowth.

The next morning, after a nervous night, we were heading downhill through a fairly open area—one of the few we'd seen—when another group of about ten Japs popped out of some brush to challenge us. PFC Slim Somerville hit them with short bursts from his BAR, and Corporal Leland Paine and I joined in with our M-1s until all the Japs went down.

We thought at first it was just another brief skirmish like the one the night before. We were wrong.

Just as we approached another strip of dripping-wet, livid-green jungle along the bank of a creek, our platoon leader, Lieutenant Dykstra, was hit by a volley of automatic weapons fire that damn near chewed his right arm off. At least four or five rounds tore through it between his shoulder and his wrist.

"Down! Down!" a couple of guys hollered as a corpsman ran to the lieutenant and tried to get a tourniquet on his mangled arm. He was in bad shape, and I said a quick "Our Father" for him after I hit the dirt and rolled behind a large tree. It was the first of at least a dozen times I said the Lord's Prayer that day.

Then, before I could blink my eyes, all hell broke loose. Gunfire erupted all around me, but I couldn't see a damn thing to shoot at. Just to my right, no more than an arm's length away, Corporal Horace E. "Tex" Goodwin of K/3/5's machine gun section had just set his .30-caliber weapon on its tripod when a bullet struck him squarely in the chest.

His eyes were wide open, and he looked straight at me for a second. It seemed like he was trying to say something, but then he fell without making a sound, and I could tell he was dead before he hit the ground. The sniper who got him must've been in one of the trees right above us, and I felt the need to move to safer ground in a hurry.

As I scrambled away, a corpsman jumped up and ran toward Goodwin's body, but I tackled him before he got there and pulled him down.

"It's no use, Doc," I said. "He's gone. You can't help him. You'll only get yourself killed if you try."

The corpsman nodded and backed off. He'd have plenty of other wounded to deal with soon enough. Out of nowhere, we were caught up in one of the hottest firefights any of us had ever seen.

A few seconds later, my buddy Lou Gargano, who was hunkered down right next to me, took a sniper's bullet through his canteen. Before we left Oro Bay, Lou had been promoted to platoon sergeant and taken over as our platoon guide, replacing Sergeant John Kelly, who'd been severely wounded in one of our last scraps on Guadalcanal.

Now, with Lieutenant Dykstra wounded, we couldn't afford to lose Lou, too.

Luckily, he wasn't hurt, just stunned a little and with a good-sized bruise on his backside. But the force of the bullet had knocked him down, and he'd dropped his carbine as he fell. Now it was lying out in the open a few feet from where I was crouching.

Lou turned to me and frowned. "Hey, Mac," he said, "can you grab my carbine for me? I can't reach it."

I barely heard him above the rising roar of rifle fire, but I hugged the muddy ground and slithered forward on my belly.

I was reaching for the carbine when I heard a Marine yell from behind me. "Don't go there, Mac! They've got the range on you!"

I grabbed the carbine anyway, made a fast retreat without getting hit, and handed the weapon back to Lou.

"You okay?" I said.

"Yeah," he said, still sounding a little dazed. "But I don't know what the hell I'm doing sitting here. Jesus, with the lieutenant down, I'm the platoon leader now. Let's go!"

Lou got to his feet and waved us forward toward the trees lining the bank of a stream about twenty yards ahead of us. "Stay low and take cover in the creek," he yelled.

The stream was designated on our maps as Suicide Creek. After what happened there over the rest of that day and into the next, I decided maybe the guy who drew up the maps knew something we didn't.

I jumped up and ran for the creek bank as hard as I could go, staying in a crouch. To get out of the line of fire, I went over the bank without slowing down and hardly looking where I was going. In my hurry, I tripped on some rocks in the bottom of the creek and fell, spraining my left ankle and twisting my knee really bad.

A jolt of pain stabbed through my leg, and I could almost hear the tendons popping in there. It hurt like crazy, and I could barely walk. Even worse, my M-1 got messed up when it fell in the water.

Just to my left, Corporal Leonard Ahner, a lanky farm boy from rural Indiana, crawled up to take a look over the creek bank, and a rifle slug ripped through the shoulder of his dungaree jacket. Somehow, though, it didn't leave a wound.

"Well, that was a close shave," Ahner said quietly after he jerked his head back down behind the bank. I always admired those Hoosier boys. They hardly ever seemed to get rattled. As for me, I was rattled as hell—and hurting, too.

To my right, Corporal Paine was hugging his rifle and breathing hard as he eased up to take a look over the bank. "Now right about here," he panted, "is where I'd like to see John Wayne ride up and hit 'em with both barrels."

The words were hardly out of his mouth when a Jap bullet grazed Paine's cheek. He reached up to touch the wound, then looked down and frowned at the blood on his fingers.

"Well, hell, Mac," he said, "I don't think old John's gonna show up, do you?"

"No, man," I said. "Looks like we gotta fight this one on our own. Open your mouth and let me check that wound."

I looked to see if the bullet had gone all the way through Paine's cheek, but despite the blood running down the side of his face, there was none in his mouth that I could see.

"You're okay," I said. "Just keep your head down."

Over near where Ahner had almost been hit, I heard Gargano yelling instructions to me.

"We've got to get in position to return fire on these bastards," Lou hollered. "Start sending the men up the creek bank one at a time, and have them follow me."

The firing was so heavy by now you could hardly pick out individual shots, but I did what Lou said. Buddy or no buddy, he was the platoon leader now, and he was giving the orders.

Of the fifteen or so guys I sent over the creek bank, close to half of them came back wounded. I sent the worst cases back toward the rear and told them to leave their rifles. My leg was giving me such pain I could hardly move, but I started disabling the wounded guys' M-1s so if the Japs overran our position, they wouldn't be able to use them against us.

The Jap rifles were puny and inferior compared to ours, but they sure as hell caused us plenty of agony that day. We had at least ten guys wounded in the Third Platoon—about a third of our total strength—and it was a miracle there weren't more.

After about an hour, the Japs pulled back, and we got a little breather. I managed to haul myself out of the creek and limp back toward the company CP. On the way, I passed a wounded Marine lying unconscious and unattended on a stretcher, and a minute later, I spotted Sergeant Jim Day of K/3/5 and told him about the wounded guy.

"Don't worry, Mac, I'll take care of him," Day said. He was one of the most trustworthy guys in the company, and I knew he'd do what he said. "What's the matter with your leg?" he asked me. "Did you get hit, too?"

"Nah, hell, I fell in the creek and screwed up my knee and my rifle both," I said.

"Here, take my rifle," Day said. "I'll pick up another one at the CP."

So we traded M-1s. I'd disabled at least seven or eight weapons left by wounded men in the past hour or so without even realizing I could've replaced my own ruined rifle with one of them. That's how addled I was.

WHEN I HEADED BACK to where I'd been earlier, I could still hear quite a bit of firing in the distance, although things seemed quiet in the immediate area. But as I started downhill toward the creek, I saw Lou at the bottom, motioning me to stop.

He was giving me a thumbs-down sign and waving me away, and I knew he meant the route I was taking wasn't safe. So I stayed where I was and took cover.

It was a damn good thing I did, but nobody apparently warned the guys in the machine gun platoon from M Company. As they approached the creek, they came straight down the hill instead of following an angle that would have given them some protection, and the Japs cut them to pieces. I don't know how many casualties they took, but they were badly hurt. Their section leader, Lieutenant Elisha Atkins, was severely wounded and weak from loss of blood, but he ordered his men to leave him in the water where he'd fallen and get across the creek to safety.

Later, two enlisted men decided to go back for him, but they couldn't find him. They crouched neck-deep in the water and listened, but they couldn't hear a thing. They were afraid to call out to him for two reasons. First, the Nips might hear them and start shooting, and second, the lieutenant might think they were Nips themselves and refuse to answer. Some enemy soldiers knew a little English and were good at imitating American voices, as I'd learned firsthand at the Matanikau River on Guadalcanal.

Fortunately, the two Marines remembered a nickname that some of the machine gunners called the lieutenant—mostly behind his back—because of the Ivy League university he'd attended.

"Tommy Harvard," they started whispering. "Tommy Harvard."

After a long silence, they heard a faint voice coming from an inlet in the creek bank: "I'm down here."

"What's your real name?" they asked cautiously.

"Elisha Atkins," he said, and they hauled him out. He was in bad shape, but he made it okay.

ALL DAY ON January 2, the Third Battalions of the Fifth and Seventh Marines fought back and forth across Suicide Creek. Some of our guys crossed the stream as many as four times, but neither battalion was able to gain a solid foothold on the opposite bank.

By late afternoon, we were back on the same side of the creek where we'd started, and my sore leg was giving me fits. It was pretty swollen by now, and I had shooting pains from my knee to my toes. Since it looked like we'd be setting up right where we were for the night—and to get my mind off the leg as much as possible—I took out my trenching tool and started digging in.

I was trying to enlarge a good-sized shell crater enough to serve as a two-man foxhole, figuring Lou Gargano and I would share it that night.

And that was when the shit suddenly hit the fan all over again.

A bunch of Japs—I'd say there were at least twenty-five of them—had somehow crept up and hidden in some high grass and bushes no more than ten or fifteen yards from where I was digging. None of the Marines knew the Japs were there until one of them jumped up and screamed like a damn banshee. It didn't sound like he was hollering "Banzai!" It was more like just "Yaaaahh!"

Then the rest of the bastards jumped up, too, and they all started shooting.

I flung my shovel away and grabbed the M-1 I'd gotten from Jim Day. Then I hunkered down into that shell crater as low as I could and opened fire. I emptied a seven-round clip at the bunched-up Japs and saw a couple of them tumble. The empty clip popped out automatically, and I stuck another one in its place and got off a few more rounds.

On both sides of me, Marines were firing from crouched positions, and off to my left, one of our machine gunners started spraying the tall grass shielding the Nips with his .30-caliber weapon. I could see bodies jerking and flopping around in the grass as the slugs tore into them. He must've gotten at least four or five of them, but those that were still able to move slithered away and took cover behind a small hill.

"Come on, you guys!" I heard somebody yell from behind me and to the right. "Don't let 'em get in the creek bed. We gotta cut 'em off!"

After a second or two, I recognized the guy yelling as Lieutenant Andy Chisick, K/3/5's executive officer. I felt relieved when I realized it was him. He was a good officer, and he knew what he was doing.

I had a hard time putting weight on my bum leg, but I crawled as fast as I could through the mud and grass along with fifteen or twenty other guys until we had the Nips pretty well encircled. Then we reloaded and opened up on them again, keeping our aim low so we didn't shoot each other.

Over the next ten or fifteen minutes, we picked off most of the Nips, but there were still some left. I swear I could hear them breathing hard and rustling the grass. They were that close.

"For God's sake," Lieutenant Chisick hollered. He sounded mad and disgusted as hell. "Everybody fix bayonets, and let's get rid of these bastards!"

We trusted Chisick, and we did exactly as he ordered. All of us stayed low while we locked our bayonets into place. Then the fifteen or twenty of us—most of the unwounded guys in the Second and Third Platoons—jumped up and lunged into the tall grass where the Japs were hiding.

As we charged, we were screaming like banshees ourselves.

We shot some of the Japs, but mostly we took care of them with our bayonets. I didn't feel much of anything but the pain in my leg when I drove my bayonet into the belly of a Jap, then jerked the blade upward into his chest. I felt detached, like I was watching someone else doing it. At that moment, killing a man with a bayonet was just another hard, dirty job to me. I could've been digging another foxhole for all the emotion I felt.

In less than a minute, tops, not a single Jap was left alive.

When it was over, we just stood there panting and exhausted, covered with red blood, red mud, and sweat. It seemed impossible, but somehow, in the whole melee, we hadn't lost a man.

I LOOKED ALL AROUND for my shovel to finish the foxhole I'd been working on, but it was nowhere in sight. I never did find it, but Lou and I managed to squeeze into the hole that night the way it was. By that time, my leg was hurting so bad I couldn't bend it.

We argued over who'd take the first watch. It was an ironclad rule for Marines in combat that one guy in every two-man foxhole stayed awake at all times.

"Listen," I said, "you almost got killed today, and you led the platoon when I couldn't do shit to help you. Now go to sleep. I'm wide awake anyway."

"No way," he said. "I can tell your leg's killing you, and you gotta get some rest. So I'm standing watch, and that's that."

"But—" I started.

"Shut up, Mac," he told me. "I'm your platoon leader, remember, and that's a damn order."

I was too tired to argue anymore. I hugged my rifle with both arms and finally drifted off to sleep with my leg hanging out over the edge of the hole.

THE NEXT MORNING, January 3, the Japs opened up with mortars to start the day, giving the area a good pounding and letting us know for sure that they hadn't gone away.

If the two Marine infantry battalions drawn up along Suicide Creek were ever going to get across the stream to stay, the brass figured we were going to have to have tank support.

The problem was, the banks of the creek were too steep for tanks to negotiate, so our engineers had to bring in a bulldozer, first to cut a path through the tangled undergrowth on our side of the creek, then to shave down the banks so the tanks could cross.

The bulldozer was unarmored, and the Nip snipers started firing at it the minute they spotted it. The driver, Corporal John Capito, was brutally exposed in the 'dozer's high seat, and as he tried to push his fourth load of creek bank into the stream, a bullet hit him in the mouth.

Two other volunteers, Sergeant Kerry Lane and PFC Randall Johnson, took Capito's place and tried at first to operate the 'dozer from the side by using an axe handle to work the levers. When this failed, Lane climbed into the driver's seat. He was soon hit by Jap fire, but he stuck with the job until the bank was cut down enough for the tanks to cross. The whole operation took most of the day.

Both Capito and Lane survived their wounds and were awarded Silver Stars for their work.

On the morning of January 4, three Sherman tanks made the crossing with rounds from Jap field pieces and machine guns bouncing off them like Ping-Pong balls. They pulverized the enemy bunkers on the other side of the stream, clearing the way for the riflemen of 3/5 and 3/7 to finally make it across.

I was sorry that I wasn't able to go with them. About noon the previous day, I'd struggled back to an aid station and asked a corpsman to take a look at my leg. He didn't like what he saw at all.

"Man, you need to go to sick bay and get some treatment for this thing," he said. "Looks like you've got torn ligaments in there, and the more you try to walk on it, the worse it's gonna get. You ain't worth a damn on the line in the shape you're in anyhow."

He sent me to a hospital tent in the rear, where they gave me some painkiller and bandaged my leg from mid-thigh all the way down to my toes. I was there for over a week, so I missed the rest of the Suicide Creek action and some of the hard fighting that followed.

Beyond Suicide Creek was a series of Jap-infested hills and

ridges, and the farther the Marines penetrated into them, the stronger the Japs resisted. Over the next few days, the Third Battalion, Fifth, lost both its commanding officer, Lieutenant Colonel David McDougal, and its executive officer, Major Joseph Skocczylas, there. McDougal was killed, and Skocczylas was wounded.

On January 8, Lieutenant Colonel Lewis W. "Silent Lew" Walt, a brawny, barrel-chested, square-faced guy who looked more like a prizefighter than a Marine officer, replaced Colonel McDougal as Third Battalion CO. Then, within hours of his appointment, the new commander found himself in the fight of his life at a place known at the time as Aogiri Ridge.

At just after 1:30 AM on January 10, the Japs launched their first banzai charge against 3/5's position on the opposite side of the ridge, where Walt had personally helped manhandle a 37-millimeter field piece into place earlier that day.

Walt ordered the Marines to hold their fire till the Japs were practically in their faces. Then they opened up with everything they had—rifles, grenades, machine guns, bayonets, Ka-Bar knives, bare hands, and that indispensable 37-millimeter gun. The charge fell apart, and the Japs were thrown back, leaving scores of bodies behind.

Before dawn, the Japs charged four more times, and each time they were beaten off with heavy losses. When daylight came, the Marines counted more than 200 Japanese dead on the slopes below the crest of the ridge.

A couple of hours later, Marine General Lemuel Shepherd, recently appointed assistant commander of the First Marine Division, visited the battlefield and decided the ridge needed a brand-new name.

"We'll call it Walt's Ridge," he said.

. . .

THE NIGHT OF January 10 may have been the most memorable one in the history of K/3/5. My Third Platoon and the rest of the company were directly in the path of those five Jap charges, and Captain Haldane, our new company commander, became a legend that night among the Marines who served under him.

"Ack-Ack was right there on the line with us every time the Nips came at us," one K/3/5 Marine told me. "He had his .45 in one hand and his Ka-Bar in the other, and he knew exactly what to do with both of them. Once when we were almost out of ammo, I saw him ram that Ka-Bar into a Jap and then pick the bastard up and throw him off the ridge the way he used to throw a damn football. He rallied us and inspired us to fight harder than we ever thought we could."

Haldane had a rare combination of learned skills, natural intelligence, and raw courage that won the respect of everybody in the company and made us proud to have him as our CO. We respected him because we could tell that he really cared about us. He richly deserved the Silver Star he was awarded for "gallantry in action and conspicuous valor" during the savage hand-to-hand combat that night on Walt's Ridge.

Today, even after all these years, I still regret not being there to fight beside him. On the other hand, maybe that corpsman who insisted that I go to sick bay saved my life.

Who knows?

WHILE I WAS in the hospital, I had a visit from Lieutenant Tom O'Neil, an old friend from New Jersey, who'd been with K/3/5 on Guadalcanal but was now with L Company. He brought me some news that hit me like a ton of bricks and left me with a pain inside that was worse than my leg had ever been.

Tom was what they called a "Mustang," meaning a guy who'd started out as a private and worked his way up through the ranks to become a commissioned officer—something that didn't happen very often—and he was one of the finest Marines I ever knew. I was pretty sure he hadn't come all the way back to the hospital just to pass the time of day, and I could tell there was something gnawing at him even before he broke down and told me.

"We lost three real good men a couple of days ago," he said finally. "It was a freakish thing. They were all hit by a short round fired by one of our own 105s. I thought you'd want to know."

The tone of Tom's voice gave me a queasy feeling in my gut. "Well, sure, I do," I said. "Who was it?"

"Dutch Schantunbach and Norm Thompson had come back to the Third Platoon CP to hand out grenades to guys to take back to their squads when the round hit," Tom said. "They were both apparently killed instantly, and several other guys were wounded, too, but—"

"You said there were three killed," I interrupted. "Who was the third one?"

Tom looked away. "Lou Gargano was a few feet away from the others, but he got hit by a bunch of fragments, and . . . well, he didn't make it, Mac."

"Oh shit," I said. As well as I remember, I said it several times.

Dutch and Norm had been in K/3/5 ever since I joined the company, and they were part of its heart and soul. I could never forget Schantunbach leading a Higgins boat full of scared young Marines in singing "Roll Out the Barrel" as we headed into shore at Guadalcanal. And no squad leader I ever knew was more respected by the men he led than Thompson.

But Lou Gargano's death was something my mind refused to accept for a few seconds. I wanted to yell at Tom O'Neil and tell him to quit kidding around.

Lou can't be dead, I told myself. *How could a guy who went through what he did at Suicide Creek be cut down by a short round from one of our own howitzers? Tom's got to be wrong!*

Only he wasn't. Lou was gone, and the realization hit me as hard as anything that ever happened to me. I couldn't stand to think about the wife and the baby daughter he'd never seen waiting for him at home. I thought I'd go nuts if I did, so I forced myself to think about something else.

ON JANUARY 12, 1944, I was released from the field hospital and rejoined K/3/5 and the Third Platoon. The doctors at the field hospital had worked wonders on my bum leg. When they took the thigh-to-toes bandage off, the pain and swelling were almost gone.

Physically, I was feeling better than I had since we'd left Melbourne. My malaria was dormant, at least for the time being, and my budding case of jungle rot had cleared up. Even the overall situation on Cape Gloucester was looking brighter than it had since we got there. Walt's Ridge was secure, and the only remaining Jap stronghold around Borgen Bay was a rocky knob designated as Hill 660. By January 16, the Japs' last attempt at a counterattack had been wiped out, and the hill belonged to the Marines.

But there was no jubilation on my part. There was only an emptiness inside me that would take a long time to go away.

When I got back to where K/3/5 was bivouacked, I was named Lou's replacement as platoon guide. It was a promotion that once would've made me feel good, but as it was I didn't feel much of anything.

Our platoon guides weren't lasting long these days. It was like being handed a time bomb to wear around your neck.

With so many good friends in the company dead now, I couldn't help but wonder what would come first for me. Would it be a trip home or a bullet—or maybe a short artillery round—with my name on it?

I tried not to waste my time and energy thinking about stuff like that. If you dwelled on it too much, it'd mess up your mind really bad.

I wasn't sure I ever wanted to make any more close friends like Lou Gargano and Remi Balduck had been. It hurt too damn much when you lost them.

I was almost afraid to think about Charlie Smith, my boyhood friend from Brooklyn who'd joined the Marines with me on a day that seemed like a lifetime ago. I could only hope Charlie was okay— wherever he was.

Right now, all I wanted was to do my job at Cape Gloucester, get it over with as soon as possible, and get the hell out of there.

For reasons that those of us who were there never fully understood—and still don't to this day—it would take three and a half more miserable months in that "Green Hell" to complete this assignment.

•   •   •

ON FEBRUARY 3, General Rupertus informed the Army that the Japs on our end of New Britain were no longer capable of mounting a counterattack against the Cape Gloucester airfield—or, for that matter, any of the area west of Borgen Bay that they'd fought so hard to hold in January.

At this point, the Japs were in general retreat to the east, and the only thing left for us to do was hunt down and destroy as many of them as we could.

Personally, I think if we'd just left the bastards alone, most of them would've probably died on their own without any help from us. They were in that bad shape. Most of them were sick with tropical diseases, and a lot of them were wounded. All of them were starving and dead on their feet from exhaustion, so they weren't capable of putting up much of a fight.

They'd demonstrate that fact again and again in the weeks ahead, but unfortunately for K/3/5, General Rupertus had other ideas. He wanted the Fifth Marines to give the Nips as much assistance as possible in the dying process, and he assigned all three battalions of us—more than 5,000 troops—to go after them.

The first problem we had, though, was that the brass couldn't decide how we were supposed to travel. At first, we were told we'd be using Higgins boats to sail along the coast to a point east of Borgen Bay, then go ashore and try to find somebody to fight, but this plan was dumped before it could happen.

Instead, we marched overland on a government trail that more or less followed the northern coastline of New Britain. K/3/5 went without its machine gun and mortar sections, and, of course, with no artillery support. BARs, M-1s, and hand grenades were the strongest weapons we had, and a group of natives went along to carry extra ammo for us.

To help us sniff out Japs, we were also joined by some Army war dogs and their trainers, and I have to admit they knew their business.

I worked directly with one of those dogs for a day or two. It was a Doberman, and I was amazed at how it could pinpoint Nips who were doing their best to hide. It was almost like a bird dog setting a covey of quail, except that when the dog spotted the Japs, it let out this loud howl like a coonhound on the scent.

At one point, that howling dog flushed over a dozen Nips out of a single hole. They didn't shoot at us or anything. They just tried to get away, but we killed them all, mostly with our bayonets.

At times, it seemed like we ran across small groups of Nips at nearly every turn in the trail, and we were always wary of ambushes. Usually, they were either too lazy or worn out to try to surprise us, but a few times they did—and one of those times cost the life of Lieutenant James Lynch, who'd just taken over as our platoon leader.

The lieutenant was a replacement who hadn't seen much action, and he made the mistake of walking right up to a line of Jap foxholes, thinking they were all empty. One of them wasn't, and the Jap inside shot Lynch dead.

After that, Lieutenant Bill Bauerschmidt took over as our platoon leader. He was another one of many green officers who were joining our ranks at that time. Most of them came in as platoon leaders, who as I said were by far the likeliest officers to be killed in action.

Bauerschmidt was the son of a World War I veteran, and he carried the "hog-leg" revolver that his father had carried in France. He developed into a damn fine Marine officer, but during his first few days with the platoon, he sent me out on a mission that could've easily gotten me killed.

We were moving into a native village when we came on a bunch of foxholes. The villagers assured us they were all empty, that the Japs who'd used them had all left, but Bauerschmidt wasn't so sure, and I wasn't either.

"Hey, Mac," he told me. "Go up there and check out those foxholes. I'll cover you."

I didn't relish going up there by myself, and I was sweating a little, but I did as Bauerschmidt ordered. Sure enough, the holes were empty, and the Nips were long gone.

Later, the lieutenant called me aside and apologized. "That was a bad move on my part, Mac," he said, "and I'm sorry. I put you at risk, and I shouldn't have done it. We should've just grenaded the damn holes to be on the safe side."

EVEN WHEN THE NIPS did try to pull an ambush on us, they seemed almost halfhearted about it. More often, they just scattered into the jungle without firing a shot. Sometimes they just sat there and let us kill them or did us a favor by killing themselves.

We didn't take any prisoners, mainly because almost none of them chose to surrender. If their situation was hopeless, they preferred to blow themselves up with grenades or fall on their own bayonets. Usually, only the wounded fell into our hands while they were still alive, and we made short work of them. We knew better than to leave any Jap wounded lying around because as long as they had breath in their bodies, they'd do their damnedest to kill us. We'd learned that lesson the hard way at Guadalcanal. I got to the point where I could shoot them without feeling anything.

To a Jap soldier, surrender was the worst disgrace imaginable. Never in any of the fights I was in did I see one drop his weapon and raise his hands, clearly signaling that he was giving up. If I ever had, I'm not sure what I would've done, but I'd probably have shot him, anyway. Most of the time, we had no secure place to put prisoners and no time to deal with them—and we knew they couldn't be trusted. If the situation was reversed, we know they'd treat us the same way.

During one of our skirmishes, a Marine scout dropped his rifle, and when he went back to get it after we finished the Japs off, he found it booby-trapped. A land mine was attached to the rifle, and a grenade was attached to the land mine.

"I think I can dismantle that thing," I told Captain Haldane. "Do you want me to try?"

"No, Mac, just stay away from it. It's safer to leave it alone," he said. So I did.

Another time, I passed the body of a Jap who had his pants pulled down and his genitals exposed. I had no idea how he'd ended up that way unless he'd died or been killed while he was trying to relieve himself.

THE PLAN WAS to rotate the Fifth Marines' three battalions so that fresh troops were going out every day. While a couple of companies marched, another one boarded landing craft to try to leapfrog the retreating Japs and get ahead of them.

But bad weather hampered us from the start. It rained buckets damn near every day, and there was such heavy cloud cover that the Grasshopper observation planes we relied on to locate Jap troop concentrations were no help at all. The surf was so rough in spots that we couldn't even land on some of the beaches.

Colonel Selden, our new battalion commander, realized what a struggle we were having, and he took it kind of easy on us. He also knew the Japs were in no condition to offer much resistance.

"With few exceptions," he explained later, "men weren't called upon to make marches on two successive days. After a one-day hike, they either remained in that camp for three or four days or made the next jump by LCM [landing craft]."

The weather and the colonel's patience were two main reasons it took us almost all of February to advance about thirty miles, from the west shore of Borgen Bay to a place called Iboki Point.

The Japs never offered any organized rearguard resistance. Most of the enemy troops we encountered were stragglers with no will to fight. Quite a few of them committed suicide as we approached by holding grenades to their heads and pulling the pins.

IT WAS DURING this time that I had one of the weirdest—and, I have to admit, one of the scariest—experiences of my life.

We were moving slowly to the east through some heavy jungle growth, and I was anchoring the extreme right flank of our advance. I was keeping an eye out for Japs to our right and also trying to stay in sight of the Marine next to me on my left, maybe fifteen or twenty yards away. But the jungle got so thick in some places that I'd go for several minutes without being able to see or hear any of the other guys.

As it got later in the day, I sort of got accustomed to being out of sight of the others, and it didn't bother me at first. But then I realized it had been a half-hour or more since I'd seen another Marine, and I started feeling a little edgy.

About that time, I passed a native woman who was bathing her young child in a shallow stream, and I moved a little farther to my right to get past her. She never looked in my direction, and I don't think she even knew I was there.

It never occurred to me then that she and her kid would be the last human beings I'd see for the next eighteen hours.

As the afternoon wore on, I started veering a little more to my left, expecting to run into one of my platoon mates. We were all familiar with the pace we were expected to keep, and I was pretty sure I was still moving parallel with the rest of the platoon.

But when I couldn't make contact with anyone, it began to bother me, especially when the daylight started getting a little dimmer, and it was obvious that darkness wasn't far away.

Several times, I considered letting out a yell, but then I thought: *What if a bunch of Japs answer?*

So I tightened my grip on my M-1 and kept my mouth shut while I veered a bit more to the left. Still, the only thing I saw was more damn trees, brush, and vines.

When it got too dark to keep going, I sat down with my back to a big tree, laid my rifle across my knees, and ate some C rations. Before long, it started to rain, as usual. The jungle was full of strange sounds, but nothing I could identify as human.

I spent that night alone in the jungle—as alone as I've ever felt. I tried to stay calm, but I had a nagging feeling that I might be seriously lost, and I actually started to wonder if I'd ever see my platoon mates again. I was soaking wet, which didn't help, and I probably didn't sleep more than a few minutes at a stretch the whole night. I kept jerking awake and feeling for the trigger of my M-1, but I had enough self-control not to fire it.

Sometime before dawn, I did drift off. When I woke up, it was daylight, but the mist was so thick I could barely see the lower limbs of the tree I was leaning against.

Okay, I told myself, *this is stupid. I've gotta find somebody—anybody!*

I stood up and started working my way to the left. After fifteen or twenty yards, the trees thinned out a little. After another twenty yards, I thought I heard low voices, and I stopped to listen. Then I saw a couple of Marines I knew sitting in a clearing and smoking cigarettes.

I went over and sat down beside them, feeling a surge of relief.

"Man, am I glad to see you guys," I said.

One of them looked at me with kind of a puzzled frown. "Why?" he asked. "Do you want to bum a cigarette?"

I didn't even try to explain.

I MADE A POINT of staying within sight of at least one of my platoon mates after that, but I've never forgotten the lost feeling I had during that night in the jungle. A couple of days later, we got to Iboki Point and took a rest.

As nasty as our job of rooting out and killing Jap stragglers was, Colonel Selden told us he was proud of us for doing it well and not having any combat losses for several weeks while "maintaining unremitting pressure on the retreating enemy."

Our last real scrap in the Cape Gloucester campaign came toward the end of the first week of March, when we moved by boat out onto the Willaumez Peninsula, which juts about twenty-five miles into the Bismarck Sea from the north coast of New Britain. A good-sized enemy force was dug in on top of a 900-foot peak called Mount Schleuchter with mortars and at least one field piece.

K/3/5 and the rest of the Third Battalion landed on a beach at the base of the peninsula near Talasea Point and the Talasea coconut plantation. We quickly occupied both areas with only minor skirmishing while 1/5 drew the tough assignment of dislodging the Nips from their fortified mountaintop.

It took four days, heavy fire from our own mortars and artillery, and hard fighting by the First Battalion, Fifth, to finish the job. But by March 9, the mountain was clear of Jap defenders, and their mortars and field piece were in the hands of the Marines.

The so-called Battle of Talasea was our last major action on New Britain, and it cost the division its first significant casualties since Hill 660—18 Marines killed and 122 wounded. Close to 200 Japanese dead were counted.

After that, enemy resistance in western New Britain was over, but the end of the fighting there didn't mean we were going to get to leave. We'd be stuck there for nearly two more months—and if Dugout Doug MacArthur had had his way, we might still be there.

"It was like pulling teeth to get the First Division from MacArthur and away from Cape Gloucester," wrote George McMillan in *The Old Breed*. "The negotiations reached their climax in the first week of April with a not altogether pleasant exchange of messages between Admiral Nimitz and MacArthur."

After all the fighting our division had been through, Dugout

Doug wanted to send us to the other end of New Britain to take on the big Jap base at Rabaul. But Nimitz and other Navy brass were convinced that Rabaul had become isolated and could now be safely bypassed, rather than made the object of a costly, pointless battle.

To apply maximum pressure, Nimitz turned for support to Admiral Ernest King, chief of naval operations, and they both advised MacArthur to forget his Rabaul campaign and relieve the First Marine Division "as soon as practicable."

In the language of top military commanders, that meant "Do it now, damn it!" and MacArthur gave in. On April 17, he made a brief visit to First Marine Division headquarters on New Britain for handshaking and picture taking that took all of about two minutes. Then he was gone. It was the only time he ever came anywhere near Cape Gloucester.

A little more than two weeks later, we were gone, too. On May 4, 1944, we boarded the USS *Elmore* at Borgen Bay, and the following day we were among the last members of the division to leave our Green Hell behind.

Other hells awaited us.

8

THE CRAB AND COCONUT WARS

WHEN WE EMBARKED from Gloucester on May 5, most of us in K/3/5 were pretty sure we were on our way back to Camp Balcombe near Melbourne for another extended stay.

Scuttlebutt to that effect had been circulating for weeks, and we'd convinced ourselves it was the straight scoop. General Rupertus himself had supposedly said so, and a feeling of excitement spread over the ship as New Britain disappeared behind us and we headed into open sea. We were like a bunch of kids on the night before Christmas.

On the deck of the *Elmore*, some guys gathered around Lieutenant Edward A. "Hillbilly" Jones, the guitar-strumming leader of the company's machine gun section, and started singing the old

Australian folk ballad "Waltzing Matilda." The tune had been adopted by the First Marine Division as our unofficial theme song when we were stationed at Balcombe back in '43, and it cheered us up to hear it again.

Lieutenant Jones was from some little burg in Maryland, up near the Pennsylvania state line, and he was one of the best-loved officers in the Corps. He was another one of those so-called Mustangs who worked their way up through the ranks, and the enlisted guys who served with him knew he'd paid his dues on his way to becoming an officer.

Jones had joined the Corps as a private in the mid-1930s and served for six years as a seagoing Marine aboard a Navy ship. He'd won a lieutenant's commission at Guadalcanal for the fine work he and his gunners did in stopping those Nip banzai charges.

He was especially popular with our southern boys in K/3/5 when he was belting out some twangy country song like "San Antonio Rose" or "Red River Valley." They were the ones who'd tagged him with the nickname "Hillbilly," but by now everybody in the company called him that.

Personally, my musical taste ran more to "Sidewalks of New York" or "My Wild Irish Rose," but I was also a big admirer of Jones. He was a damn good person as well as being a good Marine, and the way he played and sang "Waltzing Matilda" even got me to humming a few bars.

We remembered Melbourne as a peaceful, stable, *normal* kind of place—one untouched by the gruesome ugliness of war that we lived with every minute at the Cape and the 'Canal. Short of getting back to the States, there was no place else on earth we'd rather go.

If we're lucky enough to go back to Melbourne, I thought, *I may just give Marian Curtis a call when I get there.*

I guess I should've known I was only kidding myself. We were all destined to be disappointed. Very disappointed.

SOME OF MY SHIPMATES with a keen sense of direction in mid-ocean and no land in sight started to get suspicious after we'd been under way for two or three hours.

"We're headed almost due east," one of them said glumly. "We'd have veered south by now if we were going to Melbourne. Dear God, do you think they're taking us back to Guadalcanal?"

Actually, the guy wasn't far wrong. For several reasons, Marine Corps brass had seriously considered Guadalcanal as our destination for rest and recuperation. Our battleground of a year and a half ago was now the largest rear-area U.S. military complex in the South Pacific, and there were ample accommodations available for us there.

But the problem was, the 'Canal had become such a beehive of constant activity that weary Marines who got sent there were likely to spend more time working than resting.

That was exactly what had happened when the Third Marine Division was sent there after their fight at Bougainville. They'd been ordered to supply 1,000 men a day for work details on the 'Canal. After four months in the Green Hell of Cape Gloucester, we were too sick and worn out for an assignment like that, and our Marine officers knew it, even if the Guadalcanal Island Command didn't.

So the Marine decision makers, including our old friend, General Roy Geiger from the Cactus Air Force, decided to send us to an obscure, undeveloped island called Pavuvu. Nobody in the division had ever heard of it, but the name itself sent up warning flares. It sounded like something that would stick to the bottom of your shoe.

Careful! Don't step in that Pavuvu!

Geiger had recently been given command of the III Amphibious Corps, which now included our division, and he and his staff chose Pavuvu on the basis of flying over it exactly one time. Glancing down from 1,000 feet, they saw sparkling white beaches, a placid blue lagoon, and neat rows of graceful coconut palms. To them, it seemed like a perfect spot for R&R.

Believe me, they should've looked closer.

COMPARED TO GUADALCANAL, Pavuvu's just a speck in the ocean, but it's the largest of the Russell Islands, a string of tiny dots of land stretching along the southeastern edge of the Solomon group. It measures about ten miles long from east to west and six miles wide from north to south, and it lies only sixty miles from Guadalcanal.

But more important for U.S. military planners in the spring of 1944 was the fact that Pavuvu was less than half as far as Melbourne from the First Marine Division's next objective, which had already been selected for us by none other than Dugout Doug himself.

None of us knew it at the time, but that objective was Peleliu, an obscure chunk of coral in the Palau Islands that nobody in the division had ever heard of and wouldn't for several months to come. It was a long sail away from either Guadalcanal or Pavuvu—roughly 2,100 miles—but if we'd had to travel from Melbourne, the trip would've been more like 5,000.

Personally, I'm glad they kept us in the dark about where we were going next. Dealing with Pavuvu was bad enough.

• • •

EVEN FROM THE DECKS of the *Elmore*, the island could've been mistaken for a tropical paradise. As one Marine put it, "The palm trees were swaying in the breeze, and the lagoon was beautiful. Then we went ashore and found out what it was really like."

There were no docks for our ships. We had to wade ashore from landing craft through a driving rainstorm. The rainy season on Pavuvu—when more than six feet of rain (that's seventy-two inches) falls in an average year—was supposed to be over already, but it must've been running late that spring.

We expected to find at least a preliminary campsite with roads, bivouac areas, drill fields, water wells, electric generators, and tents already in place. Instead, we found nothing but a wasteland of oozy mud littered with millions of rotten coconuts and besieged by armies of rats and land crabs.

As it turned out, it was a good thing the rainy season hung around longer than usual. There was no fresh water available, and the daily afternoon downpours were our only chance to bathe or wash our muddy dungarees.

According to General Geiger, a full battalion of Seabees was already on the island and ready to assist the Marines "in every way possible." Actually, only a handful of Seabees were there, and those few were waiting restlessly to be rotated back to the States. Meanwhile, they weren't exactly eager to do any dirty, sweaty work for a bunch of Marines.

As it stood, our "rest camp" consisted of piles of ragged castoff Army tents and half-rotted canvas cots scattered on the beach, and our designated bivouac areas were under several inches of water.

Underneath a semi-solid crust, the soil was dangerously unstable. A man could sink over his shoe tops without warning. And the more it was walked and driven on, the more the surface dissolved into one giant, knee-deep quagmire.

In this mess, it soon became obvious that we were going to have to build every stinking, saturated inch of our camp from scratch.

We stood around for a while, cussing, kicking things, and shaking our heads while we asked each other the same stupid question over and over: "Whose bright idea was this, anyway?"

As usual, though, bitching and bellyaching didn't help matters a bit. So we finally started digging holes for tent poles and patching holes in the tents. We used any kind of solid material we could find—palm fronds, scraps of wood, even some of the tents and cots that were in the worst shape—to give us any kind of reliable footing against the mud.

When the sun went down that evening, it got dark in a hurry. And I do mean *dark*. In the confusion of the afternoon, we hadn't given much thought to the fact that there was no electricity on the island. As night descended, some of us scrambled around to find anything dry enough to burn and make a little light.

This was where Gunnery Sergeant Elmo M. "Pop" Haney, a World War I veteran who was close to fifty years old, came to our rescue. Haney was by far the oldest man in K/3/5. His body was hard and muscular, but he looked almost scrawny in his uniform. He only weighed about 135 pounds and was fairly short—about five-eight, I'd say—but he was as tough as one of my old leather football helmets. He was eccentric as all hell, too, no doubt about it.

Some of the stuff Pop did caused a helluva lot of laughter behind his back. Stuff like jumping up at dawn four or five times a week and conducting fifteen minutes of bayonet practice all by himself, even aboard ship. Or scrubbing his whole body—genitals included—with a stiff-bristled brush while taking a shower.

He talked to himself more than he talked to anybody else, and every now and then he'd chuckle and nod his head as if he agreed wholeheartedly with what he'd just said.

Because of such peculiar habits, a lot of the young guys in the company thought Pop was crazy as a loon and laughed at him behind his back. But as I found out when night fell that first day on Pavuvu, Haney was smart in ways the rest of us didn't understand. The longer I was around him, the more I learned.

He could deliver a lecture on hand-to-hand combat that would've done justice to any drill instructor at Parris Island—which I had a feeling he might've been at one time or another. He was a dead shot on the pistol range, where he was in charge of safety. And heaven pity anybody who tried to sneak up on him from behind. He was as agile as a monkey, and he'd turn the tables on you before you knew what hit you.

"Come here, Sergeant McEnery," he said, "and I'll show you a little trick I picked up over there in France in 1918. We didn't have much electric light in them trenches, neither."

He led me inside a tent where he had a canteen cup filled with beach sand. I watched while he cut off a piece of tent rope about six inches long and poked it down into the sand in the cup, then pressed the sand tightly around it. Next he poured a few ounces of gasoline into the cup and let it soak in good. Finally, he struck a match and touched it to the rope.

And—*poof!*—like magic, Pop Haney had made a crude little lamp that put out a fair amount of light—at least enough to eat by or write a letter by, maybe even play cards by. It sure beat stumbling around in the dark like a bunch of moles.

"Well, I'll be damned," I said.

He grinned at me and winked. "No, you won't," he told me, "not if you watch your step and learn a few more tricks."

IT WOULD TAKE about a week even to get power to the division command post, and we never had electricity in the bivouac areas during the whole three and a half months we were on Pavuvu. With enough of Haney's lamps, we had enough light to get by, but there were some dangers involved with the lamps, too.

About a month after we veterans arrived, we got a shipload of green recruits of the 46th Replacement Battalion. Many of these new guys turned out to be top-notch Marines, but I swear some of them acted like real chowderheads when they first arrived.

There was seventeen-year-old PFC Seymour Levy, for example. He was a fresh-faced Jewish boy from my hometown of Brooklyn, assigned as a rifleman in my Third Platoon. His mother had damn near disowned him for lying about his age to get in the Marines, and I could see why. He was book-smart enough that he probably made high grades in school, but in a lot of ways he was still wet behind the ears.

One of his favorite pastimes was reciting poetry by Rudyard Kipling in what he thought was a Limey accent. You know, like:

You may talk o' gin and beer
When you're quartered safe out 'ere . . .

Anyhow, when Levy heard about the gasoline lamps that Pop Haney and a few other old-timers had made, he decided to build one on his own. Unfortunately, he wasn't able to locate a wide-mouthed metal container, so he decided to use a Coke bottle instead.

Bad, bad idea.

The bottle exploded and set Levy's tent on fire. He was lucky it didn't do the same to him.

"Levy was a bright kid, but he just didn't have much common sense," said PFC Sterling Mace, another New Yorker, who was Levy's best buddy in the replacement battalion. "Other guys were a little wary of bunking with him after that."

I liked Levy. Almost all of us in the platoon liked him in spite of ourselves. He was a nice kid and a dedicated Marine who served as a morale booster for his fellow replacements and even for older guys like me. But I had serious doubts about how he was going to stack up in combat, and I spent some extra time briefing him on stuff I figured he needed to know.

Maybe it helped, because Levy turned out to be a whole lot tougher than he looked. So did PFC Bill Leyden, another boy wonder from New York City, who was as Irish as I was and a bit of a smartass, too.

Personality-wise, Leyden was as different from Levy as two people could be. Levy did some dumb things because he'd led a sheltered life and didn't know better. Leyden, on the other hand, did dumb stuff because he always wanted to see how far he could push the limits.

To get him out of the house and out of trouble, I honestly think Leyden's parents may have picked him up and carried him to the nearest Marine recruiting office the day he turned seventeen. After some of the stunts he'd already pulled, like trying to ride across Brooklyn on top of a subway train at the age of twelve—and fracturing his skull in the process—they may have thought he'd be safer in the Marine Corps than he was at home.

Leyden liked to think of himself as a daredevil, and he took pride in taking risks that other guys wouldn't. This made me kind of nervous because risk takers have a habit of dying young on a battlefield, and I knew he'd have plenty of chances to show how daring he was in the months ahead.

Also among the new replacements was PFC Eugene B. Sledge, future author of the best-selling book *With the Old Breed at Peleliu and Okinawa.* Sledge was a quiet, studious young man from Alabama, who was assigned as an ammo handler in K/3/5's mortar section.

Of all the newcomers, Sledge seemed to be the most fascinated by Pop Haney. He was always watching Haney out of the corner of his eye and, I guess, trying to figure out what was going on inside the old guy's head.

One day on the pistol range, Sledge was stunned to see Haney throw a handful of gravel squarely in the face of a green second lieutenant who'd accidentally pointed his loaded .45 in the direction of another Marine.

Any other noncom in the company might've gotten busted or even court-martialed for a stunt like that. But the green lieutenant just blushed and left the range, rubbing his eyes, and Haney went back to supervising the marksmen like nothing had happened.

"Haney was the only man I ever knew in the outfit who didn't seem to have a buddy," Sledge would later write. "He wasn't a loner in the sense that he was sullen or unfriendly. He simply lived in a world all his own. . . .

"We all cleaned our weapons daily, but Haney cleaned his M-1 before muster, at noon chow, and after dismissal in the afternoon. . . . He would sit by himself, light a cigarette, field strip his rifle, and meticulously clean every inch of it. Then he cleaned his bayonet. . . . He was like Robinson Crusoe on an island by himself."

BEFORE THE WAR, Pavuvu had been the site of a big copra plantation, but when we landed there, its coconut crops hadn't been harvested for nearly two years, and the ground in the palm groves was several feet deep in rotten coconuts.

The smell wasn't as bad as the smell of decomposing corpses on a week-old battlefield, but it came pretty damn close, and there was no way to escape from it for the first several weeks we were there.

Every day, we sent out work details to load up and haul away the putrified coconuts. They trucked them through the quagmires that passed for streets and dumped them in the huge swamp that covered about three-fourths of the island. Eventually, the smell subsided. But even Marines who'd lived on almost nothing but coconuts and rice on Guadalcanal reached the point where the very sight of a coconut made them gag.

Some guys developed such an aversion to coconuts that they started venting their anger against the trees that produced them. One classic story that made the rounds on Pavuvu was about a Marine who ran out of his tent screaming at dusk one night and threw himself against the trunk of a coconut palm and started beating it savagely with his fists.

"I hate you, goddamn it," he sobbed. "I hate you! I hate you!"

"Hit the son of a bitch once for me," somebody yelled from a nearby tent. Otherwise, there was no reaction to the screamer's outburst. It was just another typical evening on Pavuvu.

OTHER WORK PARTIES carried crushed coral from a large vein that Marine engineers located and quarried, using whatever containers they could find—pails, helmets, even mess kits—to pave walkways and streets in the endless sea of mud. Still others dug drainage ditches and collection pools to carry off and contain the rains that fell every day.

According to Marine regulations, tents in rest camps were supposed to have wooden decks, but lumber was about as scarce as gold nuggets on Pavuvu. To keep us from sinking up to our knees in the muck inside our tents, we scrounged every scrap of wood, sheet metal, or pasteboard we could find to keep at least some of our gear dry.

And then there were the tens of thousands of uninvited guests— the rats and land crabs—that invaded our tents every night.

Nobody was sure where the rats went in the daytime, but at night, they were everywhere. Herds of them ran across the tops of our tents and down the tent ropes to the ground, where they scattered in all directions, screeching wildly, darting over sleeping Marines, and devouring anything remotely edible in their path. Judging from the number of guys who were bitten by them, human flesh definitely fell into that category.

Men tried in various ways to fight back. Some made traps by placing bait in five-pound coffee cans and incinerating the rats who got caught in them with gasoline. Others created booby traps by putting percussion caps into packages of crackers.

One company commander armed his men with flamethrowers and declared all-out war against the little devils. They killed over 400 rats in a single night, but the next night there were just as many as ever, and the CO decided his offensive was wasted effort.

The land crabs also came out to prowl every night. They weren't as vicious as the rats, but they were just as repulsive and infuriating. They especially liked to crawl into our boondocker combat boots and make themselves at home. You learned pretty fast to shake out your boots in the morning before you put them on or suffer the consequences. Once I found three of the things in one of my boots. Because of the crabs and mud, some guys quit wearing shoes altogether and just squished around barefoot.

The occupants of a half-dozen tents got so sick of the crabs that they formed a crab patrol one morning and tried to exterminate them all. They routed them out of their hiding places, smashing them with sticks and rifle butts and stabbing them with bayonets, Ka-Bars, and trenching tools.

After the massacre, they counted 128 dead crabs in one tent alone. They threw the carcasses into an oil drum, drenched them with gasoline, and set them on fire—and immediately wished they hadn't.

"It was the most sickening smell in the world," one Marine said. "It was so bad we couldn't stay in our tents the rest of the day. It was a Sunday, too, so we lost all our Sunday sack time."

EXCEPT WHEN THEY'RE LUCKY enough to be dining in style aboard Navy ships, Marines always seem to complain about the chow they're served on duty, and Pavuvu was no exception to this rule.

Since there was no refrigerated storage for fresh meat, fruits, and vegetables on the island, our meals for the first month or two consisted mostly of powdered eggs, dehydrated potatoes and carrots, and three or four kinds of canned meats, all of which we called "Spam." In other words, they were the equivalent of heated C rations, and all we had to wash them down with was a bright yellow, imitation-lemon-flavored drink known as "battery acid."

During one period of several days, the cooks varied the menu by serving nothing but oatmeal—morning, noon, and night. It was monotonous, and it didn't taste all that great, but when I remembered what we survived on at Guadalcanal, I counted my blessings.

The new guys were particularly critical of the bread our cooks turned out. Gene Sledge described it as being "so heavy that when you held a slice by one side, the rest of the slice broke away of its own weight. The flour was so massively infested with weevils that each slice of bread had more of the little beetles than there are seeds in a slice of rye bread."

When combat veterans heard Sledge and other replacements bitching about the bread, some of them made a joke out of it. "Hey, those bugs are good for you," they'd say. "They put more protein in your diet."

Not all of us old hands were quite that polite, though. "What the hell are you griping about?" I remember telling one mouthy replacement. "This ain't the Waldorf-Astoria. You volunteered to be a Marine, and you're getting exactly what you asked for. If you'd been at the 'Canal, you'd know how good you've got it here."

Another veteran noncom put it even more bluntly. "Just shut up and quit whining," he told Sledge. "Things could be a damn sight worse, and besides, until you've been in combat, you got nothing to complain about."

This put-down left a deep impression on the sensitive young replacement. "He made me thoroughly ashamed," Sledge said later. "After that, I kept most of my negative remarks to myself."

It was undeniably true that Pop Haney didn't have any really close buddies. But for reasons I never fully figured out, Pop did take a liking to me, and I guess I became the closest thing he had to an actual friend in the company.

For one thing, I didn't mind listening to Pop's long explanations about the importance of one man staying awake and alert at all times in every foxhole or how to stay ready to fight off an attacker who jumped into your foxhole at night.

"You gotta keep your bayonet sharp and in your hand when there ain't room to use your rifle," he'd say. "You gotta grab that fuckin' Jap and pull him up close and cut his damn throat as quick as you can."

Usually all I had to do was nod and say "Uh-huh," and Pop would just go right on talking. But I really did listen to a lot of what he had to say because I knew he knew what he was talking about. After all, he'd been doing it since before I was born.

About once every three or four weeks, Pop came up with a pint bottle of whiskey. I never asked where it came from, and he never told me, but I figured he got it from one of the men who delivered our mail by boat every four or five days.

(The mail came from Banika, the nearest island to Pavuvu, where the Navy maintained a huge supply depot, a hospital staffed by real, live American nurses, and other major amenities. Only a handful of Pavuvu Marines ever got to go to Banika, and the ones who did talked about it like it was heaven on earth.)

Anyway, whenever Pop got a fresh bottle, he'd invite me to share it with him, and he never had to ask me twice, I can tell you. I mean, the last thing I wanted to do was hurt the old man's feelings.

He'd lead the way to a beat-up old rowboat he kept hidden in some reeds, and we'd row out to a raft anchored about a hundred feet offshore. We'd sit there for a half-hour or so, until the bottle was empty, then get in the boat and row back to shore.

After a couple of snorts from the bottle, all Pop wanted to talk about was the "old Corps" and how things were in France in World War I, where he served with the very same K Company, Third Battalion, Fifth Marines.

He'd left the Corps in the 1920s and taught school in his native Arkansas for a few years before joining back up in 1927 and getting right back in K Company again. I can't say for certain, but he may have served longer in K/3/5 than any other Marine in history.

"You'd've done all right over there, McEnery," he'd say, "because you're careful, and you don't take a lotta stupid chances. Most of these punk kids, though, they'd never of made it in the old Corps."

I always nodded and said "Thank you" a lot and kind of let it go at that. After two or three drinks of whiskey, Pop could carry on a conversation for an hour or more all by himself without any comments from me. He'd stop now and then to cuss or chuckle at something he'd said, then go right on.

But I never thought the whiskey actually had much of an effect on him. I mean, he said and did all those same things when he was dead sober, too.

One thing Pop *didn't* talk about—not ever, as far as I know—was the fact that he'd been awarded a Silver Star for heroism at Cape Gloucester. He'd made his way through heavy Jap fire to take a fresh supply of grenades to a group of pinned-down Marines who'd run out, then helped them wipe out a big nest of Nips.

I heard about all this secondhand from several guys while we were on Pavuvu, but I never said anything about it to Haney because I didn't know for sure till after the war if the story was authentic. It definitely was.

AS REST CAMPS and training areas go, Pavuvu had to rank at or near the bottom in a lot of ways. One of the major logistical problems was there was so little usable land area that it was impossible to hold large-scale maneuvers there without our skirmishes overflowing into company streets. But that was the brass's problem, as far as I could see, and when I stopped to compare Pavuvu to the other Pacific islands I'd done time on so far, I knew it could've been a whole lot worse.

To me, fighting rats, crabs, mud, and rotten coconuts was better than fighting Japs any day, but our replacement troops didn't have enough experience to realize that. They hadn't been through what the rest of us had, so they complained a lot, and some of them went nutso—"Asiatic," we called it—like the Marine who beat up the trunk of a coconut tree.

Old hands could go Asiatic, too, and frequently did. But they usually did it in quieter, more controlled ways. Like Pop Haney, for example, who always talked to himself and chuckled at things only he understood.

Stories even circulated about numerous guys getting so depressed they committed suicide on Pavuvu. In *The Old Breed*, George McMillan described how one young private finished up a four-hour stint on guard duty by putting the barrel of his M-1 in his mouth and blowing the top of his head off. I'm not saying it didn't happen, but if it did, it wasn't in K/3/5's area.

After the war, the stories got magnified even more with some guys claiming they heard guys shooting themselves almost every night. Personally, though, I think that whole thing about mass suicides was blown way out of proportion.

I never knew for sure of but one incident where somebody at Pavuvu killed himself, and the guy who did it was a young replacement who'd just gotten a "Dear John" letter from his girlfriend.

AS TIME PASSED, the situation on Pavuvu gradually became more bearable. Showers and toilets were installed where only the rain and open-pit latrines had been available before. Screened mess halls and up-to-date field kitchens were constructed, so we didn't have to wade mud as we ate or use stumps for dining tables like we had at first. The engineers also dredged out a nice swimming hole for us on the beach.

When more of the common areas of the camp were wired for electricity, we also got some large refrigerators—"reefers," we called them—for food storage. After that, we were able to have fresh meat and vegetables several times a week.

We even started having outdoor movies a couple of times a week, and we could buy chocolate bars and other concessions at a makeshift PX to eat during the show—if we could keep the rats from stealing them out of our pockets.

Toward the end of our stay on Pavuvu, we had a visit by comedian Bob Hope and his troupe of big-name entertainers, including Jerry Colonna, Frances Langford, and Patty Thomas. It was a terrific morale booster for all of us, and most of the division turned out for the show they put on.

Hope was later quoted as saying that seeing all the thousands of Marines cheering and waving from the ground as his small plane came in for a landing was one of the high points of his Pacific tour.

He even managed to make us laugh when he told a joke onstage comparing our slimy land crabs to his friend Bing Crosby's perennially losing racehorses.

"I notice they both run sideways," he said.

I SPENT TIME WITH a lot of different guys at Pavuvu. They ranged from young replacements like Seymour Levy, Sterling Mace, and Bill Leyden, to veterans like Slim Sommerville and old-timers like Pop Haney.

I also struck up a friendly relationship with Lieutenant Bill Bauerschmidt, our new platoon leader. He'd drop by my tent every day or two just to shoot the breeze, and we'd joke about how grateful we were to the good old American taxpayers for sending us on this great tropical vacation.

Bauerschmidt was a good guy and a good Marine. I liked him better than any platoon leader I'd had since Scoop Adams. But I never developed any really close friendships with anybody like I'd had with Lou Gargano or Remi Balduck or Weldon Delong. I don't exactly know why I didn't, but in a way I think it was what they call a defense mechanism on my part. I just didn't want to have to go through what I'd felt when I found out Lou and Remi were dead and Weldon was killed a few feet from me. Never again, if I could help it. It hurt too much.

I was almost glad I didn't know where Charlie Smith, my old friend from Brooklyn, was—or whether he was alive or dead, for that matter. Sometimes it was just better not to know.

Since we didn't get any liberties at Pavuvu, there weren't any special places to go, and you didn't feel as much need for special friends to go with. I spent a good bit of time writing letters home to Mom and my sister.

I even wrote some letters to my little brother, Peter Jr., who'd just turned ten. "I just hope this war's over," I told him, "before you're old enough to go."

I didn't have any regular routine assignment on Pavuvu, and sometimes it was hard to keep from getting bored. When I heard that Corporal John Teskevich, my K/3/5 comrade since 1941, was among a group of guys that Captain Haldane had picked for a two-week stay on the island paradise of Banika, I was downright envious.

If you can believe it, their only duty was to keep watch over a supply dump containing several thousand cases of beer and soft drinks. They stayed in floored tents with electric lights and took their meals on a Navy ship, where they ordered off menus and ate steaks, ice cream, and other restaurant-caliber food off real china.

As one of them told me, "We worked in shifts of about four hours on and forty-eight hours off, and we drank all the beer we could hold."

This cushy duty was intended as a reward for exceptional service at Cape Gloucester, Haldane told the guys he selected. In Teskevich's case, it was for saving the life of a wounded Marine under heavy enemy fire at Hill 660.

PFC R. R. "Railroad" Kelly was badly hit and not able to move under his own power when John found him and came to his aid while Jap bullets were hitting all around them.

"Can you put your arms around me and hang on?" Teskevich asked. "If you can, I'll pull you out of here."

"I think so," Kelly said, "but I'm pretty weak."

With Kelly clinging to him, John somehow managed to drag him to safety through a volley of Nip fire. Along the way, Kelly was hit again, but he survived.

I always thought Teskevich should've gotten a medal for rescuing Kelly like that, but I guess two weeks at Banika was better than nothing.

The only time I saw John on Pavuvu was sometime in early August 1944, after both of us were assigned to the Third Platoon of K/3/5—me as platoon guide and John as a squad leader.

The last time I'd seen him before that, he was sporting a handlebar mustache about a foot wide that he'd been cultivating for months. Now it was gone, and he was so clean-shaven I barely recognized him.

I didn't say anything about the missing mustache, and I guess it was a good thing I didn't. Another Marine told me later what had happened.

"He said some sneaky bastard slipped up on him while he was asleep and shaved half his mustache off," this other guy said. "He said he couldn't go around with just one side of it, so he shaved the other side off, too. He said, 'If I ever catch the asshole that did it, I'll kill him. I swear to God I will.'"

At that point, John and I had both been in the Pacific for twenty-six months, and if the so-called twenty-four-month rule was still in effect, I thought there was an outside chance we might get shipped stateside before our next Jap scrap came along.

Sending a guy home after he'd spent two years or more in the combat zone was supposed to be standard procedure for the Marine Corps. But I'd heard they were setting the rule aside for senior NCOs like John and me—and for commissioned officers like Captain Haldane and Lieutenant Jones, too—because they didn't have enough of us to go around. The way I read it, this meant we'd probably have to land on at least one more damn island before they'd let us go.

General Rupertus and Colonel Selden, who was now chief of staff of the division, put in a strong pitch with Marine Corps headquarters in Washington to get some of the old-timers relieved. As a result, 260 officers and 4,600 enlisted men were approved for rotation. But as far as I know, nobody in K/3/5 was on that list. John and I were among 264 officers and 5,750 enlisted men who'd have to go through a third campaign before we'd see the U.S.A. again.

For Teskevich, as he was fond of saying, this meant "another golden opportunity for my old man to collect twenty grand off my GI insurance."

ALTHOUGH I WASN'T AMONG the lucky group selected to guard the beer on Banika, Captain Haldane did write a letter of commendation about me to the commandant of the Marine Corps while we were on Pavuvu.

It was in regard to a new kind of sight that I'd developed in my free time for firing rifle grenades from the M-1. I submitted the idea accompanied by a drawing, some photos, and a record of tests performed with the sight. I've always enjoyed tinkering with mechanical things, and I considered it quite an honor for Haldane to recommend my device for use by Marines everywhere.

I still have a copy of the letter that Ack-Ack gave me. It's dated August 24, 1944, just two days before we shipped out for the Peleliu operation, and I still treasure it.

The letter reads in part:

"On his own time and initiative, based on former experience in the field, Sergeant McEnery has developed a new, improved anti-tank grenade sight for the U.S. Rifle, caliber .30 M-1. Although primarily an anti-tank grenade sight, it is easily adapted to other rifle grenades and has proven effective and practical in use. . . . Sergeant McEnery's devotion to duty is a credit to the naval service, and the adoption of the sight is a benefit to the personnel of the Marine Corps."

It's signed "Andrew A. Haldane."

DURING THE LAST THREE WEEKS of August, the brass got dead serious about maneuvers. We had them just about every day, and although most of them overflowed into other units' bivouac areas, we felt a new sense of urgency about getting the new replacements ready for combat.

On August 26, K/3/5 boarded LST 661 and bade a not particularly fond farewell to the rat and land crab capital of the Pacific. We headed straight for Guadalcanal for more maneuvers, this time concentrating on large-scale landing exercises that we didn't have room for on Pavuvu.

A lot of us veterans wanted to visit the Guadalcanal cemetery while we were there to pay our respects to buddies who were buried there, but we weren't allowed to go. Too much training to do, we were told.

On August 31, officers and senior NCOs of the division's three infantry regiments—the First, Fifth, and Seventh Marines—met in a movie area on Guadalcanal to hear a briefing and pep talk on our upcoming mission by General Rupertus.

The general made it clear that Peleliu wasn't going to be another long, drawn-out affair like Guadalcanal and Cape Gloucester, and he could hardly have sounded more confident.

"We're going to have some casualties," he said, "but let me assure you this is going to be a short one, a quickie. Rough but fast. We'll be through in three days. It might take only two."

On September 4, the thirty LSTs carrying the division's 9,000 infantry troops sailed for Peleliu. On the same ships with us were the amphibious tractors (amtracks) that would carry us ashore.

D-Day was set for September 15, and H-hour was 8:30 AM.

By noon that day, with hundreds of Marines pinned down on the beaches and dozens more already dead or wounded, we'd know for sure that General Rupertus's predictions were full of shit.

9

PELELIU—"A TERRIBLE MISTAKE"

IN THE FIRST Marine Division's first two landings on enemy-held islands, the Nips hadn't fired a single shot at us on our way to the beaches or while we were establishing a beachhead onshore.

Peleliu was different. Damn different.

Jap mortar and artillery shells were hitting all around us that morning as we headed for the Fifth Marines' designated sector of Orange Beach 2, and it felt like our amtrack was standing still. It was a turtle compared to the Higgins boats we'd used before. Its top speed was only four and a half knots, about a third of what a Higgins boat could do.

The new guys in our unit huddled low behind the gunwales, and I saw a couple of them puking as near-misses rocked the amtrack and splashed us with seawater. When we got closer in, we could hear the constant rattle of Jap machine gun fire.

On both sides of us, as far as you could see down the shoreline, other amtracks—many of them still loaded with Marines—were taking direct hits, bursting into flame, and spouting plumes of black smoke.

The First Marines were on our left, and the Seventh Marines were on our right, and it looked like both of them were catching hell. But those of us in the center of the beachhead with the Fifth Marines weren't as bad off. Our amtrack clawed its way onto the beach unscathed, and we scrambled out the rear-opening ramp onto the wet sand.

For a moment, some of the replacements hesitated behind the sheltering hulk of the amtrack. Then Lieutenant Bauerschmidt started shouting at them and waving them forward with the hog-leg .45 revolver his father had carried in France in 1918.

"Don't stand there like a bunch of dummies!" he yelled. "Remember what you've been taught. Get off the beach as fast as you can. A beach is a bad place to be, so move it! Move it!"

I was running inland as hard as I could go when a young private named Jerry Sullivan stumbled and fell beside me. I thought for a second he'd been hit, but I didn't see any blood. Then he started gagging and vomiting.

"God, I'm sick as a dog," he said. "I think it's the exhaust fumes from the tractor."

I was pretty sure it was mostly nerves, but this was no time to argue the point. I grabbed Sullivan by his shirt and pulled him upright, then gave him a shove toward a strip of pale green undergrowth about forty yards ahead.

"You'll be okay," I said. "Just stay low and run, damn it, run! I'll be right behind you."

I was carrying a "Spam can" radio, hoping I'd be able to get some useful information out of it about where the rest of K Company and the Third Battalion were. But all I could hear on it was about a million voices, all talking at once and not making any sense.

The weirdest thing I saw on the beach was a dog. At first, it was running along at the edge of the surf and barking its brains out. Then it turned inland and ran past me. It didn't seem to be hurt, just spooked out of its mind, and I wondered how it had kept from getting hit with all the American bombs and shells that had exploded on the beach that morning. Our ships and planes had been pounding the island for three days, including a constant bombardment that started before dawn on D-Day and lasted right up until the first amtracks got close to shore.

If that dog can come through all those fireworks without a scratch, I thought, *what about the Japs? Is there a shitload of them waiting for us just ahead?*

I got my answer a moment later. I spotted a group of eight or ten Nips scrambling around behind a pile of rocks maybe thirty yards in front of us. I felt the hair stand up on the back of my neck when I realized they were moving a 75-millimeter field piece into position to fire toward the beach, where more Marines were pouring ashore.

I tried again to use the radio I was carrying to call for artillery support, but the damn thing was just as useless as before. I bellowed into it as loud as I could, but I couldn't get any kind of response.

Just at that moment, I heard one of my platoon mates yelling at me.

"Hey, Mac," he said, "there's one of our tanks heading this way!"

I turned around and saw an amphibious tank, with its own 75-millimeter cannon jutting out from its turret, grinding slowly toward us.

Thank you, Lord, I thought.

"We're looking for the Seventh Marines," the tank commander shouted, stopping beside me.

"They're not in this sector," I shouted back, "but stay with us if you can. We need your help." I pointed toward the pile of rocks and that Jap 75. "Can you take that thing out?"

The tank commander's eyes followed my pointing finger, and he nodded. "Consider it done, Sergeant," he said and ducked down to talk to his gunner.

About ten seconds later, a flash of flame erupted from the tank's cannon with a deafening roar. The first round struck the target dead-center, knocking the Jap field piece onto its side. It was followed almost instantly by a second round that flung up a cloud of dust, chunks of coral, and several enemy bodies.

Some of the surviving Japs in the gun crew tried to run, but they didn't get far. Eight or ten of us opened up with our M-1s and dropped them in their tracks. Then we edged forward cautiously toward the wrecked gun, ready to finish off any Japs that moved.

None did.

I saluted the tank commander, and he waved as he rumbled away.

FOR ANY READER who hasn't guessed it by now, our primary objective on Peleliu was taking control of the island's airfield—the same as it had been at Guadalcanal and Cape Gloucester.

We were supposed to seize the airfield and get rid of the Japs defending it before nightfall on D-Day. But because of the fierce enemy resistance, it was obvious by afternoon that this wasn't going to happen.

The edge of the airfield that faced us on the seaward side was only about 300 yards from the water. The field itself was only about half a mile wide, so when we first saw maps of the layout, we didn't think it'd be that hard to get control of it the first day.

After all, General Rupertus expected us to secure the whole island in two or three days. So advancing half a mile plus 300 yards on the first day shouldn't be such a big deal, right?

We should've known better, but nobody told us going in that the steep ridges that rose up just beyond the airfield were bristling with Jap artillery, all of it zeroed-in on the field itself and the area between the field and the water. Now we were bogged down, and some of our Fifth Marines guys had gotten lost and wandered over into Seventh Marines territory.

The First Marines, now commanded by Colonel Chesty Puller, who'd won multiple Navy Crosses with the Seventh Marines at the 'Canal, were in a really bad way up on the White Beaches to our left. One battalion of the First was supposed to help the Fifth secure the airfield, but at the moment, Chesty's whole regiment was having to fight like crazy just to keep from being driven into the sea. We heard they'd taken hundreds of casualties, and several of their companies were pinned down on the beach, while others were clinging by their fingernails to a rocky knob of high ground called the Point.

Once K/3/5 got past the beach, the ground was solid coral that was next to impossible to even dent with a trenching tool, and the only natural cover between the beach and the field was some scrubby brush and a few low outcroppings of coral. Some of the men were able to find enough rocks to pile up and crawl behind, but many others were basically out in the open with nothing to protect them.

All this was tough enough on infantry trying to advance, but the airfield itself was going to be the real ballbuster. Except for some shell holes and the carcasses of a few wrecked Jap planes, it didn't offer us any cover at all. Once we started across, there'd be no turning back. We'd be like a bunch of clay pigeons in a shooting gallery. It was actually a big relief when Lieutenant Bauerschmidt told me we'd been ordered to hold the ground we had and wait till tomorrow morning to make the crossing.

They'd warned us it'd be hot on Peleliu, but we weren't prepared for the kind of heat we were getting. By mid-afternoon on D-Day, the temperature was close to 115 degrees. The only way to keep from getting heat stroke was to drink water. For that reason, each Marine had come ashore with two quart-size canteens filled to the brim.

It wasn't nearly enough, though, and a lot of Marines drank up their water way too fast. Within the first few hours, some guys had drained their first canteen and were dipping deep into the second one. I guess they thought we'd get resupplied with water before the day was over.

They were wrong.

THAT AFTERNOON, INSTEAD of the banzai charge we'd been half-expecting, the Nips sent a squadron of thirteen light tanks rolling across the airfield toward the Fifth Marines' loosely organized lines. They were supported by at least 500 infantry troops, and they aimed the center of their attack at a gap between the First and Second Battalions, hoping for a breakthrough that might throw one or both battalions back onto the beach.

We'd had a bunch of our own tanks knocked out by enemy artillery fire during the landings that morning, and I guess the Japs thought we'd lost every bit of armor we had. Fortunately, we hadn't. A platoon of Sherman tanks from Colonel Jeb Stuart's First Marine Tank Battalion were clustered just fifty yards from Major Gordon Gayle's Second Battalion command post, and Gayle was able to send them out to intercept the Jap force in the nick of time.

The Shermans were too heavily armored and packed too much firepower for those little Jap sardine cans. Between our tanks and a battery of 75-millimeter pack howitzers that the 11th Marines had just moved into position, the attackers never had a chance.

Our Shermans and artillery shredded the Nip tanks like tinfoil, and we used machine guns, bazookas, grenade launchers, and BARs to take care of the enemy foot soldiers. I'm not sure any of them got away.

One of our Shermans was disabled, but it kept right on firing and took out at least six of the Jap tanks, all of which were destroyed in a matter of minutes.

"The battle was so easy for us once it was joined," wrote Marine historian George McMillan, "that the whole affair [was] . . . something like a comic opera."

It could've turned out much differently, though, if our Shermans had arrived just a few minutes later.

•　•　•

THE ENEMY MORTAR and artillery fire slacked off at times that first day, but it never really stopped, and before the day was done, it robbed our Third Battalion of several of its key commanders. We found out that afternoon that our executive officer, Major Robert M. Ash, had been killed on the beach that morning, just a couple of minutes after he landed.

Then, about dusk, our Third Battalion CO, Lieutenant Colonel Austin "Shifty" Shofner, who'd been captured by the Japs on Corregidor, then escaped to fight again, was seriously wounded when an enemy round slammed into the battalion CP.

Shofner was hit by shell fragments at a very bad time—just as he was trying to contact our scattered companies with instructions on how to deploy for the night. PFC Bill Leyden, whose First Platoon was much closer to the CP than my Third Platoon was, told me later he heard Shofner screaming after he was hit.

"He was cussin' loud enough to put a platoon sergeant to shame." Leyden said, "but he sounded more mad than hurt."

Shofner was a former star halfback at the University of Tennessee—where he'd picked up the nickname "Shifty"—and as tough a Marine as you'd ever want to meet. But his wounds were severe enough that he had to be evacuated to a hospital ship, and Lieutenant Colonel Lewis "Silent Lew" Walt, executive officer of the Fifth Marines, was sent over to take Shofner's place.

It was getting dark by the time Walt got to the 3/5 CP, where he found radio and phone connections with I, K, and L Companies so undependable that he decided to contact the company commanders in person. He set out alone, except for a runner, and by the time he got all three companies formed up in a circle of defense, it was black as pitch outside.

What followed was one of the longest and uneasiest nights I ever spent, and our replacements in K/3/5 were really antsy. We were running low on ammo, and the fact that most of the new guys were completely out of water by now didn't help, either.

"What's gonna happen tonight, Mac?" PFC Seymour Levy asked me. "Are the Nips gonna pull one of those banzai charges?"

"I don't know, kid," I told him. "If they do, they'll let you know they're coming long before they get here, and we'll blow their asses off. Infiltrators are a bigger problem 'cause you can't hear 'em coming. Just stay down and keep your rifle and Ka-Bar ready."

As it happened, it stayed quiet that night in K/3/5's immediate area—quiet enough that you could hear men praying up and down the line. I said quite a few "Our Fathers" myself.

It wasn't nearly so quiet, though, at Fifth Marines' headquarters. Our regimental commander, Colonel Harold "Bucky" Harris, was slightly injured, and a Marine on his staff was killed when a mortar shell hit right in the middle of their CP. Major Walter McIlhenny, who'd won a Navy Cross at Guadalcanal and whose family owned the company that makes Tabasco sauce, was wounded by the same shell and evacuated.

A LITTLE BEFORE 8:30 the next morning (D-plus-1), Lieutenant Bauerschmidt came over to where I was "dug in" behind a small pile of rocks and brush, and told me to get the platoon ready to move on the double.

"It's time to do what we came here for," he said, "and capture that damn airfield."

We were about to take part in one of the largest offensive ground operations of the Pacific war. The whole Fifth Regiment was going to jump off together and charge across the airfield at the same time. North of us, to our left, elements of the Second Battalion, First Marines, would be charging, too. And to our right, near the edge of the scrubby jungle at the south end of the airfield, the Third Battalion, Seventh Marines, would also be advancing abreast of us.

In other words, a total of about 4,500 Marines would be on the move in the open—all of them exposed to intense enemy fire for as long as it took them to get north of the field.

It didn't sound like a stroll in the park—and it wasn't.

"We'll do this just like we practiced it on Pavuvu," Bauerschmidt said. "Stay down till I give the signal. Then run at a crouch and keep moving. Try not to stop for anything. Put some distance between yourself and the other guys around you, so you don't make as big a target."

I nodded and said "Okay," but as I relayed the lieutenant's orders to the guys around me, I damn sure wasn't *feeling* okay. I don't know to this day what caused it, but I was getting a sudden, urgent call from nature at the most inopportune moment of my life.

Suddenly, all the guys in the platoon were on their feet, and Bauerschmidt was jabbing the air with his hog-leg revolver.

"Move out!" he yelled. "Move out!

We went forward in a wave, then scattered out, like we'd been told. From the ridges on the far side of the field, the Japs must've been watching and waiting, because dirty little mushrooms of dirt and smoke started blossoming around us almost instantly. The air was full of blue tracer bullets from Nip machine guns.

I saw PFCs Sterling Mace and Seymour Levy running parallel to me. I saw Corporal John Teskevich directly ahead. I saw Private Dan

Lawler, one of the ammo handlers in our machine gun section, cry out and fall, clutching a bloody leg.

"Keep moving!" I shouted. "Don't slow down!"

I was at the outer edge of the main runway when I knew for sure that I wasn't going to be able to obey my own commands.

I *HAD* to stop. I had to stop *NOW*. Because I had to *GO!*

So I dropped my britches and took a crap right there in the middle of the runway while my platoon mates ran past, hardly seeming to notice me, and bullets smacked the tarmac a few feet away.

It probably didn't take me over thirty seconds to get done, yank up my pants, and start running again. But those were the longest, most helpless-feeling thirty seconds of my life.

Even if we'd had time to pause and aim and fire, there wasn't a damn thing for us to shoot at. The Japs that were raking us with everything from 75s and heavy mortars to machine gun and rifle fire were hidden in deep holes among the distant high ground.

The real name of that high ground was the Umurbrogol Plateau, but we came to call the whole thing Bloody Nose Ridge. It more than lived up to that name, but it was actually dozens of ridges, sheer cliffs, and steep ravines honeycombed with hundreds of natural and man-made caves that the Japs had spent years fortifying.

By afternoon of D-plus-one, the Fifth Marines had gained control of the airfield. Seven members of K/3/5 had been killed in the crossing, and two dozen others wounded, but the casualties we'd taken were remarkably light, all things considered.

One thing that helped save us was that the shelling raised so much smoke and dust over the field that the Nip gunners had a hard time seeing us. Plus, the fact that we were spread out so thinly helped, too.

It was one hellacious nightmare nevertheless, especially for troops who'd never come under fire until about twenty-four hours earlier. In his book, Gene Sledge called it the "worst combat experience" he had during the whole war and described it as "terror compounded beyond the belief of anyone who wasn't there."

For several days to come, the field still wouldn't be fully secure and our planes wouldn't be able to use it because it was still coming under fire from enemy guns buried deep in that maze of high ridges to the north. Those guns had to be silenced, and a lot of Marines were destined to die before the job was done.

If it was any consolation, we could at least be sure there'd be no banzai charges on Peleliu. The terrain was much too rugged for that, and the Nips we were fighting now were using a completely different strategy from what we'd seen early in the war.

They had no hope of escaping or being reinforced, and they knew we were eventually going to kill them all. But in the two-plus years since Guadalcanal, they'd learned better than to waste their time—and their lives—trying to scare us.

Except for the enemy infiltrators who visited us almost every night, the Japs' goal now was to wait for us to come to them, then take as many of us with them as they could while we rooted them out of their hiding places, one cave at a time.

AMONG THE DIVISION'S three infantry regiments, there's no question that Chesty Puller's First Marines took the worst punishment in the early going on Peleliu. Not only did they have the toughest time on the beaches, but they were also the first regiment to tackle those damn ridges just north of the airfield.

Within the first two or three days, the First lost over 500 Marines killed and wounded, and a lot of people claim to this day that Chesty deserves a big share of the blame for those losses. I'm not sure if I'm one of those people, but I do know this much: I'm damn glad I wasn't serving with the First Marines during the third week of September 1944.

Puller had won the admiration of the whole First Marine Division for the fight he led at Guadalcanal to keep the Japs from recapturing Henderson Field. But he lost a lot of that admiration at Peleliu when he threw his troops again and again against impregnable enemy fortifications in the ridges, where hundreds of Marines were slaughtered.

It was a miracle that anyone in Captain George Hunt's K Company, Third Battalion, First, lived through the first forty-eight hours of what would become a month-long battle for Peleliu.

On D-Day, Hunt and his men stormed and captured the Point, that coral outcropping jutting out into the sea above White Beach 1 that I mentioned earlier. It was the first important piece of high ground that fell to the Marines on Peleliu, and the reason it was so important was because its field pieces and machine guns were within range of about half our beachhead. As long as it was in enemy hands, no Marine on the White Beaches and the whole north half of our beachhead was safe from its fire.

Capturing it was a great accomplishment for Hunt and his guys. But holding it turned into one of the bloodiest struggles in Marine Corps history.

Before they were finally relieved two days later, Hunt and a handful of his men fought off repeated Nip assaults that left piles of enemy dead around the base of that hollowed-out chunk of coral.

In my opinion, Chesty Puller can't be faulted for the heavy casualties suffered by the First Marines in their landing area on D-day and D-plus-1. The regiment—especially its Third Battalion—simply found itself trapped in a Jap hornet's nest, and most of those losses couldn't have been prevented, no matter who was in charge.

But it was over the next four or five days after the White Beaches were secured that Puller pushed his troops too hard, and a lot of men died who shouldn't have. He sent companies that were already beaten up and shorthanded into those ridges north of the airfield, and he ordered them to keep attacking when he knew they were hopelessly outgunned and getting chewed to pieces.

One glaring example of this was what happened to C Company, First Battalion, First Marines, commanded by Captain Everett Pope—who, by the way, was a close friend and former college classmate of K/3/5's Captain Haldane.

Pope's outfit had taken a terrible beating on the beaches, where close to two-thirds of the 235 men who landed with C/1/1 were either killed or evacuated with serious wounds.

But on September 19 (D-plus-4), Pope and his ninety remaining troops were ordered to capture a knob of rock designated on our maps as Hill 100.

Once again, the maps were wrong. Hill 100 wasn't actually a separate hill at all. It was part of a long, twisting ridge, dominated by higher ridges just to the north and west, all of them packed with Jap riflemen, machine guns, mortars, and even small artillery.

Pope and about twenty-five guys easily made it to the top of Hill 100—which was only a little larger than a tennis court and offered almost no cover—only to find themselves trapped and surrounded.

Except for their M-1s and three or four dozen hand grenades, their only weapons were a couple of tommy guns, a few BARs, and one .30-caliber machine gun. Since they'd had to travel light while climbing the hill, they were critically short of all types of ammo.

They also didn't have any reliable contact with battalion headquarters or C/1/1's own mortar and machine gun squads. With nightfall closing in, they were on their own and in "one helluva bad spot," as Pope put it.

"Let's gather up plenty of rocks," he told his NCOs. "The idea's to throw three or four rocks over the side of the cliff when the Japs start trying to come up, then follow them with one grenade. In the dark, they won't know which is which, and they'll take cover just as fast for a rock as they will for a grenade."

Hand-to-hand fighting raged on Hill 100 from just after dark till dawn. By then, the Marines had fought off dozens of Nip attacks, using not only rocks but Ka-Bar knives, rifle butts, empty ammo boxes, thrown-back Nip grenades, and bare fists. Several Japs were thrown bodily off the sheer edge of the cliff.

When daylight came and the Japs broke off their attacks, only nine of the twenty-five Marines who'd reached the crest of Hill 100 were still alive, and most of them were wounded. Battalion finally got through to Pope by radio and ordered him to withdraw, but his radio operator was killed by Jap machine gun fire on the way down, and Pope had to throw himself behind a stone wall to keep from being killed, too. He'd already been hit in the leg by several chunks of shrapnel, which he later pulled out with a pair of pliers.

On September 22, a week and a day after our landing on Peleliu, the First Marines were finally pulled off the line. By that time, the regiment had lost over 1,600 killed and wounded—56 percent of its total strength—and Captain Pope was the only company commander who wasn't dead or seriously wounded.

Chesty Puller's reputation was permanently tarnished by the slaughter of his Marines in those ridges. In *The Old Breed*, George McMillan called Puller "a tragic caricature of Marine aggressiveness," who "crossed the line that separates courage and wasteful expenditure of lives."

Captain Pope was awarded the Medal of Honor for his valor and resourcefulness on Hill 100, but he never forgave Puller for sending his men there.

"I had no use for Puller," Pope said many years after the war. "He didn't know what was going on, and why he wanted me and my men dead on top of that hill, I don't know."

AFTER MAKING IT across the airfield, the Fifth Marines pushed on through thick jungle and swampy terrain toward the east coast of Peleliu and wound up in an area designated as Purple Beach. Along the way, we hardly encountered any Jap resistance at all—certainly nothing compared to what the First and Seventh Marines were running into. There was plenty of evidence that Nips were in the vicinity, but they seemed to be playing a cat-and-mouse game with us, at least for the time being.

On the morning of September 17 (D-plus-2) my Third Platoon was picking its way through a jungle thicket when we came across the decomposing bodies of some Japs who'd apparently been killed by our pre-invasion bombs or naval gunfire.

It doesn't take long in the tropical heat for dead bodies to start rotting and stinking like hell, so we were trying to put some distance between ourselves and those dead Nips when a sudden explosion splattered us with mud and sent us ducking for cover.

"What the hell was that?" yelled PFC Sterling Mace, swinging his BAR in the direction of the blast.

"Sounded like a grenade or maybe a booby trap," I said.

"Hey, we got a man hit over here!" somebody else hollered. "Corpsman! We need a corpsman!"

As Mace and I pushed the brush aside and moved together toward the sound, we saw PFC Seymour Levy squatting on his knees a few yards away. He was holding the lower part of his face with both hands, and I saw blood running down his neck. He was mumbling something I couldn't hear, and he seemed to be in shock.

"What happened to you, Sy?" Mace said, but Levy didn't respond.

A corpsman came up and covered Levy's chin and lower jaw with a field dressing. "There's shrapnel in there," he said. "Looks like several fragments. He needs to go to an aid station, maybe a hospital ship."

While we waited for a stretcher, Levy was barely conscious and still losing quite a bit of blood, but the shrapnel had missed his jugular vein—although not by much.

"Hey, cheer up, man," Mace said, trying to console his friend. "That looks like a million-dollar wound to me. I think you just got yourself a ticket home."

After Levy was evacuated, the platoon moved on. We were checking our route carefully now in case the Nips had left some more surprises for us, but I couldn't help noticing that Mace seemed gloomy and downcast.

"You worried about your pal?" I asked, moving up beside him.

"Nah, he'll be okay, I guess," he said. "Actually I kind of envy him, but I'm gonna miss him, too, Mac. I mean, Christ, I may never see the crazy so-and-so again."

I sort of shrugged. "Yeah, well, probably not till after the war, anyway."

For the record, Mace and I were both wrong.

AFTER JUST TEN DAYS on Peleliu, the surviving troops of the First Marines were ordered evacuated and sent back to Pavuvu to recuperate and regroup. The Seventh Marines had also taken a lot of casualties while eliminating a bunch of heavily fortified Jap bunkers down at the south end of the island. (PFC Arthur J. Jackson, a nineteen-year-old BAR man with 1/7, would earn another Medal of Honor for wiping out an even dozen enemy pillboxes.)

By now it was pretty obvious that the Fifth Marines' turn on the hot seat was coming up. We weren't exactly overjoyed about it, but we knew it was only fair. In the fighting so far, only thirty-seven members of K/3/5 had been killed or wounded in action while K/3/1, our sister company in the First Marines, had lost about 175 men.

This time, though, because of the heavy casualties the division had already suffered, the brass decided to try a different approach from the one that had bloodied Puller's regiment so badly.

And this time, the Fifth Marines would be spearheading the attack.

"We're going to the north end of the island and circle behind the main Jap defenses so we can hit them from a new direction," Captain Haldane told us. "Trucks are coming to pick us up and take us to the main road along the coast, but we'll have to hoof it from there through some pretty tough territory. The Marines who've already traveled that route have nicknamed it Sniper Alley, so be careful, and good luck."

When I looked at our maps, I could see what Ack-Ack was talking about. The narrow West Road passed within 300 yards or so of the heart of Japanese fortifications—an area called the Pocket—carved into the maze of ridges identified on our maps as the Umurbrogol Plateau.

For a distance of more than half a mile, the ocean was only a few yards to the left of the road, and the first of the ridges veered up sharply just a few yards to the right. This made it a perfect killing ground for snipers. Infantry passing that way was caught, literally, between the devil and the deep blue sea. There was almost no place to take cover.

From all indications, it was going to be a more dangerous half-mile than the one across the airport had been.

THE MOST SURPRISING THING that happened while we were on Purple Beach was that Seymour Levy suddenly showed up back in camp. His wounded chin was wrapped up in white bandages and he still had a little problem eating and talking. He looked tired and a little pale, but he seemed to feel okay.

Sterling Mace could hardly believe his eyes when the platoon came back from a patrol and he saw Levy sitting there waiting for him.

"What the heck're you doing here?" Mace said. "I thought you'd be halfway to the States by now."

"Aw, I sneaked off the hospital ship and bummed a ride to the beach on a ferry," Levy mumbled through the bandages. "I just wanted to be back with the company. I missed you guys. Besides, it's where I belong."

Mace just grinned and shook his head. "Jeez, Sy, you must be nuts. You know that?"

It was hard to tell because of the bandages, but I think Levy grinned back. Then, just like old times, he started reciting a Rudyard Kipling poem.

"It was Din! Din! Din! You 'eathen, where the mischief 'ave you been . . ."

THE EVENING BEFORE we moved out, my friend John Teskevich and I were lying on our backs beside the foxhole we were sharing and bullshitting about all the stuff we'd been through together in the past and what might happen after we finished up at Peleliu. We both agreed we'd seen some tough times but it could've been worse.

"This one hasn't been all that rough so far," John said, "and once we get done here, we'll be heading home. My God, Mac, even the Marine Corps can't put it off forever. They'll *have* to send us stateside after this crapshoot."

"Damn straight," I said. "They won't have any choice. What's the first thing you'll do when you get back to Pennsylvania?"

He laughed. "Call up my friends. Drink some beer. Hustle some broads. Maybe get in a fistfight or two. It sure as hell won't be working in no damn coal mine, I can tell you that."

"It's hard to believe," I said, "but in a week or two, this whole mess could be over, and we could actually be on our way."

"Yeah," he said, "time's runnin' low for my old man to collect that twenty grand in GI insurance, and my luck's been holdin' pretty good lately. If he gets it, the Japs're gonna have to hurry."

ON THE MORNING of September 25 (D-plus-10), K/3/5 and the rest of the Third Battalion loaded up our gear and got ready to move out. Our semi-holiday on Purple Beach was over. It was the last break we'd get at Peleliu.

As we hiked toward a rendezvous point on the East Road where some trucks were supposed to pick us up, we passed a column of men from the First Marines as they filed slowly down the other side of the road on their way to Purple Beach to board boats and begin their trip to Pavuvu.

They looked so pitiful that I couldn't help stopping for a minute to watch them. Their uniforms were torn, filthy, and bloodstained in many cases, and their faces were blank and hollow-eyed. They shambled along like walking dead men.

"Man, look at those guys," said Lieutenant Bauerschmidt, pausing beside me and shaking his head. "You can tell they've been through hell."

"Yeah, I'd been kind of envying the First Marines because they were getting relieved and we weren't," I told the lieutenant. "But now that I see the poor devils, I sure as hell don't envy 'em anymore."

"Well, don't envy us, either," Bauerschmidt said. "In a few days, we may be in the same shape. The Nips are still in firm control of those ridges where the First got beaten bloody. Now it's our job to come at 'em from a different direction and dislodge 'em, but it's still the same Japs in the same kind of ridges."

A few minutes later, we climbed onto the trucks and headed toward the West Road. On the way, we passed just north of the airfield and saw it for the first time since we'd crossed it under fire on D-plus-1. It had changed so much we could hardly tell it was the same place. All the wreckage from Jap planes and other debris had been hauled away, and all the shell craters had been filled. Crews of Seabees and service personnel in clean uniforms were calmly going about their business, using heavy equipment to grade and repair the runways.

Since the field was no longer within range of enemy mortars and artillery, our own planes would soon be flying missions from it against the Japs in the ridges. That was the most encouraging part of all.

I had a feeling we were going to need all the help we could get.

OUR CONVOY OF trucks stopped a short distance up the West Road, where the drivers told us to get off, that this was as far as they went. A bunch of Army troops—the first ones we'd seen on Peleliu—were congregated along the side of the road where we stopped. They were with the 321st Regiment of the 81st Infantry Division, and I asked a couple of them if they were going north with us.

"No, man," they said, "they told us we're relieving the First Marines, and we're staying right here in this area." They'd obviously heard the same scuttlebutt about Sniper Alley that we'd heard.

"Looks like we'll be walkin' the rest of the way from here by ourselves," said John Teskevich as he and I sat down beside the road to wait for the order to move out. "That don't sound like such a hot idea to me."

"Bauerschmidt says they're sending up some tanks to go with us," I told him, repeating something the lieutenant had just told me. "He says maybe we can hitch a ride on one of them, but that doesn't strike me as such a great idea, either."

"Beats walkin', though," John said.

"Maybe so," I said, "but it makes you a good target, too, sittin' there on the deck of a tank."

It was past noon when a platoon of Shermans showed up, and we got the order to move out. No one suggested that we bum a ride on any of the tanks, so we grabbed our weapons and started plodding up the road, which seemed to get narrower the farther we went. About a stone's throw to our left was a rocky beach and the ocean, and roughly the same distance to our right was the first of the ridges.

Some low undergrowth off to the right was about the only available cover, but it also could be the hiding place for a Jap sniper if one was nervy enough to set up that close.

We could hear the chatter of Jap machine guns in the distance, and occasionally we'd see a stream of their blue tracer bullets passing high above our heads and bound for some target in the ridges. There were also sporadic rifle shots that sounded a lot nearer.

Sure enough, it didn't take the Japs long to start picking our guys off. Before you could even hear the shot, you'd see somebody go stiff and fall. We almost never spotted a target to shoot back at, but some Marines would always fire a few rounds in the direction they thought the shot had come from.

Despite my misgivings about riding on a tank, we were sweating buckets by now, and I felt kind of relieved when Lieutenant Bauerschmidt waved one of the Shermans over and motioned to a group of us to climb aboard.

Teskevich and I climbed up on the platform to the left of the turret, putting it between us and those Jap-infested ridges. PFCs Jesse Googe, Sterling Mace, and Seymour Levy got aboard, too. Then Bauerschmidt signaled the tank driver to go on, and the big Sherman started to roll again.

We hadn't gone more than about thirty yards when I heard a shot that sounded like it came from ahead of us and to the right. I ducked instinctively and glanced at John, who was sitting about a foot from me toward the front of the tank. I thought for a second he was ducking, too. Then I realized he was doubled up with pain and clutching his belly. Blood was running out between his fingers.

Then I heard a second shot, and I heard Googe let out a howl from the other side of the tank. "God, I'm hit! I'm hit!"

"Stop the tank!" I yelled at the driver. "We got two men wounded!"

I jerked my head around to look toward Mace and Levy and asked them where Googe was hit.

"He got it in the arm," Mace said.

"Well come here and help me with Teskevich," I told him. "He's hurt bad. Corpsman! We need a corpsman!"

A medic showed up just as we got Teskevich to the ground. He took one look at John and shook his head.

"The slug went all through his intestines," he said. "Nothing much I can do."

"Then see about Googe," I said. "I think his arm's busted."

When I looked back at John, his face was gray and the front of his dungarees was solid blood. The worst part of it was that he was still conscious and looking me straight in the eye. I'll never forget how he looked at me and how he kind of smiled.

"Guess I'm gonna make my old man rich, after all, Mac," he whispered.

I tried to think of something to say to him, but I couldn't. I was afraid I'd bawl if I tried.

I wondered if I ought to inject him with one of the needle-equipped tubes of morphine we all carried, but he didn't seem to be in that much pain, so I couldn't see the point.

I stayed with John beside the road till he died a few minutes later. Mace and Levy stayed, too. Quite a few of the guys from K Company turned to look at us as they passed by, then they shook their heads and glanced quickly away.

Teskevich and I had been in the same company since the fall of 1941. It was damn hard to see somebody you'd spent so much time with get his guts blown out a few inches away from you. I remembered how we'd talked just the night before about going home, but after a few seconds I had to force the memory out of my mind.

John's eyes were still open when I covered him with a poncho, and he still looked like he was smiling a little.

"We better haul ass," I told Mace and Levy. "We got a long way to go."

I didn't look at them when I said it. I couldn't—I was too choked up. The three of us just stood up and started walking north again.

THERE WERE BIGGER, longer, costlier, and much better known land battles than Peleliu during the Pacific war. Guadalcanal lasted six times as long. Okinawa claimed twenty times as many lives. Iwo Jima involved thousands more American troops.

But Peleliu was uniquely horrible. In terms of savage fighting, agonizing battlefield conditions, impossible terrain and logistics, physical misery, and psychological heartbreak, it was in a class by itself.

It was thirty days of the meanest, around-the-clock slaughter that desperate men can inflict on each other when the last traces of humanity have been wrung out of them and all that's left is the blind urge to kill.

And as we found out afterward, the saddest, most sickening thing about Peleliu for the men who lived through it is that it never should've happened at all. Admiral Halsey was outspokenly against invading Peleliu. He knew attacks by the U.S. Navy had left the Jap garrison with only a handful of flyable planes and no offensive capability.

Even Admiral Chester Nimitz, the Navy's commander in chief in the Pacific, who initially approved the Peleliu operation, changed his mind and argued against it when he met at Hawaii with President Roosevelt and Dugout Doug MacArthur. But when MacArthur demanded that Peleliu and its airfield be taken to protect his flank when his Army troops invaded the Philippines, Roosevelt gave in and okayed it.

It was only later that almost all the big brass in Washington realized Peleliu could've easily been bypassed and its garrison left to wither.

For me—and every other living survivor of Peleliu—it hurts to know the truth. But as we know now, from a strategic standpoint, the battle was totally pointless. After the war, former Minnesota governor Harold Stassen, who served in the Pacific as assistant chief of staff to Admiral Halsey and later as a special assistant to President

Dwight Eisenhower, called it "a terrible mistake" and "a needless tragedy."

And it hurts even worse when I think of the 1,252 members of the First Marine Division who were killed in action on Peleliu and the other 5,274 Marines who left their blood there.

10

THE WORST NIGHTMARE YET

WITHOUT A DOUBT, the period between late September and mid-October 1944 was the worst time of my life. It was worse than the weeks we spent under siege at Guadalcanal. It was worse than the Green Hell of Cape Gloucester. It was the nastiest, ugliest, slimiest, nonstop fighting that a human being can experience.

Every day during that stretch was basically the same nightmare all over again. We attacked the underground Jap strongholds in the Umurbrogol Pocket and slaughtered their occupants by every means available. We incinerated them with flamethrowers. We blasted them to bits with artillery rounds fired directly into their caves. We poured grenades by the hundreds into their bunkers and pillboxes. Our planes seared them with napalm from the air. We called in bulldozers and demolition squads armed with TNT to bury them alive.

The brass at First Marine Division headquarters called it "blow-torch and corkscrew" tactics. I guess that's as good a description as any.

And, of course, we shot them and bayoneted them and cut their throats and strangled them with our bare hands when they came at us as infiltrators in the night. We gouged their eyes out and pounded their skulls to mush with rocks. We jerked them up and threw them off cliffs like screaming sacks of shit.

And still they fought on. Our intelligence estimated total enemy strength on Peleliu at 10,900 troops. When Jap resistance finally ended, only thirty of their soldiers came out to surrender. That was how hard they fought.

Because the First Marines had been evacuated, and the Seventh Marines were depleted from heavy losses, the main burden of digging, burning, and blasting the Japs out of their caves was now squarely on the shoulders of the Fifth Marines.

Our turn in the cauldron had come. Beginning when we ran the gauntlet up Sniper Alley, it would continue without letup for seventeen straight days. Every one of those days was horribly the same. We were always going uphill, always under a crossfire from Japs we couldn't see in mutually supporting caves and bunkers above us. Always inching our way up some naked, rocky cliff with Japs shooting at us from distances ranging from a quarter-mile to a few yards.

Before the struggle was over, a lot of us were dead or maimed for life. My grief over John Teskevich's death soon faded into the background because other friends and comrades were falling around me every day.

We'd hear a shot ring out from a sniper somewhere. One of us would go down, while the rest of us cursed or choked back tears. Or both. We'd try like hell to locate the sniper, but it was hard to do. If we figured out the shots came from a den of Japs in a cave, we could call in mortar or artillery fire. But sometimes the terrain was so crazy that our shells couldn't reach the target. And when it was an isolated sniper that was doing the damage, he might hit three or four of our guys, maybe more, before we could pinpoint where the son of a bitch was hiding.

None of us who survived the torment of those seventeen days would ever be the same again.

ON SEPTEMBER 27 (D-plus-12), Colonel Harold "Bucky" Harris, the Fifth Marines CO, assigned our whole Third Battalion—commanded by Major John Gustafson and including all of us in K/3/5—to make yet another amphibious assault on yet another Pacific island.

This time, our objective was a small chunk of coral just off the north coast of Peleliu. It was called Ngesebus (pronounced "Negaseebus"), and it would be my fourth amphibious operation in the Pacific. In some ways, it was also going to be the roughest.

Major Gustafson made it clear that 3/5 was expected to secure Ngesebus in twenty-four hours or less. That was a tall order because, despite its small size, the island was a miniature of Peleliu itself—with low ridges down its center that were honeycombed with Nip caves and bunkers. It even had its own airstrip that was big enough for Zeros to use to attack our positions on Peleliu.

"At 0800 tomorrow morning, we'll be boarding amtracks for a

landing on Ngesebus," Lieutenant Bauerschmidt told K/3/5's Third Platoon that afternoon. "Regiment estimates that the Nips have over 500 troops in heavy fortifications on the island, plus dozens of mortars, several 75s, and some large-caliber naval guns. They expect us to do the job in one day and without reinforcements, so be prepared for a hard fight."

Up to this point, we hadn't had a lot of trouble with sneak attacks by Jap infiltrators, but late that night while we were dug in along the north beach, we lost two Marines to nighttime visitors who crawled into their foxholes and killed them. In one case, the Jap who did the dirty work spoke perfect English and pretended to be a Marine asking about a lost rifle. It reminded me of the time on Guadalcanal when a Nip yelled at me in English across the Matanikau River and invited me to "Come on over."

I took those two Marines' deaths as a warning of what lay ahead for us, and I was right. We were entering a phase of the fight for Peleliu where the threat of enemy attack, either at close quarters or from weapons buried in some distant ridge, never let up. From now on, it would always be there—around the clock, twenty-four hours a day.

AT DAWN ON September 28 (D-plus-13), we gathered up our gear and moved down to a narrow strip of sand on the extreme north tip of Peleliu, where thirty amtracks were waiting for us.

A thousand yards away across a shallow strait, Navy guns and Marine aircraft were hitting Ngesebus with an awesome array of firepower. The battleship *Mississippi* and the heavy cruisers *Denver* and *Columbus* were raining sixteen- and fourteen-inch shells on the island and raising huge clouds of smoke and dust.

At the same time, Corsairs from Marine Fighter Squadron VMF-114, flying out of the repaired Peleliu airfield, were blasting Jap positions along the beach with bombs and rockets and raking them with machine gun fire.

Unless you'd seen it all before, it was hard to imagine how anything could live through such a massive bombardment. But the memory of the much larger fireworks display before our Peleliu landings was still fresh in our minds, and we remembered that most of the Jap defenders had come through that one untouched.

Still, it was nice to know we were getting so much support. Division had also sent thirteen amphibian tanks to spearhead our landing, and that was encouraging, too, but I had the feeling we were going to need every bit of help we could get.

Less than two weeks earlier, 3/5 had come ashore on Peleliu with 1,000 troops. Now there were only about 700 of us left in the battalion's three rifle companies. Casualties had claimed the rest.

At the moment, only God knew how many more killed and wounded we'd have before this day was over—but the rest of us would find out soon enough.

At 9 AM, the "softening-up" bombardment along the Ngesebus beaches ended. Then, with our amphibian tanks out front—each packing a 75-millimeter cannon and two .50-caliber machine guns—the tractor drivers revved their engines. Slowly, like giant turtles, our loaded amtracks rumbled down to the water's edge.

I took the .50-caliber on the right side of the amtrack's bow, but there was something wrong with it, and it wouldn't fire properly. I had to reload every few rounds, so I doubt if it did us much good, but I kept trying.

As far as I could tell, there was no return fire from the Japs.

This was a good break for us because it took almost six minutes for those slow-ass amtracks to crawl across the shallow water and reach the beach on Ngesebus. I was still wrestling with the stubborn .50-caliber gun when I discovered everybody else aboard was already ashore.

When I jumped off the tractor and ran after them, the first thing I saw right in front of me was a pillbox. After I hit the deck, I tried throwing a couple of grenades at the pillbox opening, but both of them fell a little short.

Then Corporal Thomas "Nippo" Baxter—who got that nickname from the uncanny way he could spot hiding Jap soldiers—crawled up beside me with a couple of other Marines. One had a bazooka, and another had a flamethrower, and between them they were able to cure the pillbox in short order. Two Nips ran out of it with their clothes on fire, and we put them out of their misery with our rifles.

We penetrated the rest of the Japs' first line of defenses without much further trouble and ran past the bodies of fifty or sixty dead Japs who'd probably been killed by the strafing Corsairs. We used grenades to silence a couple of Nip machine guns that were still being manned and quickly disposed of another pillbox, using the same combination of weapons as before.

One of my duties as platoon guide was to maintain contact with the units on our flanks. There was nothing but ocean on our left, so I had only our right flank to worry about. That was where the First Platoon was, and I was positioned as close to those Marines as I was to the guys in my own Third Platoon.

As we inched forward during that first hour ashore, I came across a Thompson submachine gun in perfect condition and about a hundred rounds of ammunition. The gun was just lying there behind a little knob of rock, and I had no idea at the time how it got there. Someone told me later that it was probably dropped by Sergeant Tom Rigney of the Second Platoon, who'd been killed in that area earlier that morning.

To me, it was almost like a divine gift from above.

I'd been checked out on tommy guns back at New River before the war, but I hadn't fired one since, and I was excited to have the chance now, especially in the situation we were in. My M-1 was a fine weapon—don't get me wrong about that—but with a tommy and plenty of ammunition, I could be the equivalent of a whole damn fire team all by myself. The problem was, I *didn't* have plenty of ammunition. That hundred rounds would go in a hurry in the kind of firefight we were into, but it would be great while it lasted.

The machine gun and small-arms fire that raged on both sides of me that morning were the heaviest I'd seen so far in the Pacific. We were lucky as hell to have our tanks giving us cover and fire support. Otherwise, I'm not sure we could've held our ground, much less flushed the Japs out of their pillboxes and caves. The tanks saved our bacon more times than I could count.

There were other times, though, when we infantry guys had to rescue some of the tankers. One of those times was just a few minutes after I found the tommy gun. I spotted a tank up ahead of me with Japs swarming all over it. There must've been twenty-five or thirty of them, and the tank crew was obviously in deep trouble.

I turned and saw PFCs Sterling Mace and Bill Leyden, along with two or three other Marines close beside me, and I yelled at them above the roar of the gunfire.

"We gotta get those Nips off that tank! Follow me!"

Luckily, the Japs were too intent on getting at the tankers to notice us at first. I was about thirty feet away when I turned loose the first long burst from the tommy. Mace, Leyden, and the others opened fire with their rifles at the same moment, and Jap bodies started flying off the tank in all directions.

Several Nips were still on top of the turret and trying to wrest it open when I hit them with a second burst. They all fell without firing a single shot in reply. Within ten or fifteen seconds, every Jap attacking the tank had been blasted off it. They'd all been hit, but some were still jerking around on the ground.

"Hey, you guys," I told the other Marines. "I'm running low on ammo, but we can't leave any of those sons of bitches alive. They're damn good at playing possum, so if any of 'em don't have their faces or guts blown open, shoot the bastards again."

When we moved away after a ragged volley of rifle shots, we left nothing but "good Japs" behind us.

We hadn't gone far when another Marine tank pulled up and stopped beside us. The tank commander opened the hatch and grinned at me.

"I saw what you guys did back there," he said. "Thanks for the help. Are you short of rounds for your tommy gun?"

"Yeah," I said, "I'm practically out."

"Well, here," he said. "I got way more than I need." He started handing box after box of .45-caliber ammunition down to me. By the time he got through, I had enough to kill every Jap on Ngesebus two or three times.

"Thanks, man," I said. "I promise to put this to good use."

"Go get 'em, Sergeant," he said, and closed the hatch.

I noticed that the rest of my Third Platoon had gone up a hill to my left, so I headed in that direction. On the way, I decided to make sure the ammo the tanker had given me would work in the tommy gun's magazine. I knew the gun took .45-caliber cartridges, but I wanted to be sure they'd be okay if I loaded them into the magazine manually one at a time, so I fired a few as a test, and they worked fine.

Just at that moment, Captain Haldane came along and saw what I was doing. "Hey, Mac," he said, "you'd better go slow on that ammo. Before we're done here, you may need every round you've got."

I remembered how worried I'd been just a few minutes earlier when I was almost out, and I felt kind of guilty. I guess it looked like I was being wasteful.

"Okay, I'll save the rest for the Japs," I said.

Ack-Ack waved at me and moved on.

THE REST OF that day was one long, continuous firefight. The hill complex that was the Third Platoon's major objective was a maze of interconnected caves and pillboxes, all of them crawling with Japs, and the air around them was full of bullets.

Once, when the platoon got bogged down temporarily as K and I Companies moved up together, I saw fifty-year-old Gunnery Sergeant Pop Haney jump up and rally the troops.

"Come on! Come on!" he yelled at Lieutenant Bauerschmidt. "We gotta keep movin'! We gotta move up!"

Bauerschmidt did what Pop told him, and we fought our way on up the hill, but guys were falling all around us. PFC Walter Stay was killed, and Corporal Richard Van Trump was evacuated with most of his lower jaw blown away.

I must've thrown forty or fifty grenades that day and had at least that many thrown at me. I also gave the tommy gun one helluva workout. One of our tanks would pull up close and fire its 75 straight into the opening in the side of a pillbox or Nip Baxter would call in Marines with flamethrowers and bazookas. Then, if any Japs ran out, I'd spray them with the tommy.

We repeated the process over and over. Only the Lord knows how many I killed that day. But we had plenty of casualties, too. One I remember most vividly happened after Bill Leyden and I saw four or five Japs run out of a cave and start throwing grenades at us as fast as they could pull the pins.

I dropped two of them with the tommy gun, but one Nip was a daring son of a bitch. He stopped right in front of Leyden and hollered "Kill me, Marine! Kill me!"

Well, Leyden killed him, all right, with a quick burst from his M-1. But the Jap got a grenade off just as he went down, and fragments hit Leyden square in the face. The last Jap still standing drew back his arm to throw a grenade at me, but I cut him in half with the tommy before he could release it.

Leyden's face was a bloody mess, especially the area around his left eye. As soon as we could get a corpsman to him, he was evacuated to the rear. The last thing I heard him say was, "Oh shit, oh shit, I think I'm blind!"

I said a little prayer for him right there.

Bill was barely eighteen, and he could be a wise guy at times, but he was also a damn good Marine who fought as hard and well that day as any man I ever knew. (I was glad when I learned after the war that the medics had managed to save his eyes. He recovered fast enough to get wounded even worse at Okinawa by a Jap 75, but he lived through that, too.)

• • •

By dusk on September 28, we had Ngesebus 90 percent secured, except for a few small pockets of Nips that were still holding out, so we dug in for the night and left the mopping up until the next morning.

It took us an hour or so to wipe out the last of the Jap caves. I called up a bazooka man and a flamethrower guy to help. Then, to make dead certain the cave was really cured, a demolition team moved in and sealed up the entrance with TNT charges.

After that, we turned over the rest of the cleanup chores to some Army troops and went back to the beach where the amtracks were supposed to pick us up and take us back to Peleliu.

By the time we left, 470 of the estimated 500 Jap troops on Ngesebus were either dead or captured. It seemed to me like we'd had to kill all the dead ones three or four times before they'd stay dead.

In about thirty hours on Ngesebus, K/3/5 had suffered two-thirds of the Third Battalion's total casualties there—eight men killed and twenty-four wounded.

We earned a big round of applause from division headquarters for the job we'd done. Colonel Lew Walt, who served as overall on-site commander of the operation, praised our "excellent tactics," and Major Gustafson, CO of the Third Battalion, called our tank-infantry assault "perfectly coordinated."

The division's battle diary summed up our victory on Ngesebus in these words: "Infantry and armor performed with a ruthless efficiency unequaled in any previous Pacific operation."

We weren't given much time to enjoy all this recognition, though. Two days after finishing up on Ngesebus, we were sent into the enemy-infested heart of Peleliu's Pocket to try for an encore. We'd stay there for two weeks of around-the-clock combat—until Peleliu itself was secured. Many more of K/3/5's bravest and best would give their lives before that happened.

BY **EARLY OCTOBER**, what was left of the Seventh Marines was locked in a stalemate with the Japs in the Umurbrogol's southern ridges and along the West Road. But the Seventh's lines were stretched thin as tissue paper. It was all they could do to hold the ground they had and keep the Nips from scoring a breakthrough.

They could measure any advances they made in feet, sometimes inches. In many places, their lines were within ten or twelve yards of the enemy's. There was no time for them to eat and no way for them to sleep. Except for brief, infrequent lulls, the firing never stopped.

To keep this so-called quickie battle from lasting the rest of the year, it was obvious that the Seventh Marines needed to be relieved in the ridges by fresher troops. And it was equally obvious that if the First Marine Division was going to break the Japs' grip on the Pocket, it would be up to us in the Fifth Regiment to do the job.

On the maps, most of the major ridges and rocky knobs had names—the Five Sisters, the Five Brothers, the Horseshoe, the China Wall—but they all looked the same to us. Inside each one was an anthill of Japs and stockpiles of weapons and ammo. When we managed to take one, there were always three or four more just like it looming ahead of us. They seemed to go on forever.

Lots of guys who lived to get out of those damn ridges later tried to describe them to the folks back home, but it was impossible. I think PFC Sterling Mace may have come up with the best description when he said, "This terrain's like the surface of a waffle iron, only magnified about a million times."

At this point, the stench of death hung over Peleliu like an invisible, suffocating fog. Our Marine pilots said the smell was overpowering even at 1,500 feet above the island. The Japs never made an effort to collect or bury their corpses. They just left them to rot where they fell. There was one dead enemy soldier in a sitting position just above a trail that I traveled pretty often, and I must've shot his corpse on at least a dozen different occasions. Whenever I rounded a bend in the trail and saw him sitting there, I'd hit him with a few rounds just as a reflex. Finally his corpse decomposed to the point where he didn't even look like a man anymore, and I quit shooting him.

Although we Marines took pride in taking proper care of our dead comrades, the intensity of the fighting in the ridges made any attempt to send out burial details a suicide mission. For one of the few times in Corps history, our dead were left on the field for days, even weeks. The bodies of some of Chesty Puller's men who were killed on D-plus-2 still hadn't been recovered by early October.

All these hundreds of decomposing bodies drew huge clouds of blowflies. They were so thick at times that they actually blotted out the sun, and you had to fight them for every bite of food you ate. If there was any Marine on Peleliu who didn't swallow a few flies along with his C rations, I never met him.

Meanwhile, the heat continued unabated—up to 115 degrees in the afternoons. In all the history of warfare, I don't think men have ever fought each other under more brutal conditions.

• • •

ON THE MORNING of October 1 (D-plus-16), all three battalions of the Fifth Marines climbed aboard a convoy of trucks and amtracks at a bivouac area south of the Jap stronghold known as the Five Sisters.

The first assignment for K/3/5 and the rest of the Third Battalion was to get rid of a bunch of enemy snipers who were threatening a stretch of the West Road called Dead Man's Curve. It was the same area where John Teskevich had been killed and Jesse Googe had been wounded less than a week earlier, so we figured we had a score to settle.

Within a few minutes after we got off the trucks and started moving up into the nearest ridges east of the road, we began drawing fire. It was nothing heavy or concentrated; it was just an isolated shot now and then, but almost every time it happened one of our guys fell. The Nips had obviously been watching us unload and waiting till we made the best possible targets before opening up on us.

The scariest part of all was how well the bastards seemed to see us. It didn't take but a split second of exposure to draw their fire. Fifteen or twenty minutes would go by without a shot being fired. Then some Marine would make a bad move—and *Bam!*—he'd be dead in his tracks.

My Third Platoon was inching its way along a jagged ridge—and I literally mean "inching"—when I got really worried. It had been quiet for a few minutes, but I just had a gut feeling that something was about to happen.

"Watch it now, you guys," I said. "There's no such thing as a comfort zone out here. Just take it easy and keep your heads down. Play it safe, and you'll be all right."

PFC Sterling Mace was crouching just to my left. I could tell he was itching to get a shot at something with his BAR, but I trusted him not to do anything stupid, and so far he hadn't. He was stuffing his pack and pockets with extra ammo and patiently waiting for a chance to use some of it.

"Oh, crap, I didn't leave any room for my cigs," he said, then turned to his left and nudged his buddy Seymour Levy. "Hey, Sy, you got room in your pack for this fresh pack of butts? I got no place to put 'em where they won't get mashed."

Levy had been quieter than usual since he'd gotten the wound in his chin. He hadn't even been quoting much Kipling poetry lately, and sometimes I thought he acted a little irritable, but he seemed okay at the moment.

"Sure," he said, "toss 'em over here."

"You better be careful, Mace," said PFC Frankie Opecek, who was huddled on the other side of Levy. "Levy's liable to smoke the whole pack when you're not lookin'."

"He better not," Mace warned. "It's the only pack I've got." He and Opecek both knew Levy didn't smoke.

Levy just shook his head and didn't say anything, and because of the dirty bandage he still had on his chin it was hard to tell if he was smiling or frowning. But after Mace moved on down the line with his BAR, some scattered shooting started up from the Nips again. I noticed an odd look in Levy's eyes, and it bothered me.

"Something eating you, kid?" I asked.

He shrugged again. "I guess I'm just edgy, Mac. I hate being pinned down like this. It makes me feel . . . you know, trapped. Sometimes I feel like I can't stand it."

"Just take it easy and keep your head down," I told him. "You gotta be patient at times like this. For God's sake, whatever you do, just stay down."

About that time, another shot rang out, and someone down the line yelled for a corpsman. Out of the corner of my eye, I noticed Levy fidgeting.

"Keep your damn head down," I warned again.

For a while after that, Levy seemed to get control of himself. I heard him strike up a conversation with Corporal Tom Matheny, a quiet guy from our mortar section, and I thought he was going to be all right.

But just three or four minutes later, Levy jerked up his rifle and let out a god-awful yell.

"I'm sick and tired of this shit!" he screamed. "I can't take it anymore!"

Then he jumped straight up—right into a Jap bullet. Little droplets of his blood spattered me in the face. He never knew what hit him.

By the time Mace came back looking for his cigarettes, two other Marines had risked their lives to haul Levy's body down the hill. When Mace found out what had happened, I thought I'd have to wrestle him down and hog-tie him to keep the same thing from happening to him.

"I'm gonna go up there and wipe out the whole damn bunch of those assholes," he said, gesturing at the ridge above us with his BAR.

"No, you're not," I said, grabbing him by the shoulders. "You're one of the best BAR men in the platoon, and I ain't lettin' you get yourself killed for nothin', so just cool off. You can handle this, kid. Hell's bells, you *gotta* handle it."

Mace sank down to the coral and lowered his head. "But why'd he have to come back?" he said. "Why couldn't the dummy just take his million-dollar wound and go home?"

"I don't know," I said. "And now we'll never know."

Battalion was finally able to call in artillery and mortar fire, along with some napalm shots by our Corsairs, and broke up the snipers' nests enough to get us out of the jam we were in and let us catch our breath.

But there were worse jams ahead, and the killing had only just started.

EARLY ON OCTOBER 3, we launched a battalion-strength assault from the south against the five-headed monster we'd come to know as the Five Sisters. For me, it would be one of the worst days of the war—a day when I lost three more friends from my Third Platoon, and K/3/5 suffered twenty casualties overall.

The attack by 3/5 was to be coordinated with a simultaneous strike from the east by the Second Battalion, Seventh Marines, on an adjacent strip of high ground now designated as Walt's Ridge in honor of Colonel Lew Walt, executive officer of the Fifth Marines. (This was the second time Walt had been so honored.) Actually, though, 2/7's target was the very same Hill 100 where Captain Everett Pope's men had taken such terrible losses two weeks earlier. This illustrates just how little ground we'd gained against the Jap-held Pocket since then and it shows why the fight for Peleliu was as disheartening as it was deadly. We were attacking the same damn ridges over and over again and never seeming to get anywhere.

We started our advance that morning with a network of ridges rising up on our left. To our right, we could see through a long, open

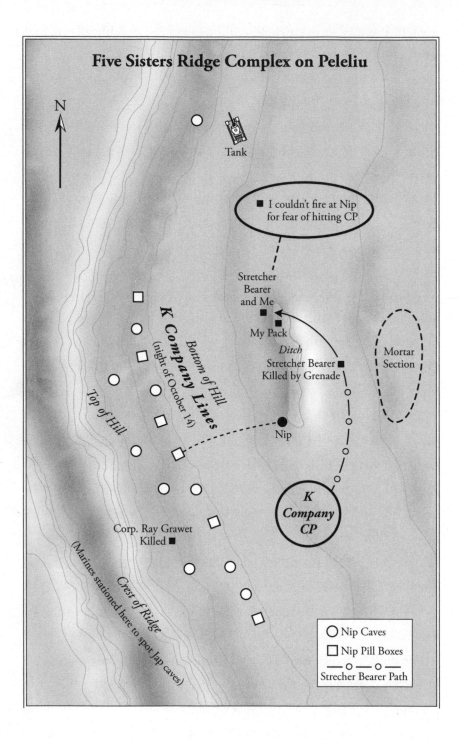

Five Sisters Ridge Complex on Peleliu

N

Tank

■ I couldn't fire at Nip for fear of hitting CP

Stretcher Bearer and Me ■

My Pack ■

Ditch
Stretcher Bearer ■
Killed by Grenade

Mortar Section

Bottom of Hill
K Company Lines
(night of October 14)

Top of Hill

Nip ●

K Company CP

Corp. Ray Grawet Killed ■

Crest of Ridge
(Marines stationed here to spot Jap caves)

○ Nip Caves
□ Nip Pill Boxes
—○—○— Strecher Bearer Path

area all the way to the airfield and our original beachhead. On our way up the slopes, we ran into some heavy fire from a string of Jap caves and pillboxes on a long ridge above us. At the right end of the ridge were the rocky knobs of the Five Sisters.

We had some tanks with us, but the terrain was so rough they could only fire at the Nip positions from a distance, so we had to spend most of the morning using bazookas, flamethrowers, and TNT charges against the caves until we thought they were all shut down. But unfortunately, we missed some, and as we moved farther up the hill, we suddenly found ourselves in a meat-grinder, catching enemy fire from both front and rear.

"Shit, they're behind us!" I heard a Marine yell. "Get down! Get down!"

Lieutenant Bill Bauerschmidt was only four or five yards from me when he was hit low in the belly by a Jap rifle bullet. I turned toward him just as he fell.

Other enemy rounds were peppering the hillside when I snaked my way up beside Bauerschmidt, and what I saw made me sick. It was like Teskevich all over again. Same kind of wound in the same area. The lieutenant was already covered with blood from the waist down, but he was still trying his best to get that hog-leg .45 of his out of its holster.

"I don't get it," he mumbled. "The shot came from behind. Are our own men shooting at us?"

"No sir, we must've missed some—" I started to say, but by then he was unconscious.

Several guys shouted for stretcher-bearers, but they were slow in coming, and who could blame them? I knew from sad experience there was no need to hurry, anyway. Within a few minutes, the lieutenant was dead.

I'd never known an officer that I liked or admired more than Bauerschmidt. He'd been an outstanding platoon leader, but he'd been a good friend, too. He'd made us grunts feel like he was one of us, and I hated what had happened to him. But at that moment, there was only one thought in my head:

A lot more of us are going to die if we stay where we are. Gotta move! Gotta move!

"We can't hold here!" I yelled at the men around me. "Fall back down the hill! Fall back!"

We lost two more guys before we made it to cover. PFC Lyman Rice was killed instantly as he tried to retreat, and PFC Raymond Grawet was cut down when he ran past one of those overlooked Jap caves. Grawet was one of those daring eighteen-year-old kids who thought he could dive off the Empire State Building into a thimbleful of water, but this time he'd moved out too far into the open and exposed himself to enemy fire once too often.

I came as close as I ever did to getting killed myself that morning when I ran back to get my pack out of a ditch where I'd accidentally dropped it when the firing started. (See map, p. 252.) One Nip threw five grenades at me, and a couple of them hit within a few feet of me, but I hunkered down in the ditch, and by the grace of God, I didn't get a single scratch. I was carrying a tommy gun again that morning, but I didn't dare shoot at the SOB because he was directly in line with the K/3/5 CP.

Then the Japs opened up on our stretcher-bearers who were trying to move some of our casualties. They killed one bearer with a grenade and wounded another one, Corporal Charles Williams, whose official job was our company "field music" or bugler. I grabbed him and pulled him down to the ground with me. Otherwise, I'm sure he would've been killed.

October 3 went into the record books as one of the costliest days of the war for K/3/5. The company lost a total of twenty killed and wounded that day.

October 4 wasn't quite so bad. We only had eight casualties that day, including PFC Alden Moore, who was KIA.

PFC Ray Rottinghaus, a tough farmhand from Iowa, fired close to 500 rounds from his BAR within a couple of minutes that morning while wiping out more than a dozen Japs caught in the open. But then a machine gun in a nearby pillbox opened up on him. One round blew off his left index finger and splintered the stock of his BAR. Another smashed into his left shoulder.

Ray calmly wrapped his shirt around the bloody remains of his left hand and started back toward an aid station on his own. He'd covered about half the distance when some stretcher bearers persuaded him to let them carry him the rest of the way. He was one of seven K/3/5 guys wounded that day.

By nightfall on October 4, the company's two-day casualty total stood at 28—or more than 20 percent of what our strength had been forty-eight hours earlier.

MEANWHILE, THE THIRD Battalion, Seventh, was faring even worse. Its L Company lost both its commanding officer, Captain James V. "Jamo" Shanley, who had been awarded a Navy Cross at the Cape, and its executive officer, Lieutenant Harold Collins, within seconds of each other. They were caught in a fierce Jap crossfire as the company tried to retreat from a jagged outcropping called Hill 120. Only eleven of the forty-eight L/3/7 Marines who attacked the hill escaped alive, and six of them were wounded.

Those two days were the swan song for Colonel Herman Hanneken's Seventh Marines on Peleliu. On October 5, General Geiger, commander of the III Amphibious Corps, ordered General Rupertus to pull the remaining troops of the Seventh off the line and get them ready for evacuation.

By now, total casualties in the Seventh had reached 1,486 killed and wounded. That was 46 percent of the regiment's authorized strength. Both L and I Companies were especially hard hit. Each of them had only about thirty able-bodied Marines left. Less than three weeks earlier, they'd landed on Peleliu with 235 men apiece.

Even under these conditions, Rupertus tried to argue with Geiger. "Just give 'em a little more time," he said. "They'll take the Pocket, and the battle will be over."

Rupertus was still kidding himself. He was the same guy, remember, who'd said the Peleliu operation would be a done deal in two or three days. Every field officer in the regiment knew the Seventh was too worn out for any kind of offensive action, but I think Rupertus's head was as deep in the sand as Chesty Puller's had been two weeks earlier.

It was true that over 95 percent of Peleliu could now be considered secure and that the Japs were bottled up in an area not much bigger than a half-dozen football fields put together.

But it was also true that we were nowhere near breaking the Jap stranglehold on the heart of the Pocket—and those of us out there on the line damn well knew it.

It was going to take a lot more dying before that happened.

Fortunately for the men of the Seventh, Rupertus eventually relented. Late on the morning of October 6, he gave in and ordered Hanneken's survivors to withdraw.

Now, if the Marines were ever going to sew up the Pocket, it'd be strictly up to the Fifth to finish the job.

We were the only ones left.

THE KILLING WENT on and on day after day, and the stink grew steadily worse. As if the odor of decaying corpses wasn't bad enough, we now had three weeks worth of human dung piled on the coral by us and our enemies. It was impossible to build latrines on the solid rock of the Umurbrogol or even gouge out a hole to bury your own waste.

The problem could've been a lot worse if so many of us hadn't lost our appetite because of the disgusting conditions we lived in. Personally, I don't ever remember being really hungry on Peleliu. Fighting the flies for every bite of food you swallow gets old in a hurry. I routinely went for two or three days without eating anything, and so did plenty of other guys.

Of course, this also meant that a lot of food got thrown out to spoil, and that added yet another element to the mix of foul smells.

We didn't sleep much, either. We went through the days like zombies because at night the Japs were always there, no more than a few feet away, and the tension never let up. Most of the Jap infiltrators wore black pajamas and rubber-soled shoes, so they were both silent and invisible in the dark. They came creeping into our lines every night, intent on killing anybody they caught unawares.

I was extremely fortunate that I never had to fight off one of the sneaky devils, but several of the Marines near me did. Maybe it was sheer luck on my part, but I still wonder if the Japs could somehow sense that I was ready and waiting for them. During those last few days in the Pocket, I barely slept at all. I kept my back against a wall of rock, my rifle or tommy gun in my hands, and my Ka-bar knife in my lap. All I thought about was what I'd do if one of the bastards jumped at me out of the dark. I forced myself not to think about home or family or anything else pleasant for fear it would lull me to sleep.

But the more the fatigue and stress built up, the more careless— and crazy—some of us became. A lot of men lost heart to the point where they didn't give a damn. I heard about guys sticking their feet or arms out into the open during firefights that never seemed to end, trying to get wounded just enough to be evacuated. I never actually saw anybody do that, but I don't doubt that it happened.

Looking back on those last ten days on Peleliu, I can't imagine how any of us lived through it—but miraculously some of us did.

Those of us in the Fifth Marines were extremely fortunate to have a CO like Colonel Bucky Harris. That was one of the most positive things going for us. Harris refused to send us on suicide missions against those Jap caves like some of the other commanders had done. Instead, he played a patient waiting game, calling in artillery, tanks, mortars, and air support and giving them time to do their work before the infantry went in to clean up with flamethrowers, bazookas, and TNT.

I truly believe that most of us in K/3/5 who left Peleliu with breath in our lungs owe our lives to Colonel Harris. If I'd been in Puller's regiment, I'm convinced I would've died there.

•   •   •

BY THE SECOND week of October, the Jap snipers in those ridges above the West Road were still giving us fits. They were a constant threat to anything or anybody trying to use the road, and they were so well concealed and so scattered out, usually firing from one-man positions, that it was next to impossible to see them, much less return their fire.

On the morning of October 10, K/3/5, along with six or seven tanks, was sent into the same general area where John Teskevich had been killed to try one more time to get rid of the snipers.

At this point, the company's casualty rate had climbed to over 40 percent, and the First Platoon, now led by Lieutenant Hillbilly Jones, was down to about fifteen riflemen—half its normal strength—with Jones as its only officer. (The lieutenant had been wounded in the hand several days earlier, but he'd insisted on staying on the line and treating the wound himself.)

Most of the snipers were firing from positions about 100 yards south of Jones's guys, and as the morning wore on, they got steadily more active. They took their time, though, and picked their targets well. PFC Charles R. McClary was hit in the gut, much like Teskevich had been, and died a short time later. Two other K/3/5 riflemen were seriously wounded within a couple of minutes of each other.

Like everybody else in the company, Jones was tired and on edge, and these latest casualties didn't help matters. If they continued at this rate, his whole platoon could be wiped out before the day was over.

"Hillbilly was one of the calmest, most levelheaded officers I ever knew," one First Platoon Marine told me, "but he was really depressed and sick about our losses. He was desperate to get back at the Japs, and that's why I think he did what he did that morning."

As Jones crouched behind one of the tanks, gripping his tommy gun and studying the sniper-infested ridge through binoculars, Major Clyde Brooks, a staff officer from Third Battalion headquarters, came running up and took cover beside him.

"Major Gustafson sent me over to see what we could do about those snipers," Brooks said. "You got any ideas?"

Jones nodded. "I'm thinking about climbing up on this tank to try to spot a target for the gunners to shoot at. They'd have a better chance of hitting something with a machine gun or a 75 than we do from the ground with rifles. What do you think?"

Brooks frowned. "It sounds awful damn risky to me," he said.

"Yeah, but I figure it's either that or sit here in this Nip shooting gallery the rest of the day."

Brooks thought about it for a moment. "Okay then," he said. "Give it a try, but watch yourself."

Jones left his tommy gun on the ground—the snipers were well out of its range, anyway—and climbed up on the rear deck of the tank, then tapped on the turret to get the tank commander's attention.

"I'm gonna try to find you a target for your .50-caliber or your 75," he said, "so get ready."

"Are you sure you want to do this?" Brooks yelled up at Jones from the protected area behind the tank.

Hillbilly shrugged. "So far, so good," he said.

Those were the last words anybody heard Jones speak. As he peered around the tank turret toward the ridge, a single shot rang out. The bullet hit Jones in the left side below his ribs, and he fell backward and slid off the side of the tank onto the ground.

Somebody yelled for a corpsman, but the other Marines were

stunned to see Jones pull himself erect and stagger back to the tank. He was obviously hurt bad and maybe delirious with pain. His shirt was soaked with blood, but somehow he climbed back onto the deck of the Sherman and tried to stand up.

Then a second shot hit him, and this one went straight through his heart.

The handsome, guitar-strumming officer described in Eugene Sledge's book as "a unique combination of bravery, leadership, ability, integrity, dignity, straightforwardness, and compassion" was gone. I think every man in the company felt a sense of personal loss when they learned of Hillbilly's death.

The snipers kept plaguing us for the rest of that day with both small-arms fire and knee mortars. But the next morning, battalion ordered every inch of that damn ridge pulverized for hours by our tanks, artillery, and mortars. Our Corsairs also came in and blistered it with napalm.

After that, the sniping in that particular area stopped. But the killing went on and on.

OVER THE NEXT day or two, with most of the Seventh Marines now in a secure rest area near the airfield, fresh Army troops were moved into the line to take over the Seventh's old positions. But these untested troops were there mainly in a defensive role, and their main job was to prevent any kind of breakout by the Japs. Carrying on the offensive against the Pocket was up to the battle-scarred Fifth Marines, who were damn near as bad off as the Seventh.

With the help of a 75-millimeter howitzer that was manhandled up a cliff to the top of a strategic ridge by sixty-eight Marines, Major

Gordon Gayle's 2/5 managed to capture the piece of high ground known as Hill 140. But because of the heavy casualties that small victory cost, it turned out to be their last organized action on Peleliu. Along with Colonel Robert Boyd's 1/5, Gayle's battalion was ordered off the line and into reserve.

Early on the morning of October 12 (D-plus-27), what was left of the Third Battalion replaced the withdrawing survivors of 2/5 on the crest of Hill 140. We were now the last infantry battalion of the First Marine Division still actively engaged with the enemy.

"You've still got Jap sharpshooters all over the place out there," one of the 2/5 Marines told me, "so be sure to warn your guys to keep their heads down. Just one quick look over the crest of the hill can be fatal."

That was demoralizing enough in itself, but I guess it was an omen of things to come. For the approximately ninety of us in K/3/5 who were still capable of combat, the most tragic day of the war lay just ahead.

BEING AS HE was an old machine gun man, Captain Ack-Ack Haldane still liked to take a personal hand in making sure the company's .30-caliber weapons were in the most effective locations.

This was especially true that morning on Hill 140, where Haldane was told that 2/5's machine gunners were kept so pinned down by Jap snipers that the only way they could take aim was by sighting along the undersides of their barrels.

For that reason, Ack-Ack called on some of his senior NCOs to go with him to an observation point on the ridge to discuss where our company machine gun section should set up.

We were running very low on commissioned officers at this point. Besides Haldane, the only two we had left were Lieutenants Thomas "Stumpy" Stanley, the company exec, and Charles "Duke" Ellington, who commanded the mortar platoon.

Because I'd been functioning as leader of the Third Platoon since Lieutenant Bauerschmidt was killed, Haldane asked me to join the group on the hilltop. Other noncoms who were there included Platoon Sergeant Johnny Marmet of the mortar section, Sergeant Dick Higgins, Haldane's personal aide, and Corporal Jim Anderson, one of the captain's most trusted runners.

Haldane was no more than four or five feet ahead of me as he crawled up to the edge of the ridgeline and raised his head a few inches to steal a look.

I heard him say something like, "We need the guns as close as we—"

In a split second, the sharp sound of a rifle shot cut off Haldane's words. It sounded less like gunfire than somebody slapping his hands together, but every one of us on that hill knew instantly what it was.

Then Ack-Ack's head vanished in a flash of red, and a shower of blood blew back in my face.

"Oh, dear God, no!" I think I whispered. Then my tongue froze in my throat as Jim Anderson and I stared at each other in shock and disbelief. Dick Higgins scrambled forward toward the body, and I seem to remember someone else pulling him back to keep him from getting hit, too. Then he whirled around and ran back down the hill, screaming for a corpsman.

There was no need for a corpsman. What Ack-Ack needed was a priest.

I can't remember what happened over the next minute or two. Whatever it was, it's still a total blank for me. When I came back to reality, Johnny Marmet had left—to tell his mortar men out on the line what had happened, I learned later. Dick Higgins was gone, too, and I understand he ended up at an aid station that morning being treated for severe shock. Two Marines were carrying the captain's body away on a stretcher. Jim Anderson was wiping his face and shaking his head.

"I can't believe this," he muttered. "I saw it, but I can't believe it."

As for me, I'd reached the point where I could believe almost anything, but there was no way to get rid of the emptiness inside me. Gradually, though, as I started to sort things out, the reality of the situation hit me like a ton of bricks:

Haldane was dead. Lieutenant Stanley was at battalion head-quarters and out of reach, and so was First Sergeant David Bailey. Lieutenant Ellington was out with his mortar squads, and Platoon Sergeant Marmet was probably out there, too, or on his way. Platoon Sergeant Harry Spiece was somewhere on the line, but nobody knew where.

"You're the highest-ranking NCO available, Mac," somebody told me. "You've gotta take charge of the company."

It was true. Whether I liked it or not. Whether I knew what to do or not. I was it. There was nobody else to do it.

So there I was, a lowly three-stripe buck sergeant, trying to take the place of one of the best COs in the Marine Corps in one of the toughest spots we'd ever been in.

What the hell was I supposed to do now?

One thing I *could* do, I decided, was get on the phone in the company CP and try to tell our artillery where those damn Jap snipers were concentrated. I was able to get in contact with an Army 105 down in the valley below Hill 140 and direct his fire on Jap positions I could see from the high ground. I also got through to a tank destroyer with a 75, and he also opened up on the Jap caves.

I sent out a few patrols and met with some aviation Marines who'd been sent up to help us. They weren't supposed to go out on the line, but when I told them about the spot we were in, they volunteered to go—all of them. I gave them a quick lesson on how to throw grenades. None of them had ever done it before, but they learned in a hurry.

When Major Gustafson, the battalion CO, found out what was going on, he phoned the company CP and asked who was directing the artillery fire.

"I am, sir," I said. "I'm the senior guy up here, and I didn't think we could afford to quit shooting till one of our officers gets back to take over."

"Okay, Sergeant," he said. "I'm sending Lieutenant Stanley back your way. In the meantime, keep doing what you're doing. Just be careful."

ON OCTOBER 14 (D-plus-29), K/3/5 was back in action in the vicinity of Hill 140 with Lieutenant Stanley in command. We spent most of the day sending out patrols, sealing caves, rooting out diehard snipers, and stringing wire to keep infiltrators away from our foxholes that night.

We also took our last two casualties on Peleliu, when Sergeant Harry Spiece and PFC Earl Shepherd were wounded and evacuated.

That afternoon, we started hearing rumors about Army troops

relieving us on the line the next morning. At first, I didn't believe it, and most of the other guys didn't either. By now, we were too damn exhausted to waste energy getting our hopes up.

But this time, to our great relief, the rumors were actually true.

About noon on October 15, we turned over our foxholes to some grim-looking replacement troops of the Army's 321st Infantry Regiment. We didn't say much to them, and they didn't say much to us, but the expressions on their faces were worth a thousand words. They were scared shitless—understandably so—and as awful as we looked, they envied us.

We made our way down the hill, still under sporadic small-arms fire, and boarded trucks for a ten-minute ride into another world—a neat, orderly bivouac area near the East Road, where the constant gunfire from the ridges was barely audible. It was so quiet that I thought for a while I was going deaf.

It was also the closest thing we'd seen to civilization in a long time. It had a well-equipped cookhouse and mess tent, showers with plenty of fresh water, decked tents, and even an outdoor movie screen. There were clean uniforms, boondocker shoes, and new white socks waiting for us to replace the filthy, rotting rags most of us had worn since D-Day.

As a precaution, we established a defensive perimeter facing the beach in case of an enemy counter-landing, but it was only a formality. Outside of the Pocket, the Japs on Peleliu were done, and for us, the fighting there was finally over.

11

GOING BACK TO THE REAL WORLD

IT TOOK US two full weeks to get away from Peleliu because the Navy had a hard time finding transportation for us, but I can't remember much of anything about that interval. From the time we were pulled off the line for good to the day we boarded ship and left the island is mostly just a blurry space in my memory.

We were all about to collapse from exhaustion, and for the first three or four days, the only thing we did was sleep. We'd wake up long enough to eat a meal or take a shower. Then we'd crawl back in the sack and sleep for another five or six hours. I didn't think I was ever going to get enough shut-eye.

On October 29, after we finally got rested up, a Marine Corps photographer lined us up on the beach to take pictures of what was left of K/3/5 and the other companies of the Third Battalion, Fifth. Showing up for the photo session was our last official duty assignment on Peleliu.

In all, only eighty-five of us were available to pose for our company portrait. The 150 others who'd landed with K/3/5 on D-Day had all been killed or wounded.

Twenty-six men from our company were either lying in freshly dug graves in a new cemetery near the airfield or had died aboard Navy hospital ships and been buried at sea, and 124 others were hospitalized with battle wounds at various locations around the Pacific. K/3/5's casualty rate of 64 percent—almost two-thirds of its D-Day strength—was among the highest in the division.

I was one of just five K/3/5 senior noncommissioned officers still standing. The other four were First Sergeant David Bailey, Sergeant Dick Higgins, Platoon Sergeant John Marmet, and Sergeant Donald Shifla. The only two commissioned officers still with the company were Lieutenant Stumpy Stanley, who took command after Captain Haldane was killed, and Lieutenant Duke Ellington of the mortar section.

Overall, the First Marine Division suffered a total of 6,336 casualties at Peleliu, including 1,121 killed in action, 5,142 wounded in action, and 73 missing in action.

I made a couple of trips down to the new cemetery, looking for the graves of guys I knew—especially John Teskevich's—but I never found any of them. Lots of graves were still unmarked, and bodies were still being hauled in for burial. It was sheer chaos, and it depressed the hell out of me.

I never knew for sure what happened to all those dead Japs. Quite a few of them were entombed in their caves, and I guess a lot of others were just left on the battlefield until much later. The impossible terrain of the Umurbrogol Pocket made it almost impossible to retrieve the thousands of enemy bodies, even if we'd had the manpower to do it.

At the time the Fifth Marines were withdrawn, it was estimated that fewer than 1,000 of the 10,900 Jap defenders were still capable of combat. But according to somebody's calculations at Marine Corps headquarters, it had taken an average of about 1,590 rounds of all types of our ammunition to kill each one of those enemy soldiers.

It would take the Army troops another six weeks—until late November—to wipe out the last Jap resistance. And it wasn't until April 1947, more than a year and a half after the end of the war, when the last group of twenty-six starving Nip survivors gave up and ventured out of their caves.

When the fighting finally stopped and U.S. forces explored the intricate system of defenses that General Sadae Inoue's troops had created, they found more than 500 caves, many of them with multiple levels and entrances. Some were equipped with sliding steel doors that opened to allow heavy artillery to fire, then closed again to hide the big guns.

One underground fortress in particular was large enough to house a whole battalion of troops—1,000 men—along with their ammo and other supplies.

As one of my comrades in K/3/5 aptly put it: "The Nips weren't just on Peleliu; they were *in* Peleliu."

AS MUCH AS I looked forward to it, the details of our long-awaited departure from that terrible island on October 30 are hard for me to sort out in my mind. I still felt tired and numb, and I didn't particularly want to talk to anybody. Most of the thoughts I can remember were recollections of friends and comrades who'd died in combat and vague feelings of relief that I hadn't.

The realization that I might never have to shoot or bayonet or grenade another human being did cross my mind at times. As John Teskevich and I had told each other the night before he was killed, the Marine Corps almost *had* to send men like us back to the States after Peleliu.

But, of course, John wouldn't be making that trip now, and there was something unreal about the idea that I would. It was almost like one of those dreams that's too good to be true. I was afraid I'd wake up and be back in a rocky hole with bullets whining around me and the smell of death in the air.

There was always the chance that somebody in Washington could change the rules, and that worried me a little. It meant I might end up in another killing spree on another damn island, so it was premature to think too much about going home. But it was also hard as hell to keep it off my mind.

One of my few clear images of the day we sailed from Peleliu is the new dock the Navy had built on the east side of the island. It was long and black and about twenty yards wide. But the water wasn't deep enough for the incoming troopships to reach it, so we had to get on Higgins boats for the short trip out to the SS *Sea Runner*, the merchant ship that was to take us to Pavuvu.

As usual, we were expected to climb cargo nets to board the ship, and even after a dozen days of rest and rehab, lots of our guys were too weak to make it to the top under their own steam. I don't recall having as much trouble with the nets as I had at Guadalcanal, but they were a real struggle for some of my comrades.

"I only got halfway before I had to stop and rest," recalled PFC Jay d'Leau, one of our bazooka men, many years later. "Three feet from the top, I was totally beat, and some sailors had to reach down and help me."

In his book, Gene Sledge remembered "feeling like a weary insect climbing a vine" and thinking it was fortunate that no Marine lost his grip and fell.

I **THINK I STAYED** in a kind of withdrawal state much of the time during our trip back to Pavuvu. It took us eight days to get there, and we crossed the equator on the way, heading south. We had comfortable quarters below decks, and the *Sea Runner*'s galley served excellent chow. We spent a lot of time on deck, just bullshitting and breathing in the fresh air, and we got in plenty of sack time, too, since we had no duties to perform.

Only a few shipboard incidents stand out in my mind. The main ones I remember were some fights that broke out between members of the Merchant Marine crew and a group of about ten Navy gunners assigned to man the five-inch gun on the aft of the ship. The Navy guys were seriously outnumbered, and they were getting the crap stomped out of them when some of the Marines decided the odds weren't very fair, and they jumped in and took care of those crewmembers.

For once in my life, I went out of my way to keep from getting involved. I just wasn't in a fighting mood.

I know the Merchant Marine did great work for our country during the war, but those guys on the *Sea Runner* were a bunch of knuckleheads, and they deserved the whipping they got.

WHEN WE ARRIVED at Pavuvu on November 7, the palm groves along the shoreline looked familiar from a distance. But as the small boats that took us from the ship to a new steel pier got closer to the beach, we hardly recognized the place.

Several decorated tables were lined up near the water's edge, and a sleek new canteen/clubhouse building was under construction in the background. There wasn't a rotten coconut or rat to be seen anywhere.

But the most shocking sight was a group of Red Cross nurses standing behind the tables and handing out doughnuts and paper cups of chilled grapefruit juice.

These were the first young, attractive white women we'd seen since our last leaves in Melbourne close to a year before, and seeing them so unexpectedly scared a bunch of us tough Marines half to death. We'd been isolated from the fair sex for so long that we didn't know how to act.

A few overeager Marines rushed up to get in line at the tables, but a good many shied away and pretended to ignore the women. They sat down on the beach, kind of sulking and looking the other way. Others just stood and gaped at the nurses like they were creatures from Mars or someplace. But some of us had enough sense just to grin and accept the refreshments they offered—and even remember to say "Thanks."

These women seemed so out of place to a lot of the guys that they actually resented them being there.

"Well, hell, I guess we'll have to wear swim trunks from now on when we take a dip," I heard one Marine say.

To me, such an attitude confirmed the old saying that "some guys will gripe about anything." The only thing the women's presence meant to me was that one little hint of civilization had finally made it to Pavuvu.

On the other hand, the odds of any of us getting really chummy with one of those Red Cross girls were as close as you could get to absolute zero. We had a better chance of flying to the moon. After all, there were only half a dozen of them, and there were 15,000 of us.

I guess that's one reason the new canteen/clubhouse building never got used very much by the Marines. After what we'd been through, maybe it was just a little too spiffy for us to be comfortable in. But all the other changes that had taken place on Pavuvu during the months we'd been gone got our full approval.

Marine engineers and Seabees had built very comfortable bivouac areas for us, complete with brand-new tents with wooden decks and electric lights. We also had access to modern showers, laundries, screened and well-lighted mess halls, plus a large PX stocked with all kinds of stateside goods.

Instead of a sea of mud, there were neatly laid-out streets and roads built of packed coral, a fifteen-acre parade ground, ball fields, and other recreational facilities. There were plenty of sodas, ice cream, candy bars, and other half-forgotten treats—including a three-can-a-week-per-man beer ration.

One of our few disappointments was that a big batch of that notorious alcoholic brew called "jungle juice," prepared by the healing wounded men from Peleliu who'd reached Pavuvu weeks before we did, had sat too long and turned to vinegar by the time we finally got there.

To MY RELIEF, I received official word a few days after reaching Pavuvu that I was scheduled for rotation back to the States within a few weeks—and a thirty-day leave once I got there. Major Gustafson, the Third Battalion commander, signed the paperwork, and it was a done deal. My departure date was originally set for November 19, but it was actually December 1 before we embarked.

Once this was settled, I went over to battalion headquarters and told the sergeant major who ran the office there that I wanted to extend my enlistment for another two years.

"You need to wait till you get stateside," the sergeant major told me.

"No way," I said. "I want to do it now, before I leave."

This may sound a little weird, but I had what I thought were good reasons for wanting to speed up the reenlistment process a little.

My current enlistment was already finished, but there was no way the Marine Corps was going to discharge a healthy NCO with my seniority and combat experience until the war was over. And, like most other Marines I knew, I expected the war to last at least another two years. (Obviously, we'd never heard of the atom bomb.)

So I figured if I extended now instead of waiting till I got stateside and wound up a thirty-day leave, it meant I might get my discharge that much earlier. In the meantime, unless I formally requested more overseas duty, I could probably serve out my time in the good old U.S.A.

Even halfway around the world, we'd heard how the Corps was now drafting guys by the tens of thousands—it was the first time in history that all Marines hadn't been volunteers—and we'd also heard how urgently they needed seasoned NCOs to train all these new boots.

I'd already completed the requirements for promotion to platoon sergeant, and I hoped I could get assigned as a drill instructor at Parris Island or some other training camp. In its own way, it would be a job that was just as vital to the war effort as shooting at Nips and getting grenades thrown at you. But at the same time, it wouldn't be nearly as dangerous and dirty as the one I'd been doing for the past twenty-eight months.

I spent the rest of my time on Pavuvu hanging around with some of the wounded Marines who'd been there a while and talking about mutual friends who didn't make it. Some of the guys from K/3/5 were trying to recover from terrible, disfiguring wounds. It almost hurt me to look at them.

One man in particular couldn't seem to get his mind off all the horrible things he'd been through. He just kept reliving them over and over. I'd try to switch the subject to something else, but he'd always come back to the bad stuff. It was like his memory was holding him prisoner.

We didn't know much about post-traumatic stress syndrome in those days, but I'm sure that's what this poor guy had. I really felt sorry for him, but I have to admit it was a relief to get away from the haunted look in his eyes when the time came for me to leave. I don't know what happened to him after that.

· · ·

ON DECEMBER 1, a large group of us boarded a Navy transport called the USS *Wharton*, and we sailed from Pavuvu that same day. Our first stop was at Guadalcanal, which was only sixty miles away. I was amazed at how peaceful and calm Iron Bottom Sound was. Not a single sea battle or air raid was going on.

I'd heard that some of the kids I'd played football with back in Gerritsen Beach were stationed at the 'Canal now, and I tried hard to find them in the short time we were there, but I didn't have any luck.

(I'd learned in a letter from my sister that my old buddy Charlie Smith was back in Brooklyn by this time. He'd been wounded twice since I'd seen him, once at the 'Canal and again, more seriously, with the Second Marines at Tarawa. That second wound got him sent home for good.)

We stopped a couple more times on our way east across the Pacific at New Hebrides and New Caledonia to take on more passengers. Then we passed Hawaii without pulling into port. We picked up some big band music on the radio from Honolulu, but that was as close as we got.

The trip got pretty monotonous after that, and I spent a lot of time at night looking up at the stars and thinking about the men we'd lost on the islands where we fought and all the different ways they'd died.

For some, it was in the heat of a firefight or as they charged a Jap cave. For some, it was when they peeked over a ridge at the wrong moment or when a Jap sneaked up in the dark and stabbed them in their foxholes. For others, it was an enemy shell or grenade—or sometimes one of our own—that came out of nowhere.

No matter how it happened, though, they were all just as dead. It made me fully aware—for the first time, I think—how lucky I was to still be breathing and heading home.

The voyage took three weeks altogether. We didn't get to San Francisco till December 21, and it didn't hit me until we were getting ready to go ashore the next morning that it was only three days till Christmas. That's how out of touch I was with the real world.

All of a sudden, I was in the mood to celebrate and in a terrific hurry to hit those legendary streets of San Francisco, but the people in charge aboard the *Wharton* had other ideas.

First the voice on the ship's intercom said, "All Army personnel prepare to disembark." Then, a few minutes later, it said, "All Navy personnel prepare to disembark."

Finally, a third announcement came over the speakers, but it didn't make any mention of disembarking. It simply said, "All Marines, stand by."

Uh-oh! What's this? I wondered. *Another ship-cleaning job?*

As it turned out, somebody was trying to do us Marines a favor. The movie actress Marie McDonald was planning to do a special welcome-home show for us on the ship.

The problem was, nobody asked us if we wanted to wait around to see her show. And—no offense—some of us didn't. I hadn't been able to write Mom and my sister that I was coming home because of the strict censorship in the Pacific, and now I was anxious to let them know I was back in the States. Once that was done, a couple of K/3/5 buddies and I were all primed to go out on the town in Frisco and reintroduce ourselves to the real world.

"Let's get off this tub," one of my buddies said. "We can catch Marie later on the silver screen."

So the three of us jumped ship. We just walked off the *Wharton*, and nobody on deck seemed to care. We didn't even take any of our gear. All we had was the clothes we were wearing—which, in my case, was a set of dungarees and a pair of boondockers—but our pockets were stuffed with back pay that we hadn't had a chance to spend in months.

I had the home address of a friend of mine, PFC Robert J. Moss, who was stationed at the Marine quartermaster base in Frisco. Bob had been wounded at the 'Canal and sent stateside. He was married to a girl from Auckland, New Zealand, and they were expecting a baby. I'd kept in touch with him by mail, and I knew he'd be glad to do me a favor.

Bob had access to a phone with priority clearance, so I asked him to call Mom and tell her I was back on American soil. At the height of the holiday season in 1944, with tens of thousands of inbound and outbound troops tying up the long-distance lines, it could take hours to complete a transcontinental call. But I gave Bob a time when I was pretty sure Mom would be home from work, and he was able to do the job in just a few minutes.

After that, my two buddies and I bought several cases of beer and spent three full days doing the town. I lost count of the parties we crashed and the bars we visited. Anytime we saw people celebrating, we just joined in. It was all kind of crazy, but nobody seemed to mind. In fact, a lot of total strangers made us feel welcome just about everywhere we went.

I don't think Americans in general ever felt more patriotic or more hospitable toward Marines and other service personnel than they did that Christmas season. We struck up a friendship with an older guy named George Brody, who drove us wherever we wanted to go in his old Plymouth.

For war-weary Marines on leave, we behaved ourselves pretty well. We only got in one small fight, and Brody, a civilian, did most of the hitting.

By Christmas night, when our nonstop celebration ended, we'd gotten a lot of the Pacific out of our systems. I think our partying was good therapy, but I was tired as hell and ready to start the long trek home to Brooklyn.

When we went back to the ship, the officer of the deck seemed unconcerned about us being AWOL. He just shrugged and told us to get our belongings and go about our business.

But when I got back to my quarters, some damn swabbie had stolen all my stuff. I had to borrow a poncho from another Marine. It was too cold that night in San Francisco to wander around in shirt-sleeves.

The next day, I caught a train for San Diego. When I got there, I was quartered alphabetically in a Quonset hut dormitory on the Marine base with about eighty guys whose last names all began with "Mc." Whenever someone stuck his head in the door and hollered "Hey, Mac!" everybody in the damn place would answer.

I was stuck there for several days, during which I got antsy and jumped the fence to take a little liberty. The people who'd been there ahead of me had been allowed liberty, but some of them got in trouble, so the privilege was canceled.

When I jumped the fence to get back in, a sentry caught me and started to write me up. I gave him a song and dance about just being back from overseas, and he finally let me go.

January 1, 1945, was an extremely happy New Year for me because that's when the train trip from San Diego to the East Coast finally started. It took a whole week because we stopped in nearly every town along the way, but the only big cities I remember going through were Kansas City and Pittsburgh. As far as I know, nobody from K/3/5 was on the train, but there was a bunch of guys from the

Fifth Marines weapons company. Almost no civilians were aboard. It was like a troop train, only it had berths, which was great because I was able to catch up on lost sleep.

One of the weapons company Marines lived in Pittsburgh, and he had a brother who was starting a wholesale food business. When we stopped there, the brother gave all of us who were continuing east a big bag of groceries. Mine was full of cheeses and other stuff that was hard to get with rationing in effect.

When I finally got to the house in Gerritsen Beach on the night of January 8, I still had that bag of groceries clutched in my arms. My heart was beating a little fast, and my palms were kind of sweaty in spite of the cold.

When the front door opened, and Mom saw me standing there, her eyes got wide, and her jaw dropped. Then she grinned and reached out for me.

"Hi, Mom," I said, "I'm home." I hugged her around the bag of groceries, and I could tell she was crying.

I have to admit I was feeling a little teary myself.

THE REST OF January was old home week in Brooklyn. It was full of family get-togethers with uncles, aunts, cousins, and plenty of Mom's great home cooking. I also made the rounds of all my old hangouts. Many of the guys I'd known as a kid were still overseas, but a few of them dropped in on furlough while I was there.

One guy I'd grown up with, Dennis Murphy, was in a cast from his toes to his hip. Naturally, I was curious about what had happened to him, but at first I hesitated to say anything, thinking he might be sensitive about it. When I finally did ask, he just shrugged and said, "SCM."

I was familiar with most of the initials we used in the service, like LST for landing ship, tank, or LCI for landing craft, infantry, but I'd never heard of an SCM.

"What the hell is that?" I asked.

"Swivel chair, mahogany," he said, and we both had a good laugh.

TOWARD THE END of January, I got some good news from the Marine Corps. I'd been accepted for the assignment I was hoping for—as a drill instructor at Parris Island—and on February 5, 1945, I reported to the DI training school for the Fourth Recruit Battalion there.

As a combat veteran of three major operations and someone who'd always liked helping younger guys become seasoned, savvy Marines, I thought I'd make a good DI, and I was really looking forward to the job. It wasn't that I got a kick out of ordering boots around or making their lives miserable. It was because I seriously believed I could teach them things that might save their lives a short time later on some godforsaken Pacific island.

The DI school was right next to where the recruits were quartered, and I'll never forget the first time I passed a new boot in a hallway. He jumped to attention and saluted me so fast I thought he was going to throw his arm out of joint.

Nothing like that had ever happened to me before, and I almost laughed out loud. But I managed to keep a straight face and told the boot, as casually as I could, to carry on.

I was assigned to a recruit platoon along with a platoon sergeant named Jim Bordenairo. Jim was a heavily experienced DI, and we got along great from day one. He was dating a lady Marine—whose name, I swear, was Grace Kelly—and when they decided to get married, he asked me to be his best man.

After the wedding, he gave me a silver cigarette lighter that had "Jim McEnery" engraved on one side and "Grace and Jim" on the other. I really treasured that lighter, and I carried it in my pocket for years. I think I still had it when I quit smoking at the age of seventy-four.

Two important things I learned from Jim were (1) never threaten a recruit and (2) never lay a hand on one. "As a DI, your main job is to teach these young men what they need to know to survive in combat," he'd say. "As green kids, they may not realize when they do something wrong, and there's plenty of nonviolent ways of making them catch on."

It was easy, for example, to lose your temper with a bunch of half-asleep recruits when you were trying to talk to them in the barracks after a hard day on the drill field. But instead of yelling at them or cussing them, I'd have them stand up and go to an open window, then take a few deep breaths of fresh air to clear their heads.

In the process of learning stuff like this, I heard a lot of stories about truly dumb things some DIs had done to their recruits. One of them marched his platoon straight into a creek, where several men drowned. This was plain stupid—and mean, too.

Some DIs also used a lot of profanity and derogatory names when they chewed out their recruits. But the worst thing I ever remember saying to one of them, even when he was arguing or being a wise guy, was: "Don't be a horse's ass. Horse's asses don't last long on a battlefield."

Some NCOs with heavy combat experience didn't like serving as DIs. They thought working with boots who knew so much less than they did was boring and a waste of time. But I never felt that way.

For one thing, I still remembered my own days in boot camp, back when I didn't know "Semper Fidelis" from "seventy-five dollars." I remembered the little things I'd learned there that had saved me a bunch of grief later on. Little details about dislodged pins in hand grenades or open bolts in '03 Springfields or keeping a sharp bayonet at your fingertips in your foxhole at night.

To me, teaching these new kids things like that was just as important as killing Nips had been on Guadalcanal, Cape Gloucester, and Peleliu. In a way, maybe it was even more important.

In that winter of 1944–45, the Marine Corps was rushing to get thousands and thousands of green troops ready to fight in two of the biggest, toughest battles of the war—Iwo Jima and Okinawa.

I'm still glad I played a small part in preparing dozens of those untested recruits for the dangers and challenges they'd soon be facing in those final Pacific campaigns.

Did it do any good? Did it save any lives?

I can't say for sure, but I'd bet my last nickel that it did.

I NEVER EXPECTED THE WAR to end so soon. I don't guess anyone else did, either, except President Harry Truman and the people who developed the atomic bomb. The first A-bomb wiped out Hiroshima on August 6, 1945, and three days later a second one hit Nagasaki. On August 15, Emperor Hirohito announced Japan's surrender.

At the time, many of my former comrades in K/3/5 were still on Okinawa, waiting for the dreaded order to invade the Japanese home islands. America's military leaders expected 1,000,000 casualties in that invasion. But, thank God, it never came.

Within a few weeks, recruit training at Parris Island came to a virtual standstill. There was no longer any need for fresh troops. On the contrary, millions of service personnel were being discharged and sent home. Unfortunately, I wasn't one of them.

On November 28, my stay at Parris Island officially came to an end. But instead of being discharged, I was reassigned to Casual Company, a military police outfit responsible for watching over Marines awaiting undesirable discharges and transporting military prisoners.

By late September 1946, I had so much unused furlough time built up that the Marines relieved me of all assignments and basically allowed me to live as a civilian while drawing my regular pay. I even got a card in the carpenters' union and went to work full-time on a veterans housing project.

But it wasn't until November 27, 1946—six years and almost three months after I enlisted in the Corps—that I officially became a civilian again.

EPILOGUE

FOR ME, THE EXPRESSION "Once a Marine, always a Marine" is a whole lot more than just another old saying.

As I mentioned at the beginning of this story, I think I've always been a Marine at heart. And today, nearly sixty-six years after I received my discharge from the Corps and returned to civilian life, I still consider myself a Marine.

The men I fought beside and shared foxholes with in World War II—especially those in K/3/5—are like members of my own family. Except for my wife, Gertrude, my daughter, Karen Cummins, and my two grandsons, Brendan and Erik, these guys are the most important people in the world. (My sister, Lillian, passed away in 2004, and my brother, Peter Jr., was killed in a car crash in the early 1980s.)

This is why I've made it a point to stay in close touch over the years with as many of my Pacific comrades as possible. I still talk regularly by phone to wartime buddies like Slim Somerville, Bob Moss, and T. I. Miller, my old platoon guide at Guadalcanal. They're as close to me as brothers, and they will be for as long as we live.

I also feel a strong kinship with all the men who ever saw combat with K/3/5, including many that I've never met. Not long ago, I read an article in *American Legion Magazine* about the major role played by the Third Battalion, Fifth Marines, in the Afghanistan war, where 3/5 had the highest casualty rate among U.S. infantry units—30 killed and 200 wounded.

Accompanying the article was a color photo of my old company in combat during the brutal fighting in Helmand Province. When I saw it, I felt such a powerful emotional connection to those young guys in the picture that it almost brought tears to my eyes. Their weapons and equipment were much more modern and sophisticated than the prehistoric stuff we used at Guadalcanal. But the point is, they were doing exactly the same kind of dirty, deadly job that we did seventy years ago.

I couldn't have felt a greater sense of pride if I'd been there myself.

In my younger days, I never missed a K/3/5 or First Marine Division Association reunion. Gertie and I traveled all over the country to see my old buddies. But travel's gotten tougher for everybody in recent years, and I'm not as young as I used to be. I turned ninety-two in September 2011, and my Pacemaker plays hell with those metal detectors in airports, so I don't go as far or as often as I'd like anymore.

Sadly, the number of World War II vets at those reunions grows smaller every year, and every time another one of my old comrades passes away, I feel a deep personal loss. This was especially true in 2001, when Gene Sledge, who did so much to immortalize the men of K/3/5 in his book *With the Old Breed at Peleliu and Okinawa*, reported for duty to the Man Upstairs.

When Gene's book was first published in 1981, he sent me a complimentary copy, along with one of the most touching notes I've ever received:

"Best wishes to one of the Old Breed—Guadalcanal, Gloucester, and Peleliu," he wrote. "With profound admiration for one of the best Marines and bravest NCOs I ever saw under fire. It was guys like you, Jim, that acted as an example to some of us 'boots' and kept us going when things got rough."

I was also deeply touched several years ago when retired Marine Major General Pat Howard promoted me to the rank of honorary captain—and later honorary major—when he met with a wonderful group I'm involved with called Vets Helping Vets.

(The head of this organization is Hank Whittier, who served as a machine gunner with the Second Marine Division many years after I left the Corps and who ranks as one of the most caring people I've ever known. Hank is never too busy to help out a fellow veteran who needs transportation to a clinic or hospital, a bit of financial assistance, a sympathetic ear in times of trouble, or any other type of helping hand. He's the living personification of Vets Helping Vets.)

I'd mentioned to General Howard that, through some sort of paperwork snafu, my promotion to platoon sergeant had never come through, although I passed all the requirements two years before my discharge.

"Maybe these promotions will help make up for that oversight," he told me, jokingly, as he presented me with a captain's gold bars and a major's gold leaf, "but you understand, of course, there's no pension involved."

Truth is, it's me who owes a debt to the Marine Corps, not the other way around. My six-plus years as a Marine gave me a totally different perspective on life and taught me a lot of practical lessons that were worth a fortune later on. As a Marine in combat, I learned to adapt to conditions that most people would find unbearable. As a result, I was able to hold down a wide range of civilian jobs after the war and even own and operate my own successful auto trim business in Hempstead, Long Island.

When a local urban renewal shopping center project claimed the land my business was located on, I took a position as a maintenance foreman at Rutgers University in New Jersey and worked there until my retirement in 1981. After that, Gertie and I bought a nice home with a swimming pool in Ocala, Florida, where we still live today.

For a kid who never went beyond the eighth grade in regular school, I think I did pretty well.

Of course, it also helped that I had a tough childhood. But remembering what I went through as a Marine gave me the strength and confidence to take on risks and challenges I probably would've avoided otherwise. Once you've lived through hell in the Pacific, you figure you can cope with whatever happens here on American soil.

Let me make one thing clear. I don't consider myself a hero. Never have and never will. Except for the presidential unit citations earned by the First Marine Division at Guadalcanal and Peleliu, I never received any valor-based decorations. I never suffered a wound in combat, so I don't even own a Purple Heart.

I'm just a journeyman Marine and damn proud of it.

• • •

I'VE OFTEN BEEN told that I have a good memory for dates, and I guess it's true. When someone asks me when a certain firefight I was in seven decades ago took place, I can usually come close to the exact date and maybe even hit it right on the nose.

But at the top of the list of dates I'll never forget is May 9, 1947. That's the night I met a girl named Gertrude Johanson, who was a friend of my sister, Lillian, and worked at the same insurance company with her.

The company was holding a dance for its employees at the Hotel New Yorker in midtown Manhattan, and Lil invited me to come.

"I'll have this friend of mine meet you at the hotel entrance and show you where to go," my sister told me.

I had a feeling I was being set up for a blind date, but once I met Gertie and danced with her a couple of times, I didn't care. She turned out to be the love of my life, and on August 30, 1947, less than four months after that first meeting, we were married.

That was sixty-five years ago, and I've never regretted it for a second—and I hope she hasn't, either. But early in our marriage, we went through some very sad and rough times trying to have children. It was especially hard for Gertie. After the normal birth of our daughter, Karen, we lost four precious babies who were born with fatal birth defects.

When we learned that an irreversible condition called the RH factor was to blame and that it was caused by the fact that our blood types weren't compatible, we realized how blessed we were to have a healthy child like Karen.

I'm equally blessed to have a wife like Gertie. Her love and her faith in me are the source of my strength. She helps and comforts me in more ways than I could ever deserve, and I thank God for her every day.

IF I HAVE any complaints relating to my service in World War II, they'd be directed at a few of the military officers and civilian leaders who controlled the fate of the millions of Americans who fought—including thousands who died—in the Pacific during that terrible time.

As you've probably gathered by now, I don't have much regard for General Dugout Doug MacArthur. I blame him for thousands of needless American casualties. When I think of the misery we endured at Peleliu and the good men who died there in a struggle that had no strategic value—all because of MacArthur—it makes me sick.

His sorry record started in the Philippines, where he let his air force be destroyed on the ground, then abandoned his sick, starving, surrounded troops on Bataan and Corregidor. After that, he spent the rest of the war in the safe haven of Australia, except for a few publicity photo ops.

President Roosevelt didn't do those of us who fought in the Pacific any big favors early in the war, either. To rescue Britain and his friend Winston Churchill, he left the defenders of the Philippines high and dry while he sent all our available manpower and best equipment to the European Theater. He promised help to Bataan's garrison, then refused to deliver any.

It's never made sense to me why Roosevelt stuck with that "Europe first" approach and let the Nips do whatever they wanted in the Pacific for months after they knifed us in the back at Pearl Harbor.

It was Japan that attacked us directly, but Roosevelt's only concern seemed to be Germany.

He fired General Walter Short and Admiral Husband Kimmel, our top Army and Navy commanders in Hawaii, and made them the scapegoats for Pearl Harbor. Kimmel tried to send a relief force to the Marines at Wake Island, but he was relieved of his command before it could get there. Then Roosevelt let Dugout Doug get away with murder.

The Marines saved MacArthur's butt in the Pacific, but he was always jealous of them. Why else wouldn't he allow a single Marine Corps general to be present at the Japanese surrender aboard the USS *Missouri* in Tokyo Bay?

This was a calculated slap in the face to men like Marine Generals Vandegrift, Roy Geiger, and Oliver Smith, who had as much to do with our victory over Japan as anyone in the U.S. military. Sixty-seven years later, I still get steamed about it.

And seventy-three years after I enlisted in the Marines, I'm still convinced it was the best damn thing I ever did.

I don't want Americans of the twenty-first century to forget what happened at Guadalcanal or Cape Gloucester or Peleliu. I want the memory of those tragic times and terrible places to live forever.

Thinking back on them sometimes causes me actual physical pain. But I truly believe that keeping the memory of them alive for future generations is the only way to make sure they never happen again.

People ask me now and then if I ever feel remorse or regret over some of the things I did in the heat of combat. My answer is a simple "No." It was kill or be killed out there, and I did what I had to do to protect my own life and the lives of the Marines around me.

I still grieve over the friends and comrades who didn't make it, and I'm sure I always will. But I've never lost sleep over the enemy soldiers I shot or bayoneted or blew to bits with grenades—not even the wounded ones I put out of their misery or the occasional prisoner who posed a potential threat. I did it the same way you'd chop off the head of a poisonous snake that was about to bite someone.

When conditions allowed, I turned captured Japs over to rear-echelon troops to be taken to a holding area, but in the midst of hostile action, that was impossible.

I feel no bitterness toward the Japanese people of today. I prayed for them as earnestly as I ever prayed for anyone after the deadly earthquake and tsunami that struck their country in early 2011. But the ones we fought at Guadalcanal, Cape Gloucester, and Peleliu were utterly ruthless and treacherous. Time after time, I saw unarmed American corpsmen—all of them clearly identified by their Red Cross armbands—deliberately shot down by enemy soldiers when all our medics were trying to do was help wounded and dying men.

The Japs we faced in the Pacific between 1942 and 1944 were instilled with hate and contempt for all Americans. They proved it countless times, and they didn't change when they were wounded or had supposedly surrendered. They forced us to learn—if we wanted to survive—that the only "good Jap" was a dead Jap.

I can only hope that God takes such things into account when Judgment Day comes—and I honestly believe He will.

For the record, I hated every minute I spent on those islands, but I'm glad I was there to fight those battles. If I had my life to live over, I'd willingly do it all again.

That's what it means to be a Marine.

Semper Fidelis!

INDEX

Adams, Arthur "Scoop," 10, 14, 15, 47, 57–58, 59, 65, 68, 113–15, 201
Afghanistan, 286
Ahner, Leonard, 160, 161
airfield: on Cape Gloucester, 153, 155, 156, 173; on Guadalcanal, 11, 15, 49, 50–51, 58–60, 73; on Ngesebus, 237; on Peleliu, 210–12, 215–16, 217, 218, 228, 239. *See also* Henderson Field
Alligator Creek (Guadalcanal), 5, 74, 80–81
Americal Division, U.S. Army. *See* 164th Infantry Regiment
amphibious tractors (amtracks), 105–6, 206, 207–8, 209, 237–38, 239, 240, 245
Anderson, Jim, 263, 264
Armistice Day (1926), 24–25
Army, U.S.: at Cape Gloucester, 174; dogs of, 174; First Marine Division transport from Australia and, 141; on Guadalcanal, 52, 109–10; McEnery thoughts of joining, 18–19, 33; on Ngesebus, 245; on Peleliu, 228, 261, 265–66, 269
Arndt, Charles C. "Monk," 5, 69
Ash, Robert M., 214
"Asiatic," going, 199

Atkins, Elisha, 162–63
atomic bomb, 283
Australia: combat training school in, 147–48; Fifth Marines depart from, 150–51; MacArthur in, 290; McEnery in, 137–52; McEnery's views about, 140; and U.S. troops-Australian relations, 141. *See also* Brisbane, Australia; Camp Balcombe; Melbourne, Australia

B Company, First Battalion, Fifth Marine Regiment (B/1/5), 75
B Company, First Marine Raider Battalion, 93, 95
Bailey, David, 264, 268
Bailey, Kenneth, 93, 95–96, 97
Balduck, Remi, 38–40, 42, 43, 100, 145–46, 172, 202
Banika: assignments on, 202–3; U.S. Navy base on, 197–98
banzai. *See* Bushido/banzai
Basilone, John, 116–17
Bataan, 44, 58, 82, 131, 138, 290
bath incident (Guadalcanal), McEnery's, 84–85
Bauerschmidt, Bill: at Cape Gloucester, 174–75; death of, 253–54, 263;

Bauerschmidt, Bill (*continued*)
McEnery recon assignment by, 175;
McEnery relationship with, 201–2;
on Ngesebus, 238, 243; on Pavuvu,
201–2; on Peleliu, 208, 212, 215–16,
227, 229, 230, 253–54; personal
background of, 175; as platoon
leader, 174
Baxter, Thomas "Nippo," 240, 244
Blakesley, Kenneth, 67–68, 86, 87–88,
89–90
Bloody Nose Ridge (Peleliu). *See*
Umurbrogol Plateau
"blow-torch and corkscrew" tactics, 236
Bordenairo, Jim, 281–82
Bors, Lou, 125
Boyd, Robert, 262
Brisbane, Australia, 137–40
British; in Pacific War, 44
Brody, George, 278
Brooklyn, New York: McEnery child-
hood and youth in, 21–33, 288;
McEnery on leave in, 39; McEn-
ery train trip from California to,
279–80; McEnery's return from
Pacific to, 280–81
Brooks, Clyde, 260
Bushido/banzai: at Cape Gloucester,
168; as double-edged sword, 72;
Ichiki Detachment and, 79–84;
meaning of term, 71–72; November
3 battle on Guadalcanal and, 119–
26; on Peleliu, 218; Puller's troops
and, 108. *See also* Edson's Ridge:
Battle of; Tenaru River: Battle of

C Company, First Battalion, First Marine Regiment (C/1/1); on Peleliu,
220–22
C Company, First Marine Raider Battalion, 93–94, 95–96
Cactus Air Force, 77, 101–3, 110, 112,
185

Camp Balcombe (Australia), 141–50,
152, 183, 184
Camp Lejeune (North Carolina), 41
Canberra (ship), 55
Cape Gloucester (New Britain): airfield
on, 153, 155, 156, 173; Army dogs
at, 174; Beach Yellow at, 154, 155;
importance of remembering, 291;
Japanese retreat/stragglers and,
173–80; maps of, 154–55; Marines
on, 152, 153–81; McEnery's leg
injury on, 160, 161–62, 163, 164,
165, 166, 167, 169, 171; McEnery's
scary experience on, 177–79; rota-
tion of Fifth Marines at, 176–77;
supplies/equipment for, 156, 174;
Talasea battle on, 180; tanks at, 155,
167; Walt's Ridge on, 168, 169, 171;
weather on, 156–57, 177
Capito, John, 167
Carl, Marion, 101
Casual Company (military police);
McEnery assignment with, 284
Cates, Clifton, 83
cemetery: on Guadalcanal, 137, 206; on
Peleliu, 268
Chisick, Andy, 164, 165
Christmas (1944), 277–78
Churchill, Winston, 44, 290
Civil War veteran; McEnery sees, 25
coast watchers, 78, 103, 107, 110
Cobb, Charles, 134, 146
coconuts, 12, 61, 193–94, 199
Collins, Harold, 255–56
Colonna, Jerry, 201
Coral Sea, Battle of, 54
corpse, Japanese; McEnery shooting
of, 247
corpsmen. *See* medics/corpsmen
Corregidor, 44, 58, 82, 138, 214, 290
Crosby, Bing, 201
Cummins, Brendan (grandson), 285
Cummins, Erik (grandson), 285

Cummins, Karen (daughter), 285, 289

Curtis, Marian, 142, 144–45, 185

Daniels, Agnes (grandmother), 22, 29

Daniels, Christopher (grandfather), 22, 29

Day, Jim, 161–62, 164

death: McEnery's reactions to, 106, 122–23, 124, 125, 172, 176, 202, 236–37, 254, 268–69, 270, 276, 291–92; stench of, 247, 257. *See also specific person*

Delong, Weldon, 120–21, 123–25, 202

Distinguished Service Cross, 133

d'Leau, Jay, 271

dogs: at Cape Gloucester, 174; on Peleliu, 209

Doolittle, Jimmy, 129

Dragons (football team), 26

dress blues, 19, 39

drill instructor: criticisms of, 282–83; McEnery as, 281–83, 284

Dykstra, Daniel, 150, 157–58, 159

Eastern Solomons, Battle of, 100

Edson, Merritt A. "Red Mike," 90–97, 105, 133, 147

Edson's Ridge (Guadalcanal): Battle of, 74, 90–97, 98; map of Guadalcanal beachhead and, 49

Eleventh Marine Regiment, 43, 89, 97, 213

Ellington, Charles "Duke," 263, 264, 268

equipment. *See* supplies/equipment

"Europe First" approach, 290–91

European Theater of Operations (ETO), 9

Few, Frank L, 68–69

Fifth Marine Regiment: advance on Guadalcanal of, 51; Battle of Edson's Ridge and, 97; at Cape Gloucester, 147, 153, 173, 176–77; defensive perimeter for, 59; departure from Australia of, 150–51; Edson as chief of staff for, 147; Edson as commander of, 133; Guadalcanal casualties in, 12; Henderson Field defense and, 100; K/3/5 clean up after departure of, 139; map of Guadalcanal beachhead and, 49; Matanikau River battles and, 104, 107, 117, 132; McEnery's San Diego—Brooklyn train trip and, 279–80; in New Guinea, 151–52; nickname for, 43; on Peleliu, 207, 208, 211, 212–13, 215, 216, 217, 222, 224, 236, 246, 248, 257, 258, 261–62; Quantico as home for, 40; relieved on Guadalcanal of, 134–35; Rupertus briefing to, 206; Seventh Marine Regiment split off from, 43; trip to Guadalcanal by, 44–45; Wellington training of, 45; in World War I, 40. *See also specific person or battalion*

First Battalion, Fifth Marine Regiment (1/5): at Cape Gloucester, 154, 173, 180; first Guadalcanal assignment of, 4–6; Matanikau battles and, 75, 117, 118–19, 120–26; on Peleliu, 213, 248, 262; Smith (Charlie) assigned to, 41

First Battalion, First Marine Regiment (1/1), 4, 80–84

First Battalion, Seventh Marine Regiment (1/7), 105, 107, 108, 115–16, 154

First Marine Air Wing, 102

First Marine Division: age among men of, 3; in Australia, 128, 137–40; Camp Lejeune as home of, 41; at Cape Gloucester, 153, 156, 168, 180, 181; casualties of, 135–36, 233, 268; command structure of, 133–34; historian for, 79; lack of experience among men in, 2; MacArthur visit

First Marine Division (*continued*) to, 181; organization of, 42–43; as part of U.S. Sixth Army, 150–51; at Pavuvu, 186–206; on Peleliu, 207–33, 236, 246, 262, 288; presidential unit citation for, 288; Rabaul campaign and, 181; Rupertus as commander of, 148; Savo Island battle and, 54, 56; total strength of, 5–6; Vandegrift as commander of, 44–45; "Waltzing Matilda" as theme song for, 184. *See also specific battalion; see also next entry*

First Marine Division—at Guadalcanal: casualties of, 135–36; first major objective of, 14; Goettge patrol and, 68; Japanese surrounding of, 57; landing of, 1–4, 10; map of beachhead and, 49; Matanikau battles and, 74–75, 76, 115; orders for, 45; presidential citation for, 288; relief of, 128, 135; strains on, 132

First Marine Division Association, 286

First Marine Parachute Battalion, 5, 89, 92, 96, 97, 99, 134–35

First Marine Raider Battalion, 5, 89, 91–97, 105, 106, 134–35

First Marine Regiment: activation of, 43; airfield mission of, 50–51; defense of Henderson Field and, 100; defensive perimeter for, 59; Edson's Ridge Battle and, 97; evacuation from Peleliu of, 224, 227; on Goodenough Island, 151; landing on Guadalcanal of, 4; at Lunga River, 16; map of Guadalcanal beachhead and, 49; Matanikau battles and, 76; at Pavuvu, 224; on Peleliu, 107–8, 208, 211, 218–19, 220–22, 228, 236, 246; Puller as commander of, 107–8, 211; Rupertus briefing to, 206. *See also specific battalion*

First Marine Tank Battalion, 213

First Recruit Battalion, 36

Five Brothers hill (Peleliu), 246

Five Sisters hill (Peleliu), 246, 248–55

Fletcher, Frank J., 53, 54, 56

Florida Island, 5, 45

food/water: on Guadalcanal, 9, 12–13, 19, 61–62, 99, 196; on Pavuvu, 195–96; on Peleliu, 212, 215, 257; steer for, 61–62

football; McEnery's interest in, 26–27, 276

46th Replacement Battalion, 190

Foss, Joe, 101

Fourth Infantry Regiment, Japanese Army, 108

Fourth Marine Regiment, 43, 138

Fourth Recruit Battalion, 281

Frank, Richard, 80

friendly fire casualties, 103–4

G Company, Second Battalion, Seventh Marine Regiment (G/2/7), 146

Gargano, Lou, 142–44, 145, 158–59, 161, 162, 163, 166, 170, 171, 172, 202

Gavutu Island, 5, 9

Gayle, Gordon, 213, 262

Geiger, Roy S., 102–3, 185, 186, 187, 256, 291

Goettge, Frank/Goettge Patrol, 49, 63–69, 82, 85, 86

Goodenough Island, 151

Goodwin, Horace E. "Tex," 158

Googe, Jesse, 230, 248

Grawet, Raymond, 254

grenade incident: dislodged pin, 7; McEnery-Jap, 105

grenades; McEnery idea for firing rifle, 205

Guadalcanal: Army and, 52, 109–10, 135; beginning of end for Japanese on, 117; "Cactus" as code name for, 77; cemetery on, 137, 206;

December 18 offensive on, 135–36; duration of battle for, 231; Edson's Ridge Battle as turning point on, 98; estimates of number of Japanese on, 51; first day for Marines on, 8–15; first Marine victory on, 51; first night for Marines on, 16–20, 32; first objective for Marines on, 10–11; as first U.S. offensive ground action in Pacific War, 4; food/water on, 9, 12–13, 19, 61–62, 99, 196; friendly fire casualties on, 103–4; importance of remembering, 291; importance of U.S. campaign for, 136; Japanese invasions of, 11, 128–29; Japanese plan for withdrawal from, 135; Japanese reinforcements on, 73, 76, 77–78, 101, 107, 131; K/3/5 maneuvers on, 205–6; K/3/5 rotation back to U.S. and, 276; location and size of, 11; map of beachhead on, 49; Marine landing on, 1–4, 6–12; as Marine rest base, 185; native settlements on, 11; November 3 battle on, 119–26; October 13 and 14 on, 109–13; as rear-area military complex, 185; Red Beach on, 1, 4; shortage of U.S. troops on, 16; stranding of Marines on, 56, 57; supplies/equipment for, 8–9, 13–14, 16, 17, 19, 43, 48, 50, 56, 57–58, 64, 85, 96, 99, 116, 129, 130; as turning point in Pacific War, 136; U.S. reinforcements for, 99, 109–10, 129; U.S. troop buildup on, 135. *See also specific person, combat unit or battle*

Guadalcanal: Starvation Island (Hammel), 12

Guadalcanal Diary (Tregaskis), 83

Gunter, Paul, 122

Gustafson, John, 237, 245, 260, 265, 274

Haldane, Andrew Allison "Ack-Ack": Australia departure of, 149; background and personality of, 146–47; and Banika assignments as rewards, 202, 203; booby-trapped rifle incident and, 176; at Cape Gloucester, 169; death of, 263–64, 268; as legend, 169; McEnery commendation letter from, 204–5; McEnery tommy gun and, 243; named K/3/5 commander, 146; on Peleliu, 224–25, 262–63; Pope and, 220; Silver Star awarded to, 169; twenty-four month rule and, 204

Halsey, William F. "Bull," 129, 131–32, 135, 141, 153, 232

Hammel, Eric, 12

Haney, Elmo M. "Pop," 188–90, 191, 192–93, 197–99, 201, 243

Hanneken, Herman, 256, 257

Harris, Harold "Bucky," 215, 237, 258

Haruna (ship), 110

Henderson, Lofton, 73

Henderson Field (Guadalcanal): Edson's Ridge Battle and, 94; first U.S. use of, 77; importance to U.S. of, 78, 136; Japanese bombing/shelling of, 73, 78–79, 94, 100–101, 103, 110–11, 112; as Japanese objective, 74, 78, 89; Naval Battle of Guadalcanal and, 131; Tenaru River Battle and, 79–84; U.S. defense of, 100, 219

Hiei (ship), 129, 131

Higgins, Dick, 263, 264, 268

Hill 100 (Peleliu), 220–22, 251

Hill 140 (Peleliu), 262, 265

Hill 660 (Cape Gloucester), 171, 180, 203

Hope, Bob, 201

Horseshoe Hill (Peleliu), 246

Howard, Pat, 287

Hughes, William, 88

Hunt, George, 219

Hunt, LeRoy P., 2, 14, 51, 133
Huskies (football team), 26
Hyakutake, Harukichi, 84

I Company, Third Battalion, Fifth
   Marine Regiment (I/3/5): food
   for, 62; friendly fire casualties and,
   103–4; Goettge patrol and, 68; map
   of Guadalcanal beachhead and,
   49; Matanikau battles and, 75, 76,
   104–5, 118, 120–26; on Ngesebus,
   243; on Peleliu, 214
I Company, Third Battalion, Seventh
   Marine Regiment (I/3/7), 256
Iboki Point (Cape Gloucester), 177, 179
Ichiki (Kiyoano) Detachment, 79–84
Imperial Japanese Army, 72, 128
Inoue, Sadae, 269
intelligence, U.S., 11, 51, 63
Iron Bottom Sound, 55, 57, 75, 85, 93,
   110, 276. *See also* Sealark Channel
Iwo Jima, 231, 283

Jackson, Arthur J., 224
Japanese: battle surrenders of, 64, 175,
   176, 236, 269, 292; final surrender
   of, 283, 291; as infiltrators, 218,
   238, 257–58, 265; kamikaze attacks
   by, 130; McEnery's feelings about,
   291–92; McEnery's first sight of, 48,
   59; suicide by, 64, 83, 84, 122, 175,
   177; "washing machine Charlie" as
   name for, 60, 77; wounded, 175–76,
   292. *See also specific person, battle,
   or location*
Johanson, Gertrude. *See* McEnery,
   Gertrude Johanson (wife)
Johnson, Randall, 167
Jones, Edward A. "Hillbilly," 183–84,
   204, 259–61
jungle; McEnery's night alone in,
   178–79
jungle rot, 157, 171

K Company, Third Battalion, Fifth
   Marine Regiment (K/3/5): Adams
   as leader of, 113–15; in Australia,
   137–51; baptism of fire for, 86–90;
   at Cape Gloucester, 153–81; casualty
   rate on Peleliu for, 268; changes in
   command structure and, 133–34;
   Cobb named commander of, 134;
   as front-line combat troop, 6;
   Haldane named commander of,
   146; Haldane's death and, 264–65;
   hopes for return to Melbourne by,
   183–85; McEnery first assigned to,
   40; McEnery kinship with, 285–86;
   McEnery of leader of, 264–65;
   McEnery as platoon guide for, 172,
   240; McEnery as Third Platoon
   leader of, 263; morale in, 58, 191;
   on New Britain, 128; on Ngesebus,
   237–44, 245; on Okinawa, 283–84;
   at Pavuvu Island, 185–205; on
   Peleliu, 128, 206, 207–33, 235–37,
   246–66; photograph of, 267–68;
   praise for Ngesebus battles of, 245;
   replacements for, 148–49; rest
   assignment of, 128; reunions of,
   286–87; rotation back to U.S. of,
   270–75, 276–77; supplies/equip-
   ment for, 149. *See also next entry;
   see also specific person*
K Company, Third Battalion, Fifth
   Marine Regiment (K/3/5)—on Guadalcanal: advance of, 57–58; Army
   troops and, 109; assignment of, 42;
   baptism of fire for, 86–90; daily life
   of, 84–86; duration of, 45; first night
   of, 15–16; food/water for, 12, 61–62;
   friendly fire casualties and, 103–4;
   Goettge patrol and, 65–69, 85, 86;
   Henderson Field and, 77; landing
   of, 3–4; maneuvers of, 205–6; map
   of beachhead and, 49; Matanikau
   battles and, 74–75, 104–5, 118,

120–26; McEnery as reconnaisance
sergeant for, 104–5, 113, 118–19,
134; and October bombings by Japanese, 113; recon patrol of, 47–48, 50;
search for F4F Wildcat fighter by,
65; shortage of supplies/equipment
for, 57–58, 60

K Company, Third Battalion, First Marine Regiment (K/3/1), 219, 224

Ka-Bar knives, 149, 168, 195, 215, 221,
258

kamikaze attacks, 130

Kelly, Grace, 282

Kelly, John, 125, 159

Kelly, R. R. "Railroad," 203

Kimmel, Charles J., 120, 122

Kimmel, Husband, 291

King, Ernest, 181

Kipling, Rudyard, 190, 226, 249

Kirishima (ship), 129, 132

Kokumbona (Guadalcanal village),
117

Kongo (ship), 110

Korean construction workers; on Guadalcanal, 51

Krueger, Walter, 153, 156

Kukum (Guadalcanal village), 51, 111

L Company, Third Battalion, Fifth
Marine Regiment (L/3/5), 68, 75,
76, 118, 170, 214

L Company, Third Battalion, Seventh
Marine Regiment (L/3/7), 255–56

lamp, Haney, 189–90, 191

land crabs; on Pavuvu, 194, 195, 199,
201

Landrum, Bill, 16–17, 19, 122, 123, 125

Lane, Kerry, 167

Langford, Frances, 201

Lawler, Dan, 216–17

Lefebvre, J. J., 142

leg injury, McEnery's, 160, 161–62, 163,
164, 165, 166, 167, 169, 171

Levy, Seymour, 190–91, 201, 215, 216,
223, 225–26, 230, 231, 249–51

Leyden, Bill, 191–92, 201, 214, 241–42,
244

Lunga River (Guadalcanal): Balduck
death near, 146; Battle of Edson's
Ridge and, 93; First Marine Regiment at, 16; importance of, 74; map
of Guadalcanal beachhead and, 49

Lynch, James, 174

M Company, Third Battalion, Fifth
Marine Regiment (M/3/5), 162–63

MacArthur, Douglas "Dugout Doug,"
14, 138, 139, 140, 153, 180–81, 186,
232, 290, 291

Mace, Sterling, 191, 201, 216, 223–24,
225–26, 230, 231, 241–42, 246–47,
249, 250–51

machine gun training; McEnery's,
41–42

mail service, 69, 93, 197–98

malaria, 114–15, 127–28, 132, 139, 140,
146, 147, 171

Mangrum, Richard, 101

maps: of Cape Gloucester, 154–55, 159;
of Guadalcanal, 50, 80; inaccuracy
of, 50, 80, 154–55, 159; of Peleliu,
225, 246

Marine Corps, U.S.: draft for, 275;
language of, 36; McEnery joins, 19,
33, 34; McEnery reenlistment in,
274–75; McEnery's feelings about,
288, 291–92; McEnery's last days
with, 284; organization of divisions
in, 42–43; punishments in, 36–37;
recovery of dead soldiers by, 247;
shortages in, 43; twenty-four month
rule for, 204, 270; in World War I,
138

Marine Fighter Squadron VMF—114,
239

Marmet, Johnny, 263, 264, 268

Marshall, George C., 136

Matanikau River (Guadalcanal): battles along, 74–75, 104–6, 107–9, 115–26, 163; importance of, 74; Japanese patrols along, 128; Japanese withdrawal from, 89; K and I Companies friendly fire incident along, 103–4; map of Guadalcanal beachhead and, 49; U.S.–Japanese fights along, 74–77

Matanikau Village (Guadalcanal), 75, 119

Matheny, Tom, 250

McClary, Charles R., 259

McDonald, Marie, 277

McDougal, David, 168

McEnery, Gertrude (wife), 145, 285, 286, 288, 289–90

McEnery, Jim: baptism of fire on Guadalcanal for, 87; birth of, 21; childhood and youth of, 21–33, 288; death of father of, 28–29; drinking of, 32; early jobs of, 29–30, 32–33; education of, 29–30; family background of, 21–22; fights of, 26, 30–32, 39, 148, 271–72, 278; financial affairs of, 17, 19, 33, 34, 38, 278; Haldane commendation letter for, 204–5; leadership skills of, 3; leg injury of, 160, 161–62, 163, 164, 165, 166, 167, 169, 171; as Marine at heart, 21, 285; marriage of, 145, 289; motivation for joining military of, 17–18; physical appearance of, 27; post-war life of, 288; promotions of, 3, 85, 172, 275, 287–88; reenlistment of, 274–75; religion and, 28; return to civilian life of, 284; rifle/shooting skills of, 37, 41–42; robbery of, 279; scary experience of, 177–79; sees first military uniform, 24–25; self-image of, 288; sports and, 26–27, 40, 148; worst day/time of life for, 125, 235. See also specific topic

McEnery, Lillian (mother): McEnery in Australia and, 142; McEnery childhood and youth and, 22, 24, 28, 29, 30–32, 33; McEnery Guadalcanal letters to, 69, 73; McEnery Guadalcanal memories of, 6, 32, 112; McEnery as helping support, 17, 33; McEnery on Pavuvu and, 202; McEnery return to U.S. and, 277, 278, 280; Muroski marriage of, 30–31, 32; Murosky–McEnery fight and, 30–32; refuses permission for McEnery to join Navy, 18, 32; religion and, 28; as single parent, 17–18, 22, 28, 29

McEnery, Lillian (sister): childhood and youth of, 22, 24, 28, 29, 30, 33; death of, 285; Gertrude as friend of, 289; McEnery Guadalcanal letters to, 69; McEnery Guadalcanal memories of, 6; McEnery as helping support, 17, 33; McEnery on Pavuvu and, 202; McEnery return to U.S. and, 277; Muroski as step-father to, 30; news about McEnery's friends from, 276

McEnery, Thomas (father), 28–29, 30, 32

McIlhenny, Walter, 215

McIlvaine, Rex, 113–14

McMillan, George, 56, 79, 98, 108, 180, 200, 213, 222

Mead, George, 75

Medal of Honor, 97, 101, 116, 133, 222, 224

medics/corpsmen: on Cape Gloucester, 158, 169; on Guadalcanal, 88–89, 125, 132; McEnery's feelings about Japanese shooting, 292; on Ngesebus, 244; on Peleliu, 223, 230, 253–55, 260–61

Melbourne, Australia: First Marine Division in, 141–45; K/3/5 hopes for return to, 183–85

Merchant Marine crew; Navy gunners fight with, 271–72

Midway, Battle of, 10, 54, 73

military, U.S.: McEnery motivation for joining, 17–18; McEnery's dreams of joining, 25. *See also specific branch*

military uniform; McEnery sees first, 24–25

Miller, T. I., 114, 286

Milne Bay (New Guinea); Fifth Marine Regiment at, 151–52

Moore, Alden, 255

morale: on Guadalcanal, 58, 73, 98, 100; on Pavuvu, 191, 201; on Peleliu, 258

Moss, Robert J., 278, 286

Muroski, Peter Paul, 30–32

Muroski, Peter Paul Jr., 30, 32, 202, 285

Murphy, Dennis, 280–81

Murray, William, 7, 134

National Guard troops, 109

Naval Battle of Guadalcanal, 129–32

Naval Operating Base (Norfolk, Virginia); McEnery assignment at, 38–40

Navy, Japanese, 101–3, 136

Navy, U.S.: Banika base of, 197–98; Battle of Midway and, 10; First Marine Division in Australia and, 141; as Guadalcanal backup, 6; Guadalcanal departure of, 16, 73; Japanese air raids on, 13–14, 16, 56; McEnery thoughts of joining, 18, 32; Merchant Marine crew fight with, 271–72; Paleliu battle and, 232; Peleliu dock of, 270; Rabaul campaign and, 181; supplies for Guadalcanal and, 9; support for troops on Guadalcanal and, 100, 129. *See also specific person, battle or vessel*

Navy Cross, 101, 124, 133, 146, 211, 215

New Britain: K/3/5 assignment to, 128, 153–81; MacArthur visit to, 181. *See also* Cape Gloucester

New Caledonia, 56, 93, 129, 131, 276

New River, North Carolina; McEnery field training at, 15, 41, 42, 142

Ngesebus; Battle for, 237–44, 245

Nimitz, Chester, 180–81, 232

nurses, Red Cross, 272–73

officers: code names for, 15. *See also specific person*

Okinawa, 231, 244, 283–84

O'Neil, Tom, 169–71

164th Infantry Regiment, Americal Division, 109–13, 115, 116, 117

182nd Infantry Regiment, U.S. Army, 129

Opecek, Frankie, 249

Oro Bay (New Guinea); Seventh Marine Regiment at, 151

Pacific War: British in, 44; Guadalcanal as turning point in, 136; weapons and equipment for, 9. *See also specific topic*

Paine, Leland, 157, 160–61

Parris Island, South Carolina: McEnery in boot camp at, 35–37, 283; McEnery cruise to, 34; McEnery as drill instructor at, 281–83, 284; McEnery hopes for appointment as DI at, 275

Patch, Alexander, 135

Patterson, Lawrence V., 14, 86, 105, 121–22, 133–34

Pavuvu Island: changes on, 272–74; coconuts on, 193–94, 199; entertainment troupe at, 201; food/water on, 195–96; and Haldane commendation letter for McEnery, 204–5; K/3/5 rotation back to U.S. and, 270–75, 276; as Marine rest camp, 185–205, 224; Marine suicides on,

Pavuvu Island (*continued*)
200; morale at, 191, 201; rats/land crabs on, 194–95, 199, 201; weather on, 187

Pearl Harbor: Battle of Tenaru River as payback for, 82; Japanese attack on, 10, 43; Short and Kimmel as scapegoats for, 291

Peleliu: airfield on, 210–12, 215–16, 217, 218, 228, 239; Army troops on, 228, 261, 265–66, 269; cemetery on, 268; death stench on, 247, 257; as First Marine Division objective, 186; food/water on, 212, 215, 257; importance of remembering, 291; Japanese infiltrators on, 218, 257–58, 265; Japanese strength on, 236, 269; Japanese surrender on, 236; K/3/5 departure from, 270–71; last duty assignment on, 268; MacArthur role in battle for, 232, 290; maps of, 225, 246; Marine casualties/wounded on, 268; Marine landing on, 206, 207–10; most tragic day and, 262–64; Orange Beach on, 207; as pointless battle, 232–33; Rupertus comments about, 206, 256; Sniper Alley on, 225, 236; supplies/equipment on, 215; tanks on, 209–10, 212–13, 229–30, 253, 258, 260–61, 265; Umurbrogol Pocket/Bloody Nose Ridge battles on, 216–18, 225, 235–37, 246–66, 269; as uniquely horrible and worst time of McEnery's life, 231–32, 235; weather on, 212, 247. *See also* Ngesebus

Philippines, 43, 290

photograph: of 3/5, 268; of K/3/5, 267–68, 286

platoon leaders: as tough job, 114, 174. *See also specific person*

Point Cruz (Guadalcanal), 49, 118

Pollock, Edwin, 80, 81

Pope, Everett, 220–22, 251

post-traumatic stress syndrome, 275

Pratt, Malcolm, 64

prisoners of war: at Battle of Tenaru River, 83; Bushido and, 72; Japanese as, 51, 83; at Singapore, 72

Prohibition, 23, 29

Puller, Lewis B. "Chesty," 107–8, 115–16, 211, 218–20, 222, 247, 256, 258

Quantico, Virginia; McEnergy assignment at, 40–42

Rabaul; Japanese base at, 78, 103, 153, 181

rats; on Pavuvu, 194–95, 199, 206

Red Cross nurses, 272–73

Resurrection Catholic Church (Brooklyn, New York), 28

Rice, Lyman, 254

Rickenbacker, Eddie, 101

rifle incident: bolt problem, 36–37, 89–90; booby-trapped, 176

Rigney, Tom, 241

Rivers, John, 82

Roosevelt, Franklin D., 44, 138, 232, 290–91

Rottinghaus, Ray, 255

Royal Life Saving Society, 148

Rupertus, William, 148, 150, 156, 173, 183, 204, 206, 211, 256–57

Rutgers University, 288

Samoa, 18, 42, 43

San Diego, California; McEnery in, 279

San Francisco, California; McEnery in, 277–79

Santa Cruz Island, 49, 129

Saunders, Captain , 40

Savo Island, 52–56, 91

Schantunbach, Norman "Dutch," 8, 170–71

Schmid, Al, 82

Scott, Raymond, 88

Seabees, 187, 228, 273

Sealark Channel: Japanese air raids on U.S. ships in, 13–14, 48, 52–55. *See also* Iron Bottom Sound

Second Battalion, Fifth Marine Regiment (2/5), 5, 94, 104, 105–6, 117–18, 154, 173, 213, 248, 262

Second Battalion, First Marine Regiment (2/1), 4, 48, 80–84, 216

Second Battalion, Seventh Marine Regiment (2/7), 105, 107, 155–56, 251

Second Marine Division, 133, 135, 147

Second Marine Raider Battalion, 135

Second Marine Regiment, 18, 104, 276

Selden, John T., 147, 177, 179, 204

17th Army, Japanese, 79, 84, 117

Seventh Marine Regiment: in Australia, 145–46; Balduck with, 42, 43, 100, 145–46; at Cape Gloucester, 153, 157; casualties of, 256; evacuation from Peleliu of, 256; Matanikau River battles and, 104, 107, 115, 117; at Oro Bay (New Guinea), 151; on Peleliu, 208, 210, 211, 222, 224, 236, 246, 256–57, 261; as reinforcements on Guadalcanal, 99, 100; Rupertus briefing to, 206; in Samoa, 42, 43; as split off from Fifth Marine Regiment, 43. *See also specific battalion*

Shanley, James V. "Jamo," 255–56

Shea, John, 82

Shepherd, Earl, 265

Shepherd, Lemuel, 168

Shifla, Donald, 268

Shofner, Austin "Shifty," 214

Short, Walter, 291

Silver Star, 133, 167, 169, 199

Singapore, 44, 72

singing: on Armistice Day, 24; Guadal-canal landing and, 8, 171; by Jones, 183–84

Sixth Army, U.S., 150–51, 153

Sixth Marine Regiment, 43

Skocczylas, Joseph, 168

Sledge, Eugene B., 192–93, 196–97, 218, 261, 271, 287

Smith, Charlie, 18–19, 33, 34, 36–37, 38, 41, 172, 202, 276

Smith, John L., 101, 102

Smith, Oliver, 291

Sniper Alley (Peleliu), 225, 236

Snodgrass, Jimmy, 104

Somerville, Charles "Slim," 121, 124, 157, 201, 286

Spaulding, Joseph A., 69

Spiece, Harry, 264, 265

sports; McEnery's interest in, 26–27, 40, 148

Spurlock, Lyman, 75–76

SS *America* (ship), 141

SS *B.F. Shaw* (ship), 151

SS *Manhattan* (ship), 44

SS *Sea Runner* (ship), 270–72

Stanley, Thomas "Stumpy," 263, 264, 265, 268

Stassen, Harold, 232–33

Stay, Walter, 243

Stuart, Jeb, 213

Student, Emil, 106

Suicide Creek (Cape Gloucester), 159–60, 161, 163, 166–68, 171

Sullivan, Jerry, 208–9

supplies/equipment: Battle of Edson's Ridge and, 96; at Cape Gloucester, 156, 174; Goettge patrol and, 64; for Guadalcanal, 8–9, 13–14, 16, 17, 19, 43, 48, 50, 56, 57–58, 64, 85, 96, 99, 116, 129, 130; Japanese air raids on U.S. ships and, 13–14, 48, 85, 130; for K/3/5, 139, 149; K/3/5 recon patrol and, 50; on Peleliu, 215; Savo Island battle and, 54, 56;

supplies/equipment (*continued*)
on Tulugi Island, 56; U.S. capture
of Japanese, 51, 91; World War I
leftover, 43
surrender story; Goettge patrol and,
63–69

Talasea (Cape Gloucester), Battle of,
180
Tanambogo Island, 5
tanks: at Cape Gloucester, 155, 167; at
Guadalcanal, 83, 99; on Ngesebus,
241–42; on Peleliu, 209–10, 212–13,
229–30, 253, 258, 260–61, 265. *See
also* amphibious tractors
Tarawa, 276
Task Force 62 (U.S. Navy), 6
Tenaru River (Guadalcanal): Battle of
the, 74, 79–84, 98; importance of,
74; landing of Marines on Guadalcanal and, 5; map of Guadalcanal
beachhead and, 49
Teskevich, John: Banika assignment
of, 202, 203; at Cape Gloucester,
202, 203–4; death of, 230–31, 236,
248, 253, 259; grave of, 268; on
Guadalcanal, 121, 125; mustache
of, 203–4; on Peleliu, 216, 226–27,
228–29, 230–31; personality of,
121; twenty-four month rule and,
204, 270
The Old Breed (McMillan), 56, 98, 108,
180, 200, 222
III Amphibious Corps, U.S., 186, 256
Third Battalion, Eleventh Marine Regiment (3/11), 83
Third Battalion, Fifth Marine Regiment
(3/5): in Afghanistan, 286; Battle of
Edson's Ridge and, 94, 97; at Cape
Gloucester, 163, 167, 168, 173, 180;
first assignment on Guadalcanal of,
4–6; first night on Guadalcanal of,
15–16; Goettge patrol and, 65; Gua-

dalcanal landing of, 4; Gustafson
as commander of, 237; Matanikau
River battles and, 75, 104, 105–6,
117, 118, 119; on Ngesebus, 237–44,
245; at Oro Bay, 154; on Peleliu, 209,
214, 227, 248, 262; photographs of,
268, 286; praise for, 245; rumors
about Japanese capture of women
and, 62; Savo Island Battle and, 52;
supplies/equipment and, 57, 60
Third Battalion, First Marine Regiment
(3/1), 4, 115, 155, 220
Third Battalion, Seventh Marine
Regiment (3/7), 154, 163, 167, 216,
255–56
Third Marine Division, 185
Thomas, Patty, 201
Thompson, Norm, 170, 171
321st Regiment, 81st Infantry Division,
U.S. Army, 228, 266
Tokyo; U.S. bombings of, 10, 129
tommy gun: McEnery's finding and use
of, 240–41, 242–43, 244; McEnery's
training in use of, 41–42
Torgerson, Harry, 96
train trip, McEnery's San Diego—
Brooklyn, 279–80
Tregaskis, Richard, 83
trench foot, 157
Truk; as Japanese base, 78, 79
Truman, Harry, 283
Tulagi Island, 5, 9, 45, 56, 93
Tunney, Gene, 40
Turner, Richmond K., 53–54, 55–56
Tweedie, Dick, 104
twenty-four month rule, 204, 270

Umurbrogol Plateau (Peleliu), 216–18,
225, 235–37, 246–66, 269
USS *Astoria* (ship), 55
USS *Atlanta* (ship), 130
USS *Balduck* (ship), 146
USS *Chicago* (ship), 55

USS *Colhoun,* 85
USS *Columbus* (ship); 238.
USS *Denver* (ship); 238.
USS *Elmore* (ship), 181, 183, 187
USS *Enterprise* (ship), 100, 129, 131
USS *George Elliott* (ship), 48
USS *Hornet* (ship), 100, 129
USS *Jarvis* (ship), 55
USS *Juneau* (ship), 130
USS *McCauley* (ship), 54
USS *Mississippi* (ship); 238.
USS *Missouri* (ship), 291
USS *North Carolina* (ship), 100
USS *O'Brien* (ship), 100
USS *Patterson* (ship), 55
USS *President Jackson* (ship), 137, 139
USS *Quincy* (ship), 55
USS *Ralph Talbot* (ship), 55
USS *San Francisco* (ship), 130
USS *South Dakota* (ship), 129, 132
USS *Vincennes* (ship), 55
USS *Wakefield* (ship), 44, 45
USS *Washington* (ship), 129, 132
USS *Wasp* (ship), 100, 129
USS *West Point* (ship), 141
USS *Wharton* (ship), 276, 277
USS *Zeilin* (ship), 130

Van Trump, Richard, 243
Vandegrift, Alexander A.: Battle of
    Tenaru River and, 83; Bushido
    fighting and, 84; as commander
    of First Marine Division, 44–45;
    commendation for Marine fliers by,
    78; Edson's Raiders and, 91; First
    Marine Division in Australia and,
    140; and importance of Guadalcanal
    campaign, 136; landing on Guadal-
    canal and, 4; and Marines at Japa-
    nese surrender on USS *Missouri,*
    291; Matanikau River battles and,
    75, 115; orders relief of Fifth Marine
    Division, 132; Rupertus takes over
    command of First Marine Division
    from, 148; Savo Island battle and,
    54; trip to Guadalcanal of, 44–45;
    turns over Guadalcanal command
    to Patch, 135
Vets Helping Vets, 287

Wake Island, 44, 82, 291
Walt, Lewis W. "Silent Lew," 168, 214,
    245, 251
Walt's Ridge (Cape Gloucester), 168,
    169, 171
Walt's Ridge (Peleliu), 251
"Waltzing Matilda" (song), 184
"washing-machine Charlie," 60, 77
water. *See* food/water
Wellington, New Zealand; Fifth Ma-
    rines in training at, 45
Wells, Captain , 121, 122
Whaling, William J., 106, 107
Whittier, Hank, 287
Williams, Charles, 254
Wilson, Dean, 82
*With the Old Breed at Peleliu and Oki-
    nawa* (Sledge), 192, 287
women; rumor about Japanese capture
    of, 62–63
World War I: aerial combat in, 101,
    102; Fifth Marines in, 40; Haney in,
    188, 189, 198; K/3/5 in, 198; leftover
    equipment from, 43; MacArthur's
    comments about Marines in, 138;
    Rickenbacker record in, 101
World War II: beginning of, 33–34;
    most tragic day for K/3/5, 262–64.
    See also specific topic

Young & Jackson's Pub (Australia),
    141–42

Zimmerman, John, 136